MULTIMEDIA

CS-66

For

Bachelor of Computer Applications [B.C.A.]

S.ROY

MCA,B.SC.,DECM,DCPA,DECOM

Academic Counsellor - ARSD College,Delhi University

Guest Lecturer - Delhi College,Delhi University

Visiting Faculty - Punjab Technical University

Dinesh Verma

MCA, BCA, 'A' & 'O' Level, SCJP(USA), JP

CLOSER TO NATURE

WE USE RECYCLED PAPER

Valid For

IGNOU, Vinayaka Mission University, IP University, Delhi University, CCS University, JMI University, B. M. V. Open University (KOTA), M. P. Bhoj Open University(M.P.), Tamilnadu Open University, YCM Open University (Maharashtra), Mahatma Gandhi University (Kottyam), M. D. University, and all other Indian Universities.

GULLYBABA PUBLISHING HOUSE (P) Ltd.

AN ISO 9001:2008 CERTIFIED CO.

GullyBaba Publishing House (P) Ltd.

2525/193, Ist Floor, Onkar Nagar-A,
Tri Nagar, Delhi-110035
Ph: 9350849407, 9312235086, 011-27387998
E-mail: info@gullybaba.com / info@degreewala.com
Website: www.gullybaba.com / www.ignouonline.com

First Edition : March, 2012

ISBN : 978-81-89086-35-0

Preface

This book is mainly targeted for BCA exam of Multimedia. It has been introduced in market after seeing the huge demand of ready to grasp material for exams with high level of quality, and its un-availability in market. We the GullyBaba Publishing House took a step ahead to publish the quality material focusing on exams at the same time giving you indepth knowledge about the subject.

GPH Book is the pioneer effort that provides a unique methodology so as to perform better in exams. If your goal is to attain higher grade use this powerful study tool independently or along with your text.

On the Web : ***www.gullybaba.com*** *is the vital resource for your exams acting as catalyst to boost up your preparation. Gullybaba.com has been Listed* ***no.1*** *in www.google.com and www.yahoo.com when you search "IGNOU MCA BCA MBA". Now you can access us on the net through* ***www.doctorignou.com, www.doeacconline.com, www.gphindia.com, and www.gullybabapublishinghouse.com.***

Feedback about the book can be sent at **cs66writers@gullybaba.com.**

Acknowledgments :

We appreciate the staff and facility support provided by GullyBaba Publishing House. In particular, we appreciate the encouragement and professional advises received from Mr. Ajay Saini, Mr. Tarun Sharma, B. K. Krishna and many more.

Also we would like to thank typesetting and designing team Mrs. Bhawna Verma, Mr. Shravan Vats, Mr. Parveen Kumar, and Mr. Mukesh.

We gratefully acknowledges the significant contributions of Mr. Mahesh Chand, Mrs. Bimla Devi, Mrs. Bhawna Verma and our experts in bringing out this publication.

New Delhi ***Publisher***

Contents

Question Papers

CHAPTER 1

AN OVERVIEW OF MULTIMEDIA

- **Introduction**
- **Objectives**
- **Multimedia-The Concept**
- **Hardware for Multimedia Computer**
  - ✓*The CPU*
  - ✓*The Monitor*
  - ✓*Input-Out Devices*
  - ✓*CD-ROM*
  - ✓*Sound Card*
  - ✓*Laser Disc*
  - ✓*DVD*
- **Software for Multimedia**
- **Components of Multimedia**
  - ✓*Textual information*
  - ✓*Images Animation*
  - ✓*Digital Audio*
  - ✓*Digital Video*
- **Multimedia-Design, Production and Distribution**
  - ✓*Planning/Design of Multimedia*
  - ✓*Production of Multimedia*
  - ✓*Distribution of Multimedia*

Just look back few years ago when multimedia was nowhere in the scene. The computers which were available in the market had black & white analog / manual monitors & a simple keyboard as input/ output devices. Then came GUI (Graphical User Interface) which gave birth to mouse. Now every computer today whether it be a multimedia computer or simple computer has a mouse. But as time passing by & with latest technologies there has been a considerable change in the input / out devices in a multimedia computer. And more newer devices are covering the market daily.

Q1. What is Multimedia? Explain its features. What are the components of Multimedia ?

Multimedia is an integration of various media, which convey the information with computing technology. Various media such as text, graphics, animation, sound, audio, video etc.

Multimedia is a computer itself or a computer software product. In practically we can say that multimedia is a combination of both hardware and software. Another much used term is "hypermedia". The term hypermedia refers to the information structure of the content. If the texts, pictures, and sounds are linked to each other by associative links the applications may be called "hypermedia".

Multimedia systems support the physical and logical coexistence and interactive use of heterogeneous media classes such as print, audio and video in specific application environments.

One of the key features of multimedia is "**Interactivity**". Hypermedia and virtual reality applications are based on multimedia systems. Hypermedia extends the **media-oriented features** of multimedia systems by the concept of hyperlinks, i.e.; logical structures that provide means for organizing media objects in a flexible, logically coherent, network-oriented and non-sequential way. Virtual reality extends the interaction **oriented features** of multimedia by the concept of cyberspace, i.e. modeling objects and their behaviour in virtual environments. The basic advantage of multimedia over the conventional form of media, which uses sound, graphics, and text etc. is the interactive feature of multimedia.

The basic components of multimedia are:

(i) The text can be used for adding emphasis.

(ii) Graphics provides a visual impact.

(iii) Voice tries to enhance a presentation.

(iv) The animation can be used effectively for attracting attention.

(v) The video part of multimedia can be used as a powerful communicator providing clear cut instruction.

In general, by using multimedia in the applications, we can produce applications that are:

• **Efficient :**

We can replace information you read with information you can see and hear, such as a video clip.

• **Direct :**

You can deliver information using the best medium, such as a language teaching applications that plays a native speaker's voice to demonstrate pronunciation.

• **Interactive :**

It is easier to construct genuine and multilevel user interaction with pictures and sounds than with plain text only.

In a complete sense, pictures, graphics, text and sound is the essence of multimedia and it provides the user friendly environment with most flexible interactive facilities.

Q2. Whether multimedia is a computer itself or a computer software product?
 # "Multimedia is not just Hardware but also Software". Comment on the above statement. [JUN02,Q1(a)]

Apart from hardware (many devices) required for a multimedia. Many software are also required to make an application with the help of multimedia. Just imagine if one has a P.C. with all the hardware but no software he is like on a boat but with no water in the sea. Thus in multimedia hardware and software goes hand in hand. There are different softwares available for different purposes. Some of them are as under:

- Photoshop for image & graphic editing.
- Premier & after FX for production.
- Director & authorware for authoring.
- Sound Forge for sound editing.
- 3DS max for special effects & 3D animation.
- Flash for web animation.
- Apart from the above softwares there are many other softwares available for multimedia applications.

Q3. What is the basic advantage of multimedia over the conventional form of media?

The basic advantage of multimedia over the conventional from of media, which uses sound graphics and text for example, TV, audio etc. is the interactive feature of multimedia. For example, a multimedia version of news bulletin would be the situation where you can request the broadcaster the type of news you are interested in, when you want to hear it, and with the press of a button or click of the mouse you can hear the news.

Non-availability of a wide range of multimedia products in the market was one of the strong reason that it remained a mystery to the general public. However, as the costs have reduced and product functionality increasing, the multimedia is here to stay and now become easily available and more accessible. It may become part of our everyday life just like the PCs. For achieving these goals, several important technologies are being developed to solve, the problems associated with multimedia applications and interactive TV services to the home.

Some of these technologies are video servers, multimedia groupware, network resource management, and hypermedia courseware etc. Some of the new products are being equipped with real-time video-compression system. A newer broadband systems based on MPEG (Moving Picture Expert Group) standard, will allow transmission of several video signals using a single satellite transponder. Flow communication terminals, also know as digital set-top boxes, are equipped with computer capabilities offering features such as on-screen interactive program guides, movie on-demand capability, and personalized information channels. These home communication terminals will soon feature robust and full user interactivity as well as MPEG-based video, all controlled and managed by an open architecture operating system running on a set-top box.

Q4. How multimedia is creeping into our day to day life in various form?

Multimedia has started creeping into our day to day life in various forms, and information has started becoming available; in the digital format. Please note, when the information is available in the digital format we get a lot of flexibility in handling it. It can be edited according to specific requirement processed and produced in various style and taste.

Multimedia is interactive, non-linear media in comparison to broadcast television. In addition, it may provide a user with several meaningful paths. Thus, it is the interaction between user and information that makes it a very powerful media for activities that require the process of communicating information, such as education and training, reference material, business presentations, manuals, multimedia database, geographic information system, advertising, documentaries and so on.

Q5. In what sense we can use the component of multimedia?

The basic component of multimedia can be used for :

✓ The text can be used for adding emphasis.

✓ Graphics provides a visual impact. It is generally said that a picture is worth a thousands words. Thus, graphics can be used for enhancing a presentation.

✓ Voice tries to enhance a presentation to the extent that a presentation moves on to the form of persuasion. Many people want to listen about a particular topic rather than reading about it.

✓ The animation can be used effectively for attracting attention. Animation also makes a presentation light, thus, can be used for presentation of several complex subjects. It is also a tool, which helps in focusing attention; for example, a chart if drawn through animation may be focused on to quickly.

✓ The video part of multimedia can be used as a powerful communicator providing clear-cut instructions.

Q6. What is the use of multimedia in business?

Multimedia is widely used now a days in various applications and business is one of them. As the market competition is increasing with the introduction of better products in the market everyday, it has become absolutely necessary to provide service and timely information to your client in a brief, necessary and more understandable manner in a short time. Multimedia provides various ways to maintain a competitive edge for a company especially in training, market speculation, and public relation.

Now let us see the different aspects of business where multimedia is used.

✓ **The global team :** Multimedia technology with communication technology has opened the door to form global work group team, members may be working anywhere and do there work. These team members can be in different cities and may also speak different languages.

✓ **Voice mail :** Voice mail is a tool which communicates voice over lines. This can be phone lines or the Internet. A voice mail system is not dependent. The only draw back for a voice mail is that it only hurdles audio information, voice mail system is time & location independent but it offers no interactivity.

✓ **Multimedia based fax :** Fax is more famous and more used rather than the voice mail for the following reasons.

(i) Used to send detailed information.

(ii) Easier to use.

(iii) Handles graphic information

(iv) Provides a printed copy of information.

(v) Also fax is non interactive option for the user. Even a fax modem can be used to send & receive fax.

Audio conferencing: This technology allows out of town people to participate in a formal meeting. This technology can also be used by a group of people to meet frequently whatsoever is the physical distance among them. Audio conferencing is quite effective means of communication as it is used to discuss anything regarding everything. The only disadvantage regarding this type of conferencing is that one cannot see the other person. This may also cause problem if the other person is not well conversant & is not able to speak clearly. Audio conferencing technology was just available only in the conference room.

Video conferencing: Video conferencing is generally used in large corporate sectors. In foreign countries the use of video conferencing is a high success. Video conference is just like any office meetings thus require setting of time, preparing rooms & place, agenda, followed by discussion etc. Video conferencing brings people together naturally & tries to simulate a real life meeting environment. Video conferencing works with the help of a TV & a camera. The same hardware should be available with all the people who are participating in video conferencing. They are looking at the camera & the other person can see in the T.V. Now a days video conferencing can be done through a PC also. But setup for a video conferencing is high. It is very expensive. Video conferencing is done through high speed network connection also known as broadband technology.

Advantages :

✓ Save time & money for big corporate houses when they have to go out of country to attend meetings.

✓ Very effective & powerful means of communication.

Document conferencing : The other name of document conferencing is Audio-graphic conferencing. A PC & a telephone line is required for document conferencing. The PC is the information hub and telephone connection is used to connect two PC. Due to these telephone connections two people can share information from each others PC which is stored in it.

Apart from sharing information it also allows online editing of a document by several participating people in the conference this conference facility has been adopted by many big companies, specially in the IT industry and the education industry. In the education industry it has been great catalyst with the help of this technology it is possible to bring the education classroom or the corporate environment to the community. A document that can be used in the conference may consist of text, graphics, sound or even video clips.

Advantages :

✓ As now even the common men have a PC at their home, it becomes very easy to go for document conferencing.

✓ This is very easy to use.

✓ It is less expensive.

✓ Basic setup is not very high.

✓ Every common man can use it.

Website Hosting and Publishing : Website is one of the very important place where multimedia is used streaming Audio, Video, millions of people daily enjoys like on demand audio and video from rich, media web sites. Streaming media is a method of making audio, video and other multimedia available in real-time with no downloads. Streaming media elements have five elements namely.

- Encoders & tools
- Data types
- Servers
- Networks
- Players

✓ **E-commerce based application:** Electronic commerce is an upcoming model of new selling and merchandising tools in which buyers are able to participate in all phases of a purchase decision, while stepping through process electronically rather in physical stores. The multimedia technologies may be used for presentation of information through the web for such systems.

Q7. What is the use of multimedia in educational sector?

 # "Multimedia is the tool for teaching tomorrow." Comment on the above statement. [JUN03,Q1(a)]

 # How can multimedia be used in education ? Describe an example of multimedia in education ? How is it going to be an advantageous in comparison to printed books. ? [JAN01,Q2]

Another critical application of multimedia is educational sector. Multimedia enhances the quality of education. It provides new way for teachers to encourage one of the most rare and important elements of learning i.e., curiosity to know and explore. Topics can be linked with other related information. Linking is possible with graphics, text and sound (may be a lecture session from the subject teacher and so on).
With a large screen projector and a multimedia playback system, teachers can use multimedia as a way to enhance their standard lesson plan and stimulate questions. On the other hand students will be able to further explore the topics using standard multimedia platform. The assignments, which require students to make their own interpretation of facts, can be represented in the multimedia topics, there are several applications possible in this area of education using multimedia. The use of multimedia in education would go a long way.
In a complete sense pictures, graphics, text and sound is the essence of multimedia and it provides the user friendly environment with most flexible interactive facilities. Multimedia is very important in all the field but from education point of view it has done wonders. Education with the help of entertainment is provided by multimedia. This is also known as edutainment, i.e. fun with education. Now let us understand the whole process of education & see where multimedia is useful. For teaching books are required & thus the use of multimedia also begins here. Right from the designing of books to the content & the outer look multimedia is used. To enhance the learning experience proper text highlights, graphics are used. Apart from the books now a days. One gets the facility of learning through CBT. To develop this CBT different elements of multimedia like text, graphics, animation etc. are used. This CBIT is useful for the students and also to the tutors. With latest technology of distributed computing multimedia education can also be helpful over the network.

The use of multimedia in education are many ways. Lets take one example of an encyclopedia. Now we all know that encyclopedia is used for all round education. Encyclopedia has all the information of everything. They come in the sets of 5 to 10 books. Now just imagine that if these books were boring black & white text only. Naturally the interest automatically goes. But the books now being more graphical and colourful becomes very simple to learn & fun to read also. You can get the whole book on an interactive CD. This is very exciting & great fun as its like playing game when you are learning. This has many advantage as compared to a text book as per the following ways:

- Very interactive
- Very colourful & attractive.
- Made more powerful by adding sound & video where needed.
- Easy to browse through the content.
- Its fun and easy just like game.
- Visual presentation helps to remember more.
- Entertains you even when you are learning that is edutainment.

Thus we can see that multimedia definitely helps in education.

Q8. What are the hardware components needed for professional multimedia development platforms? Define the purpose of each of the hardware components.

[DEC02,Q1(b)]

#: What are the various hardware components needed for Multimedia display and development? Describe the usage of these components. [DEC01,Q1(b)]

#: What are the various multimedia hardware components? What additional components of hardware will be needed in case you want to download multimedia contents from the Internet?

#: Give various input/output devices for multimedia applications.[JAN01,Q1(ii)]

#: Give various storage devices for multimedia. [JUN02,Q1(b)]

#: A multimedia hardware platform is to be used for delivering multimedia based tutorials available on the CD. What will be the configuration of such multimedia computers. Describe the purpose of each component in your selection.

[JUN03,Q1(b)]

A typical multimedia computer usually include devices like **CD-ROM** player, sound card such 7777as Sound Blaster, Master Blaster and sometimes a microphone and a range of multimedia softwares. And probably with either MIDI (Musical Instrument Digital Interface) a standard interface can be in hardware or software which is used for playing a digital instrument through PC interface on the card as an add-on utility. Let us look into the requirements of hardware for a multimedia PC. Figure follows gives the diagram of such requirements.

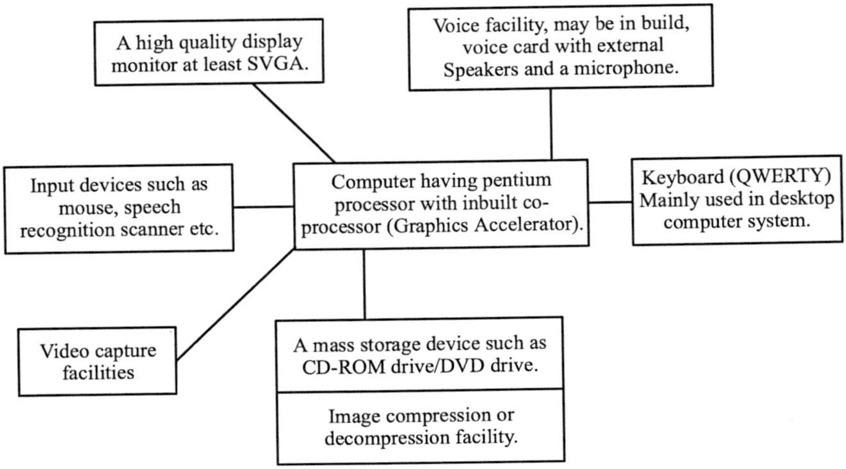

Requirements of Multimedia Computer

One cannot record video using such a system. For doing recording one require additional equipments such as digital video camera. However, once various components of multimedia are recorded in the required format, this machine can be used to put various pieces together to form a multimedia information system. Many multimedia machines however are equipped to record sound. Let us explore more about the hardware related to multimedia technology

🗁 **The CPU :** The CPU which is recommended for a multimedia computer should be Pentium processor on a PC or other advanced chips such as PowerPC etc. Apple Macintosh and Silicon graphics have their own set of powerful processors for multimedia. However, the CPU of multimedia computer should be at lest 486 with math co-processor attached otherwise the response time of multimedia will be poor. The co-processor chip greatly reduces the load of the CPU. The powerful co-processor chip added for supporting graphics is called graphics accelerator. The memory capacity for such a machine should be 8 MB or above. A 16 MB memory enhances the performance of a multimedia machine by 50% over 8 MB machines. Now a days PCs with 2.3 GHz of CPU speed are available in market. With 256 MB RAM. One can get best multimedia performance over those PCs. Moreover, the latest applications / softwares for multimedia coming in market runs over these high configuration PCs only.

🗁 **The Monitor :** The multimedia PC should be equipped with a monitor having Super video Graphics Arrays (SVGS) card. The basic advantage of having SVGA is that it has a better resolution, thus the display will be of better quality for the graphics and pictures. A typical representation which may be used in multimedia can be 720×640 or 1200×680 etc.

🗁 **Input-Output Devices :** Keyboard and Mouse are two important components for any multimedia PC. Since multimedia computer are accessed using a graphical user interface, therefore mouse is an essential input device for it. Here special mention is to be made about two important input-output devices. These are the sound speakers, which produce sound output and microphones, which are used for on-line recording of sound using various multimedia softwares. In addition to this, multimedia also supports MIDI interface, thus a digital musical instrument can be connected to it on this socket provided for it. Thus, a audio interface normally allows data transmission using DMA channels, that is it does not require the intervention of the CPU while transferring digital data to memory.

Some of the newer machines are coming up with a TV board which is installed inside the computer and allows connection of VCR/Video Camera/Cable connection. This TV board can be operated with the help of software, which are normally provided with this board. Thus you can watch TV programmes on the multimedia machine. However, please note that this interface does not allows digital recording of video on to your computer. This interface is meant only for the purpose of display. If you want to capture these video frames a video capture board is to be added in the multimedia PC.

CD-ROM is a very important storage device, which has become an essential component of multimedia computer of its mass storage capacity and portability. A CD-ROM drive is a common hardware component of a multimedia computer. A scanner can also be used along with a multimedia PC for scanning the pictures and putting them in digitized form in the computer.

🗁 **CD-ROM :** Multimedia uses digitized audio and video not only take huge amount of storage space, but also require high speed storage media, which can store large amount of data back and forth quickly to keep audio and video playing recording smoothly.

Because of this requirement most of multimedia packages use hard disk drive, which offer high speed, high data throughput, and plenty of storage devices like 40 to 80 GB or more. Sometimes two or more hard disk drives are used as array to work together so that they act like a single hard drive. However using array of two or more disk for multimedia storage, can no doubt boost the processing speed for the multimedia element, but these are not durable in nature. Magnetic optical disk media offer large amount of storage in a durable package. CD-ROM is widely used for multimedia storage as it has an amazing amount of flexibility and potential as multimedia storage and distribution medium. One CD-ROM can hold up to one and half hour of digital audio or around 700 to 750 MB of computer data for that matter. As far CD-ROM is concerned, the main feature of it is huge storage space and very high immunity from damage. It can easily locate different pieces of data in CD-ROMs, so that comparatively simple software can be used to guide the laser beam to find what is required.

🗁 **Sound Card :** Sound output from a computer has been feature of machines usually used for sending warning error message or games. If better quality and capabilities for sound output or inputs are required, then there must be a device, which can be added to the basic machine. This device is know as Sound Card, which is attached to the basic machine by inserting it in free slot. The most common reason for adding a sound card to a PC is to be able to use multimedia fully by recording and playing back the digital audio. While selecting an add on sound card, quality of sound from the loudspeaker has to be taken into consideration and the software provided with a sound card should be adequate enough to suit your requirements for handling sound effects in multimedia

🗁 **Laser Disc :** Like CD-ROM, a laser disc uses the same recording media. It can record and play back high quality digital audio files. As compared to the CD-ROM, a laser disc can play back four channels at a time (two digital and two analog channels) whereas CD-ROM can play only two channels at a time. CD-ROM stores digital data on only one side of the disk, whereas the laser disc stores an analog video signal on both side of the disc. But the biggest difference between them is that laser disc stores video in analog form.

The disadvantages of using a laser disc are like any other video source. The only plus point

being that you can access video from any location on the disk. The older multimedia system used to have a laser disc under computer control for playing video they used to have a separate TV screen in addition to a computer screen. Laser Disc is old technology; the DVD has replaced it.

🗁 **DVD :** DVD is the cohesion of multimedia and digital video player, movies and interactivity. By employing the latest advances in digital technology, DVD can hold up 25 times more digital info than a CD-ROM and DVD can be used to create innovative cutting edge video-discs with all sorts of data including director's cuts, photo galleries, interview with actors in fact practically anything today's video producers can imagine. Using DVD technology. Besides multilingual capabilities of DVD the producers can create a limitless range of interactive titles, instead of watching a video in the linear fashion as with traditional videotape.

Originally it was felt that DVD is the short for Digital Video Disc now it is more commonly referred to as "digital Versatile Disc" as it has many potential applications than video. The new multimedia storage format of choice, DVD is more that just a high quality video formatting DVD-ROM can combine hours of stunning video, audio and music with computer data and instructions to offer high-capacity media-rich games with exceptional video quality, specialized educational and entertainment programs, software libraries, and training programs, digitized photo collections and, of course, high quality interactive encyclopedias and interactive experiences, all on a single disk. Even today's most popular games consoles have DVD at the core of their technology. A single-sided, single-layer DVD can contain up to 133 minutes of video enough to handle 95% of all movies, without the interruption of flipping the disc over changing discs. DVD was designed to be the next generation of home video entertainment. DVDs offer digital sound and picture and high video resolution. However, our object is to use it as rich multimedia source.

DVD is the first standard designed specifically with the consumer and computer electronic industries in mind. Consumers will be able to enjoy the benefits and enhanced performance of DVD and PC users can turn their PC into genuine multimedia machines. The main advantage for PC uses is the enormous capacity of 4.7 to 17 GB that DVD offers. More storage intensive graphics and video sequences can be incorporated into software applications. A PC equipped with the necessary hardware and appropriate playback software can then DVD-Video discs. Thus PC users can take advantage of the consumer side of DVD.

For the computer world, the main type of DVD disc used is called the DVD-ROM. This is a real only disc similar to the CD-ROM. In order to real DVD-ROM discs, PC users will also need a special DVD-ROM drive. With this equipment, PC users can access any data in standard PC formats or even video in MPEG-1 format, It is possible to use a PC for cross platform applications with a wide variety of audio video material.

🗁 **DVD-ROM drives :** DVD-ROM driver are designed to read both CDs and DVD discs. The drives have seek time ranging from 150-200 ms, access time between 200 and 250 ms, and data transfer rates of 1.2 to 1.4 Mbps with burst transfer rated of up to 17 Mbps. This is the data equivalent of an 8x CD-ROM drive. Hence, when reading CD-ROMs, DVD-ROM driver transfer data at 3x speed. For PC users, upgrading to a DVD-ROM does not involve complicated installation procedures or exotic hardware. Connectivity is similar to CD-ROM drive DVD-ROM drive are available with standard interfaces such as EDIE (ATAPI) and SCSI-2. Audio connections allow playback of audio CDs. With the correct audio deciding equipment, a PC can produce DVD-audio quality sound.

🗁 **DVD-RAM for writing and deleting many times :** Another DVD product for PCs is DVD-RAM. These discs and drive have a capacity of 2.6 GB can be rewritten many times. It includes functions and applications similar to those of floppy discs or MO (magneto optical) discs. DVD-RAM is an efficient rewrite-able medium for handling and storing any data the requires a large capacity, such as moving pictures. Because ultra precise writing is necessary, even a fingerprint left on the disc's recording side before writing would change the optical intensity so that accurate writing could not be achieved. Therefore, a DVD-RAM (rewrite-able) disc must be contained in a special cartridge.

Q9.What is the difference between CD-ROM and DVD-ROM?

CD-ROM Vs DVD-ROM

	CD-ROM	**DVD-ROM**
Diameter	120 mm	120 mm
Thickness	1.2 mm	1.2 mm (0.6mm per layer)
Track Pitch (distance between successive turns of a spiral	1.6 μm	0.74 μm
Min. Pit length	0.83 μm	0.40 μm
Laser Wavelenght	780 mm	640nm
Layers	1	1,2 or 4
Data Capacity	0.65 GB	4.7 GB
Data Capacity (per layer)	0.650 GB	4.7 Gigabytes 92 hours 15 minutes) - Single side, single layer 8.5 Gigabytes (4 hours) - Single side, dual layer 9.4 Gigabytes (4 hours) 30 minutes0 -Double side, single layer 17 Gigabytes (8 hours) -Double side, double layer

Q10. What are the software requirement for multimedia?

Using multimedia always means using multimedia software. Multimedia applications need good operating system as their platform. Currently the operating system is typically windows 95/98. It is important that the operating system provides smooth handling of sound, video, graphics, and network communication.

Making multimedia applications or "multimedia components", requires special software. Graphics programmes such as Photoshop are specialized for processing and manipulating bitmaps, while Corel Draw is a programme for vector graphics. Cake Walk and Cool Edit are applications for making and manipulating music and sound.

Similarly other multimedia related software also work on the same type of working environment, but they have their own features to experiment upon. Some of the recent software used in multimedia industry are:

✓ **Photoshop :** Industry standard digital imaging software.
✓ **Director :** Authoring multimedia for CD-ROM & the Web.
✓ **Premiere :** Digital video and post-production tool.
✓ **Sound Edit :** Sound capture and editing for multimedia, music or the net.
✓ **Flash :** Vector-based animation tool.
✓ **Frontpage :** Authoring tool for intranet and the WWW.
✓ **Alias | Wavefront :** 3d tools for games, films.

Q11. How we can extend multimedia in Windows?

To provide all PC same standard multimedia, Microsoft developed multimedia extension for Windows operating environment. This feature add several multimedia capabilities to the Windows operating system, including Resource Interchange File Format (RIFF), a standard format for multimedia data including Bitmap, graphics, animation, digital video and audio recording and playback facility for digital audio. It also includes MIDI (Musical Instrument Digital Interface) file and MCI (Media Control Interface) to interface one's work with external devices such as CD-ROM, sound card, laser disc players etc. most of the multimedia extension software for windows works in the background. The utilities like MIDI mapper, sound recorder and media player are the direct interface to the software the multimedia extension for windows.

Most standard window graphics are limited to 256 colors if it is not interfaced with any external device outside the multimedia extension for windows are controlled by MCI for windows. The main interface to MCI is the media player which in turns control any external devices such as CD-ROM, Video player, and Laser Disc Player etc. Whereas sound recorder utility provided facility to playback and record digital audio as ".WAV" files, directly into the PC with the external sound device such as sound card. It has the function liked start record, stop, play etc. Similarly MIDI mapper makes sure that events that are specified in the MIDI file are sent to the correct MIDI instruments.

The video for windows is a external set of software works along multimedia extension for windows. It has feature for digitised video recording, playback and editing. The videocap utility of this software is used to capture the video and audio clips using external hardware. The captured sequence can be viewed in a number of frame. Video for windows has four different colour palates scan be created for individual frame. Video for windows has four different of editing features named as VidEdit, PalEdit, WavEdit and BitEdit. As the name suggests VidEdit is used to cut and paste captured video segments together, WavEdit is the feature which work with the recorded digital audio and helps you to edit it. Where as PalEdit is the work with the colour plates within the captured video to improve the colour BitEdit helps clean up the rough patches in the images. It also has the interface to the media control panel to control digital video files.

In the present environment there are many files formats existing for multimedia in Windows and Internet. The following table shows the details on these multimedia formats.

Multimedia File Format Table

File Extension	Description
MOV (Quick time)	Video: A video format that originated on Apples macintosh computers, now in windows too.
MPG (MPG: Motion Expert Group)	Video: A highly compressed format Requiring special pictures hardware and software for DOS playback and recording.
PCD (Photo CD)	Photos: Photographs stored on Kodak Photos CDs, accessible by Kodak's own software.
PCX (Picture Paintbrush)	Graphics: A popular format accessible by Most graphics program, including paintbrush.
Tif (TIFF: Tagged Image File Format)	Graphics: A format Popularized by Aldus PageMaker for moving graphics between different types of software and computers, often used by scanners.
VOC (Creative Voice)	Sound: Sound Blaster cards records sounds in the format.
Wav (Waveform)	Sound: Windows preferred format for Storing recorded sounds.

Multimedia File Format Table

File Extension	Description
AVI (Audio interleaved)	Video With Sound track accessible through Windows media player.
BMP (Bitmap)	Graphics, accessible through windows paintbrush
CGM (Computer Graphics Metafile)	16 Color graphics. An international Standard for moving simple graphics between families of Corel Draw and most major graphics package.
FLC, FLI (Flick)	Animation, a format started by Autodesk. That can be played back form a wide variety of graphics software.
JPG (JPEG: Joint Photo Expert Group)	Photos: High quality photographs stored Using a special graphics compression format.
MFF (MIDI File Format)	Music: A slightly abbreviated MIDI Format designed for Microsoft windows, accessible

Q12. What are the components of multimedia? Explain.

After discussing about the definition, hardware and basic software requirements for multimedia, we still face a question: "What are the various components of multimedia in computer and how create them?" Let us try to answer this question in this section.

🗁 **Textual Information :** All multimedia productions contain some amount of text, and even some might contain a large amount of textual matter. The text can have various types fonts and type sizes to suit the professional presentation of the multimedia software. The standard software interface which is now a days provided on multimedia is the windows interface. This interface allow large amount of fonts to be stored in multimedia.

🗁 **Images :** Another important and interesting components of multimedia is graphics. One of the basic facets in multimedia production is that people do not like reading large amount of textual matter on the screen. Also, it is a myth about human nature that a subject is better explained to them when represented in pictorial or graphical form, instead of textual matter i.e., graphics are used more often than text to explain a concept present background information etc.

Unlike text that is represented in universal ASCII format, graphics does not have any single agreed format. To start with these are two different ways in which graphs or images can described, Bitmap and vectors.

🗁 **Bitmap Images :** A bitmap images assumes an image to consist of two-dimensional squares, which are called the pixel or dots on the screen. The size and the quality of such a image depends on the pixel density and number of colors it user. For example, a standard VGA screen uses 640×480 i.e., a total of 307200 dots or pixel to display an image. If your image is in black and white, then only one digital bit is required to store this information about the image for each dot (0 for black and 1 for white), and the position to the dots can be taken as the order in which they are produced. As byte consists of 8 bits one can store a black and white image of this type in ((640×480)/8 = 38400 bytes = 37.5 KB, so imagine the storage place required to store all the image involved in multimedia production. If you are using colour .for the images then the size of the bitmap image become larger depending upon the number of colour used. A standard VGA, which uses 16 colours, needs 4 bit of storage to store the information, so only two dots can be coded in a single byte. Hence ((640×480).2) = 153600 bytes of space is required to store a single image with 16 colours. Similarly for an image with 256 colours (8 bit per dot), 32000 colours (16 bit per dot) or 16,000,000 colours (24 bit per dot) storage requirement will be very high. So a standard image with 16 colours will be ideal solution for a low cost multimedia package. These bit map files can be edited easily, however, require large memory space for editing purposes.

As bitmap images are stored as large files and you require large amount of disk space to deal with it. To avoid this constraint, the images can be compressed, which make the use of the fact that many entries in a bitmap files has repeated information or contain very little information. But there is no single standard compression method for image files. There are various formats such as PCX, TIF, BMP, and GIF etc., in which images are stored.

The software packages, which normally are used for creation of bitmap images, are called Painting programs. This program allows drawing of object using a paintbrush. Free hand drawings can easily be produced using these packages. One such package is the Paintbrush program available in Windows.

🗁 **Vector Images :** Other formats for storing images vector or object oriented format. In this format, an image is formed as a set of straight or curved lines instead of dots. A line can be represented by a mathematical equation, whose number can be stored as a set of binary codes. This form of coding is potentially more economical for disk storage space. The drawback is that it requires software to produce the image that is time consuming. CAD package use this type of images. A vector image file is always of the same size no matter how large a image is. Thus, for display clarity this type of images should be projected on better resolution display units.

🗁 **Animation :** There are several technology and sources available to produce image or graphics for multimedia package. Image can be created by using a Paint program, by scanning photographs using a scanner and by drawing artwork. You can generate 3D graphics and animation using various sophisticated software. You can combine these images using image manipulation programs that can combine many different types of graphics files, to create new images.

🗁 **Morphing :** Morphing takes two images and seamlessly changes one image to another. The second image actually seems to grow out of the first one. Morphing can also be used to show the pace of changes more clearly that photos. Warping is variation of the morphing where one image is used to show various changes that is take place. It uses the key points of one image to create different effects, instead of mixing up two images.

In 3-D animation mathematical model of 3-D object is created to realistically portray with depth. Now it has become a common media element in film, video and multimedia packages. 3-D animations follow mainly three steps; modelling, animation and rendering. Of these three first +-two are crucial and take long time to finish. Modelling is the design phase where a 3-D object is created. **In a 2-D animation** an object can move up (called Y axis) and sideways (called X axis). But in the case of a 3-D model, a third axis is used; depth or the Z-axis. Once an object is created along these three axes, colour, shading and light source can be added to the image to make it more realistic.

In the second phase, the 3-D image moved along a motion path which is defined using key frames of the animation sequence. These key frames are used to create the in-between frames in the sequence automatically.

And in the final stage, the entire sequence is rendered to create a 3-D animation. Blending texture maps into the model to add realism causes one of the main slow downs during rendering. A texture map is wallpaper for 3-D models, in which a graphics images is wrapped over the surface of a model. When a 3-D animation program renders an images, it mix up intimately all the colour, texture maps, light source and surface attributes in each frame of the 3-D animation sequence. The rendering process is computationally intensive step.

🗁 🗁**Digital Audio :** The most common reason for using digital audio in computer is to be able to use multimedia in its full potential. The most common requirement is to be able to input sound such as a spoken commentary on image or a document. The sound is a repeated pattern of pressure in the air and a microphone converts a sound wave into an electrical wave. The shape and frequency of the electrical wave is identical to the shape and frequency of the sound wave and the clarity of what we hear is entirely to the dependent on the shape and frequency of the sound wave. Sound can also be recorded and reproduced using digital signals and the errors can be reduced drastically in digital recording of the sound. For replaying the sound, audio has to be converted into digital form to produce digital audio in order to use it in the multimedia. And the digital audio system will then reconvert the entire digitised audio into analog form, which can be heard on the speaker. This two-way transformation of audio is know as analog-to-digital conversion and digital to analog conversion respectively. But the storage space required for digital audio is huge, somewhere around more that 1 MB for one minute of audio. The entire process of digitization is simple process of converting analog or electrical signal of audio to computer data file in the digital format. The microphone (which is normally used for recording) convert the voice into electrical signal or analog audio signal. Then the analog signal is passed into the audio input of a digital card or sound card. Once inside, the signal is fed into the analog to digital converter, which convert the analog audio signal to digital form and store it as computer data file. Playing back a digital audio file is just the reverse process of converting analog to digital. Once the digital audio file is sent to the sound card for playback the file is channelled through a converter and the digitised version of the original file is converted into analog and put into speaker. As constant or frequent conversions can reduce the sound quality, it is always advisable to keep all audio in digital format while working on a multimedia program.

A Digital signal processor is always embedded in the sound card to provide additional capabilities without affecting the CPU. A simple recording of digital sound can be done and may be compressed if desired. A common digital sound file existing in personal computers are know as. WAV files. The MIDI sound saves disk space as it only stores the instructions about how to play a musical instrument. It prestores the sound relating to the sound notes of various instruments and reproduces it when a voice signal asks for it. Several software which are used for creation of digital sound files (may be as. WAV file) are media player for windows.

🗁 **Digital Video :** Digitised video is one of the many technologies used in the development of interactive multimedia. It is one of the ways to play back and record video in multimedia program. It offers a wide range of flexibility as compared to standard video signal.

It is one of the ways to play back and record video in multimedia program. It offers a wide range of flexibility as compared to standard video signal. Video projects are created in two main phases : production and post production.

Capturing footage on video tape, once the footage has been host, the post production has started. The function of the post production phase is : editing creating effects, and adding titles.

Digital video editing involves converting video taped footage into data that can be stored on, and accessed from a computer hard disk. Digital video editing is non linear. Permitting any video clip, sound, edit, or effect to be removed without overwriting or changing the original clip. A non linear, open architecture digital video system is based on multi-step process that includes logging and digitizing source video, editing and post production and transferring final output to the video tape, CD-ROM, DVD or hard disk. These process are :

✓ Logging
✓ Capturing or digitizing
✓ Visual effects
✓ Composing
✓ Animation
✓ Titles
✓ Motion control
✓ Transitions
✓ Image processing and
✓ Digital video applications

Unlike regular video, quality of image would not degrade from copy to copy as digital video is make up of digital code and not an electrical analog signal. However, the final output depends on how the video image are converted to digital form during the development phase. Video signal comes from an external source such as TV or VCR or camera to the video-digitizer-card inside the system. Some systems use a digitizer card, which has dual function for both audio and video conversion. The process of converting analog video signal to digital format is called 'sampling'. Using this process, the converter card in the system converts the analog video signals into digital data streams so that these signals can be stored in the binary data structure format of 1s and 0s. the digital data file is them compressed to a considerable amount using some compression program. During this process the digitizer fuses the digital video into a digital movie format and saves all the sections of the compressed movie in the hard disk. Once the conversion and compression process is complete, the file can be played back on the computer screen. These digitised files can also be edited according to requirement using various video editing software. However, you may find that the video if used as full screen video may be jerky in certain machines. The main reason for this is that to present a moving picture, we have to store and process enormous amount of data, as we need to show 30 frames of continuous pictures per second considering one frame itself requires lot of data a moving pictures requires 30 times of it per second. However, standard such as Moving Pictures Expert Group (MPEG) have specified compression standards, which have enabled a full screen video. MPEG compression only records the frames and tries to predict the remaining frames from this key frame by comparing the changes of missing frame from key frames. Another technology, which is using this kind of compression, is video conferencing. ".AVI" files in windows basically contains interleaved data for audio/video. This compressed data can be decompressed and passed through a digital to analog converter to produce the video. These components of a multimedia system are integrated after they have been stored digitally by using Authoring software, which provide the necessary interactivity in the overall mix of information.

Q13. Explain the planning/designing, production and distribution phase of multimedia?

All the development works are based on these basic principles; planning and design, production and distribution of the final product, this is also true for multimedia development.

Planning/Design——————————>Production——————————>Distribution

- **Planning/Design of Multimedia :** During the initial design phase all the aspects of the related multimedia project is carefully thought about and planned, well before the production start. Every key element involved is discuss. There are various tools available to plan the project. A flowchart is one of them. If is one of the commonly used tools to prepare a blue print of the plan during the design phase. It shows how all the elements involved in the project are related to each other, with adequate information about their controlling features.

Like any other video program or movie, multimedia programs require a script a script on the subject involved. The script and flowchart works together to provide a printed version of text, graphics and sound to be used in the production of the multimedia program.

- **Production of Multimedia :** The process of creating the related media elements in multimedia project including graphics, sound, animation and digital video is called production. In multimedia all these creation of media elements, can even be independent in terms of tools used to produce them. For example, graphic elements are created independently using various computer graphic package such as Paintbrush, 3D studio etc. These are created and modified accordingly so as to work under various multimedia platforms. All the video scenes of the project are digitised and editing into various sequences and when the digitised video sequences has all the required scenes, titles and transitions, they are compressed to playback in the required speed and pre-defined sequence. The sound and music effect relevant to the project, and digitised scene sequences are created using digital recording system and MIDI (Musical Instrument Design Interface) equipment in a music studio, edited and converted into ASCII format and then modified later and placed at the appropriate location within the scene sequences. One of the most important production tasks in a project is regular checking of all the sequences.

Once, all the related media elements are created and digitised according to the specifications, then come the final stage of the production process i.e., joining or combining these media elements which is also know as authoring. This process is used to join all the independent media elements such as graphics, text, animation and sound to produce an interactive framework. The testing and debugging of the entire package is done at the stage before putting into distribution media. The first step authoring is to bring all the independent media elements used in the multimedia project, as each of them are developed using various graphics, audio, video and animation tools.

Once all graphics, text, animation and digital video are combined together, different relationship and action each of the media element can be worked out by adding interactive control. When multimedia program is executed, the interpreter part of the authoring. Program takes all necessary commands and relationships that has been define for each media elements and convert them into binary code or machine code that computer operating system can understand. The converted program is then executed by the CPU of the computer system, which sends out instructions to the system to play the music or audio, display the text, video and animation.

Multimedia productions are tailored to specifically meet the users needs, whether your needs include employee training, customer service, or product development and marketing. The basic facilities needed for multimedia production include video capture, video editing, photograph scanning and editing picture digitization morphing, of 2D and 3D models, and animation and authoring.

🗁 **Distribution of Multimedia :** Once all the media elements are combined together using authoring software they are bundled into package and stored in various storage media for distribution. Creating multimedia package for various platforms is one the most crucial stages that multimedia development procedure faces today. There are many platforms available for multimedia, each of which has their own advantages. To work with full potential, multimedia packages need to be available in as many platforms as possible. The main storage media used to store multimedia package is the CD-ROM. Distribution of Multimedia can also be made through Word Wide Web.

Q14. What is morphing? Describe a situation where it can be used.

[DEC02Q,1(c)]

#: What is Morphing? How is it similar/different to that of warping?

[DEC01,Q1(d)]

First of all morphing and warping are two different techniques of animation. The suitable work would be effects used for production. There is a lot of difference in both.

🗁 **Morphing:** Morphing takes two images and seamlessly changes one image to another. The second image actually seems to grow out of the first one. Morphing can also be used to show the pace of changes more clearly than photos. Morphing is used in Ads & Movies. Morphing is quite different than Warping.

Warping: Warping is variation of the morphing where one image is used to show various changes that is take place. It uses the key points of one image to create different effects, instead of mixing up two images.

Q15. What are the various sound formats that may be allowed in multimedia? Describe in detail any one of them. [JUN03,Q1(c)]

The various sound formats that may be allowed in multimedia are :

✓ CDA
✓RAM
✓ MIDI
✓ MJF
✓XM
✓S3M
✓ STM
✓ MOD
✓ DSM
✓ WAV
✓ WMA
✓ M3U
✓ DAT
✓ MP3

MIDI Description:

🗁 **MIDI :** MIDI or musical system interface is the second most popular type of PC sound. MIDI was not designed for the PC; it was created for the Musicians, to allow them to create, store and play a broad cross Section of instruments, including those invented on synthesizers. A MIDI file can be best described as " electronic sheet music".

Role and Subsystems : The sound card is part of the multimedia subsystem. It plays music and sound from digital files within the PC, and also plays audio from audio CDs played on an optical drive. The speakers connect to the sound card to actually play the music.

Related Components : The sound card is most closely related to the optical drive and the motherboard.

Key Compatibility Selection Criteria : Here are the key criteria to consider in selecting a sound card and speakers

Interface : Sound cards can connect to the system using either an ISA slot or a PCI slot. ISA slots are more commonly found on older machines PCI is the trend for the future. If you are planning to reuse an older ISA card in a new system, be sure there is an available ISA slot in the motherboard.

Resource Availability : Sound cards are notorious for using a large number of system resources interrupt request lines (IRQs), direct memory access channels (DMAs) and I/ O addresses. On a new system the PC maker will take care of these issues, but if you are upgrading or adding a card to a system, be sure to check for availability of resources. The fancier the card, the more likely it will require a lot of resources.

SoundBlaster Compatibility : The SoundBlaster was one of the first sound cards and became a virtual standard in the PC world. Virtually all cards are compatible with at least one version of the SoundBlaster family, and this is something you want to make sure you have, especially for games.

Performance and Capacity Selection Criteria : Generally speaking, the more you spend on the card, the more performance you get from it, but it's debatable as to how important this really is. You want to be sure to look for a card that supports wave table playback, not just FM synthesis, as this will give you much better sound. Beyond that, you are paying for support for more simultaneous "voices", faster processing and so on. As I have mentioned, these are really of primary interest if you are heavily into gaming, otherwise virtually any sound card will do the job.

Speakers are pretty much the same story : paying more gets you more power (volume) and better quality. Virtually any speakers will work for occasional gaming, but if you want the full gaming experience you need to use either good speakers or a home stereo system.

Quality Selection Criteria : Name-brand cards are all fairly reliable and quality problems are not great. Sound cards usually come down to a comparison of features, and just avoiding the "really cheap" ones that can be of poor quality.

As for speakers, this is one place where you really do get only what you pay for. Cheap speakers generally sound like junk; if all you can afford is $20 for a couple of teeny speakers then you will be able to hear what sounds and music your software is producing, but that's about it. If you can, consider using a patch cord from the sound card to the auxiliary input of a stereo system; the sound produced by even an economy portable stereo will be much better than what you get from most inexpensive computer speakers. If you can't do this and you are on a budget, I personally would spend more on the speakers and less on sound card features.

To test if a PC's sound system sounds good or bad due to its sound card or its speakers, try using a good pair of headphones in the output jack of the sound card. Or better, try different sets of speakers with the same sound card on the same system.

Q16. What is MIDI in the context of multimedia? Describe one application of it. [JUN02,Q1(c)]

Musical Instrument Digital Interface, or MIDI, is a system designed to transmit information between electronic musical instruments.

MIDI allows computers, synthesizers, sound cards and drum machines to control one another, and to exchange system information. Though modern computer sound-cards are MIDI-compatible and capable of creating realistic instrument sounds, the fact that sound cards' MIDI synthesizers have historically produced sounds of dubious quality has tarnished the image of a general purpose computer as a MIDI instrument.

MIDI is almost directly responsible for bringing an end to the "wall of synthesizers" phenomenon in 1970s-80s rock music concerts, when musical keyboard perfomers were sometimes hidden behind banks of various instruments. Following the advent of MIDI, many synthesizers were released in rack-mount versions, enabling performers to control multiple instruments from a single keyboard. Another important effect of MIDI has been the development of hardware and computer-based sequencers, which can be used to record, edit and play back performances. Synchronisation of MIDI sequences is made possible by the use of MIDI timecode, an implementation of the SMPTE time code standard using MIDI messages, and MIDI timecode has become the standard for digital music synchronization.

MIDI can also be used for applications other than music:

theatre lighting

special effects

recording system synchronization

audio processor control

computer networking, as demonstrated by the early first-person shooter game.

Q17. What is MIDI Messages? Explain its functioning.

MIDI messages transmit information between MIDI devices and determine what kinds of musical events can be passed from device to device. The format of MIDI messages consists of the *status byte* (the first byte of ant MIDI message) which describes the kind of message, and *data bytes* (the following bytes). MIDI messages are divided into two different types :

🗁 **MUSIC**

✓ **Channel Messages :** Channel messages go only to specified devices. There are two types of channel message:

Channel voice messages send actual performance data between MIDI devices, describing keyboard action and control panel changes. They describe music by defining pitch, amplitude, timbre, duration and other sound qualities. Each message has at least one and usually two data bytes that accompany the status byte to describe these sound qualities. Examples of channel voice messages are *Note On, Note Off, Channel Pressure, Control Change, etc*.

Channel mode messages determine the way that a receiving MIDI device responds to channel voice messages. They set the MIDI channel receiving modes for different Midi devices, stop spurious notes from playing and affect local control of a device. Examples of such messages are *Local Control, All Notes Off, Omni Mode Off, etc.*

✓ **System Messages :** System Messages go to all devices in a MIDI system because no channel numbers are specified. There are three types of system messages:

System real-time messages are very short and simple, consisting of only one byte. They carry extra data with the. These messages synchronize that timing of MIDI devices in performance; therefore, it is important that they be sent at precisely the time they are required. To avoid delays, these messages are sent in the middle of other messages, if necessary. Examples of such messages are System Reset, Timing Clock (MIDI clock), etc

System exclusive messages allow MIDI manufacturers to be create customized MIDI messages to send between their MIDI devices. This coding starts with a system-exclusive-message, where the manufacturer is specified, and *ends with an end-of-exclusive* message.

The main issue in current MIDI-based computer music system is *interactivity.* Music is a temporal art, and any computer program dealing with music must have sophisticated facilities for representing point in time. This capability of music applications became possible because of increased computational speeds (e.g., the computational). Therefore, current computer music systems are able to modify their behavior in response to input from other performing musicians.

Q18. What is Multimedia? What are its advantages? Where can one use Multimedia? [DEC01,Q1(a)]

The term multimedia is often associated with the information superhighway, or with interactive TV that can produce videos (information on demand) or with hypermedia. However, multimedia can be considered as text, graphics, images video and audio in computer. One of the key features of multimedia is Interactivity. It may, convey enriched interactive information to its users.

Multimedia system support the physical and logical coexistance and interactive use of heterogeneous media classes such as print, audio and video in specific application environments.

About the above definitions the question is whether multimedia is a computer itself or a computer software product. In practical sense it is the combination of both. The fact remains that it has best potential to be one of the most powerful form of communicating ideas, searching for information and experiencing new concept of common media ever developed.

Advantage of Multimedia :

The basic advantage of multimedia over the conventional from of media, which uses sound graphics and text for example, TV, audio etc. is the interactive feature of multimedia. For example, a multimedia version of news bulletin would be the situation where you can request the broadcaster the type of news you are interested in, when you want to hear it, and with the press of a button or click of the mouse you can hear the news.

Multimedia can be used in various fields :

- ✓ Education
- ✓ Corporate Training
- ✓ Medical and health care
- ✓ Entertainment
- ✓ Marketing
- ✓ Publishing
- ✓ Web etc.

Q19. What do you mean by animation ? Describe two applications of animation.

[JUN01,Q1(ii)]

Animation : The word animation comes from a latin word Anima meaning to breath. If anything breaths means it has life & thus animation means to bring life i.e. to make or give moments to any object or thing. This can be any object created on computer. An animation is just a continuous series of still images that are displayed in a sequence. There are mainly two types of animation used in multimedia, namely, 2D and 3D animation. 2D animation also known as cell (pixel based) animation, is the most common kind of animation, where flat images are drawn one frame at a time. This process is very time consuming but result obtained is spectacular in nature. Computer animation has increased the efficiency, and enhanced the results of cell animation with introduction of wide ranges of colour and speed. In 3-D animation mathematical model of 3-D object is created to realistically portray with depth. Now it has become a common media element in film, video and multimedia packages. 3-D animations follow mainly three steps; modelling, animation and rendering.

There are endless examples of the applications of animation. Two examples where it is used are following :

In Analysis and Understanding British Telecom for example uses a sophisticated program that plots on a map of the U.K. the density of telephone fault reports using different colours. When a storm was plotted on top of this map, and the whole system was animated it could be seen that the density of the faults increased at areas from which the storm had just passed. It would have been very difficult to visualise this in a different way.

Astronomers also rely on computers to do animations of high speed jets penetrating different gases in order to determine why a few galaxies flare dramatically. This research has given out valuable information about why some galaxies flare into broad plumes and why some others remain extremely straight and narrow.

In Teaching

On of the most difficult things in teaching, is communicating ideas effectively. This might be very difficult in complex situations, and here is where animation might help to convey information. For example there are many programs that show the planetary system in action in three dimensions - an idea that would be very difficult to grasp otherwise.

Q20. Compare and contrast the following in the context of Multimedia:
(a) CD-ROM and DVD **[JUN01,Q1(i)]**

🗁 **CD-ROM :** CDROM is widely used for multimedia storage as it has an amazing amount of flexibility and potential as multimedia storage and distribution medium. One CD-ROM can hold up to one and half hour of digital audio or around 700 to 750 MS of computer data for that matter.

To install a CD-ROM drive, there must be a free bay and the computer system also have a sound card installed or a square slot into either a card or CD-ROM drive can be placed. Before installation all the jumper setting should be properly done according to the specification. Once the CD-ROM drive is fitted in the drive bay with proper jumper setting, necessary software can be installed to make the CD-ROM drive work.

🗁 **DVD :** DVD is the short for Digital Video Disc now it is more commonly referred to as "digital Versatile Disc" as it has many potential applications than video. DVD is the cohesion of multimedia and digital video player, movies and interactivity. By employing the latest advances in digital technology, DVD can hold up 25 times more digital info than a CD-ROM and DVD can be used to create innovative cutting edge video-discs with all sorts of data including director's cuts, photo galleries, interview with actors in fact practically anything today's video producers can imagine. Using DVD technology. Besides multilingual capabilities of DVD the producers can create a limitless range of interactive titles, instead of watching a video in the linear fashion as with traditional videotape.

(b) Analog Video and Digital Video **[JUN01,Q1(i)][JAN01,Q1(i)]**

	Analog video		**Digital video**
1.	Analog video can be classified as interlaced.	1.	Digital video can be classified as non-interlaced.
2.	Video programs like SECAM(broad casting standards) are interlaced where each frame consisting two fields displayed in two passes.	2.	Most PC displays uses progressive slams in which all lines in a frame are displayed in one pass from top to bottom before next frame.
3.	A frame of an interlaced video is divided into fields. Each field contains every horizontal line.	3	While for the digital video frame, the whole frame is read from top to bottom then to the next.
4.	Due to the analog we see a flicker affect (horizontal line moving down.	4.	Due to the digital format the flicker effect is eliminated.
5.	Due to our T.V. being analog devices all the broadcasting is done on analog video.	5.	Computer related work & post production work is done using digital videos.
6.	VHS are examples of analog videos.	6.	VCD, DVD,are examples of digital video.
7.	Analog cameras are used to capture the shots.	7.	Now we get digital cameras to capture the shot.

(c) Icon based and Time based multimedia authoring softwares. **[JUN01,Q1(d)]**

With **icon-based** authoring tools, non-technical multimedia authors can build sophisticated applications without scripting. By placing icons on a flow line, you can quickly sequence events and activities, including decisions and user interactions. These tools are useful for story boarding, as you can change sequences, add options, and restructure interactions by simply dragging and dropping icons. You can print out your navigation map or flowchart, an annotated project index with or without associated icons, design and presentation windows, and a cross-reference table of variables.

Time-based systems are popular multimedia authoring tools. Each uses its own distinctive approach and user interface for managing events over time. Many use a visual timeline for sequencing the events of a multimedia presentation, often displaying layers of various media elements or events alongside the scale in increments as precise as one second. Others arrange long sequences of graphic frames and add the time component by adjusting each frame's duration of play.

(d) Analog audio and Digital audio **[JAN01,Q1(i)]**

	Analog Audio		Digital Audio
1.	When we hold a microphone up. in the air & screen, the microph one connects the changes in the air & connects into a electric voltage.This is known as analog signal	1.	Digital audio is a technological process whereby an analog audio is first converted into a continous stream of numbers.This is known as digital audio
2.	Analog audio when plotted on a paper it would look like a graph	2.	But where as digital audio give the output in series of 0 & 1
3.	The recording is done on a magnatic tape for further play modes	3.	The recording done on a hard disk or any media which supports digital format
4.	The output device for an analog sound is a simple speakers.	4.	The output device of a digitized audio is amplified speakers which are built in.
5.	The quality of the sound output is less	5.	Here the sound quality is excellent.
6.	Editing a analog audio piece is quite difficult & time consuming & less accurate.	6.	Digital audio editing gives high quality output with less complexi ty & less time consuming. Accuracy level is high.

(e) Analog image and Digital image **[JAN01,Q1(i)]**

	Analog Image		Digital Image
1.	A normal image which is sketched or even has been printed is a Analog Image	1.	When any image created on a computer or scanned into the PC becomes a Digital Image.
2.	Analog images are in one format only	2.	Digital images are in many formats like Triff,JPEG,etc.
3.	Analog images are in only of one type	3.	While there are two types of Digital Images.Bitmap & Vector image.
4.	Examples of Analog Image are paintings , Sketches,Cartoons etc.	4.	Examples of Dogital Images are all images which are in computers.

(f) JPEG and MPEG **[JAN01,Q1(i)]**

The JPEG (joint photographic expert group) standard is for compressing continuous still pictures. It is normally used to encode 24-bit RGB video images and will leave out some of the minor picture details for the sake of simplicity. It produces a compression ration of 20:1 for still images without any appreciable degradation of pictures. This is a popular standard on Macintosh and Amiga platforms.

MPEG (Moving Picture Expert Group) is compression standard for compressing video since 1993. MPEG was developed specifically for motion images. MPEG can compress both audio and video. It produces a compression ration of 50:1 before the degradation in picture quality occurs. MPEG standard allows fast video and audio compression, and real time decompression. MPEG allows a decompression data rate of 1.2 to 1.5 M per second, thus, allowing full motion, full screen video.

	JPEG		MPEG
1.	JPEG-joint people exprt group.	1.	MPEG-motion picture expert group.
2.	Digital format for an image.	2.	Digital format for a movie chip.
3.	Compressed format for a digital image.	3.	Compressed format for a digital video.
4.	High compression rate but the quality is same for image.	4.	Quality does not reduce a seven then compression is done.
5.	Used for image on web & multimedia presentation.	5.	Used for movies on the web & of course for multimedia presentation.

Q21. Describe the features that you will consider while selecting a development

tool for the following multimedia components: **[DEC02,Q3]**

(a) Sound/Audio

(b) Graphics

(c) Animation

(a) Various features can be kept in mind while selecting a development tool for **Sound / Audio :** (i) Quality, how much efficient is the tool for processing the sound quality ?. How much sample rate supported by the software? What are the formats supported by the software? and one more important feature is whether it is able to support cross platform files or not.

Because multimedia applications use audio in the form of music and /or speech, music and its MIDI standard, as well as speech synthesis, speech recognition and speech transmission so all these should also be kept in mind while selecting the tool.

(b) Various features can be kept in mind while selecting a development tool for **Graphics :** Graphics is the most predominant component of a multimedia. Graphics may be used in many form such as photos, charts for illustration and summarizing numerical data, environments simulation, logos, and colors that illustrate the content of the application.

So it is kept in mind whether all these features should be available in the tool. Besides all these graphics specific features others are also important like, Quality, how much efficient is the tool for processing the image quality ?. What are the formats supported by the software? and one more important feature is whether it is able to support cross platform files or not.

(c) Various features can be kept in mind while selecting a development tool for **Animation :** Animation also plays vital part in the multimedia program. The dedicated hardware and software built into the system increases the animation speed.

Support of 2D and 3D animation should be there as day by day 3D is the most demanded among the users.

Quality, how much efficient is the tool for processing the animation quality ?. How much frame rate supported by the software? What are the formats supported by the software? and one more important feature is whether it is able to support cross platform files or not.

NOTE : And for tools for all the three discussed above SPEED and PRICE are also the two of the concern while selecting development tool. As tool should be price efficient means we should get "value for money" and at the same time speed also matters.

CHAPTER 2

APPLICATIONS OF MULTIMEDIA

- **Introduction**
- **Objectives**
- **Application Areas for Multimedia**
  - ✓*Entertainment*
  - ✓*Edutainment*
  - ✓*Business Communications*
  - ✓*Knowledge Transfer*
  - ✓*Public Access*
- **Publishing Industry and Multimedia**
- **Communication Technology and Multimedia Services**
- **Multimedia in Business**
- **Multimedia Pedagogues: Interactive Systems for Teaching and Learning**
  - ✓*Simulations*
  - ✓*Multimedia Composition*
  - ✓*Multimedia and Explanatory Systems*
  - ✓*Technological Challenge for Developers*
- **Concepts for Distributed Learning Environment**
- **A Medical Application: Mednet-A Medical Collaboration and Consultation System**

In the First chapter, we have discussed about the digital multimedia-system technology that is, hardware and software for multimedia. We have also presented, in brief, the development methodology for multimedia packages, and gave you hints about the applications of multimedia. The multimedia technology as a standalone technology is quite useful, however, the use of multimedia system is only partial if we do not integrate it with communication technology. The integration of multimedia and communication technology has resulted in bringing down the geographical distances.

In this chapter, we will present various scenarios where multimedia technology is used along with communication technology to form powerful applications. Please not that all the applications mentioned in this chapter involve multimedia. However, you may find many similar kind of applications which do not use multimedia technology.

In fact, boundary between multimedia and non-multimedia products is getting blurred and will cease to exist in near future then all the applications will have multimedia facility. We have not covered all the applications of multimedia in this chapter; only a representative sample is presented.

In this chapter, we have presented a broad overview of various types of applications that may be available on networked or standalone multimedia platforms. Our discussions are focussed on only few applications, but it does not mean that these are the only applications currently available. Many people are working in this area for bringing out more and more applications. The areas of application may be very different, however, they may be incorporating some of the concepts discussed in this chapter. You should also keep on exploring about newer applications and newer ideas, specially relating to Multimedia on Internet, where lot of newer applications are appearing.

Q1. What are the application areas for multimedia?
 # Explain the use of multimedia in the following areas:
Entertainment, Edutainment, Business Communications, Knowledge Transfer, Public Access.
 # What are the application areas for multimedia?

With the advancement of technology many applications are evident for the multimedia technology. The advancement of technology has opened up news field for the application development. One such fields, which is having tremendous potential and falls under the broad preview of multimedia, is virtual reality, may be the tool of tomorrow. Today, virtual reality is primarily used in applications in entertainment industry but is going to be very useful tool for performing simulative, remote control applications. Virtual reality will have a tremendous impact on on-job training sector. In the following sections we well present a board categorization multimedia applications.

✓***Entertainment*** **:** The entertainment industry has used this technology the most create real life like games. Several developers have used graphics, sound animation of multimedia to create variety of games. The special technologies such as virtual reality have made these games just like experiences of real life. Our such example is flight simulator which creates a real-life imaging

Many multimedia games are now available on computers. The children can enjoy these experiences, for example, they can drive cars of different variety, fly aircraft, play any musical instrument, golf etc. Multimedia productions are also using creation of many movies where the multimedia components are mixed with real life pictures to create powerful entertainment atmosphere.

✓***Edutainment*** **:** Edutainment is nothing but educational entertainment. Many computer games with focus on education are now available. Example, in this case is an educational game, which plays various rhymes for little kids. In addition to playing rhymes, the child can paint the pictures, increase reduce size of various objects etc. Similarly many other edutainment packages, which provide a lot of details information of kids, are available. Microsoft has produced many such CD-based multimedia such as Sierra, Knowledge Adventure etc. Which in addition to play provide some sort of learning component. The latest in this series is a package, which teaches about the computer using games playing. There are many more companies which have specialized in entertainment sector you may explore the list of such companies on the net.

✓***Business Communications*** : Multimedia is a very powerful tool for enhancing the quality of business communications. The business communications such as employee related communications, product promotions, customer information, and reports for investors can be presented in multimedia form. All these business communications are required to be structures such that a formal level of content structure exists in the communication. Other common business application involving multimedia requires access to database of multimedia information about a company. The multimedia technology of today can easily support this application as natural language enquiry systems do exit for making queries.

The options available for business presentation are varied but which one would work best for the suggested application depends on how multimedia is used. Some of the presentation types are:

- Keyboard Interactive Station
- Interactive Touch screen Kiosk
- Sequential Playback
- Continuous Loop Playback

Interactive kiosks are probably one of the most versatile of the multimedia tools currently available. They allow the user direct and active control over the information being given, making kiosks perfect for applications such as navigational guides and product information displays. They combine the strengths of speed and accessibility with sight and sound to create not only an effective means of information dissemination, but also a memorable and fun to use method great for all ages and levels of computer experience.

Keyboard Stations allow the user, usually an employee, to step through the presentation with a customer, giving visual backups to the verbal information that the speaker is bestowing. Because this type of presentation waits for the operator, it allows the customer to ask as many questions as they need to without having the presentation run ahead. It works more like a slide show that a movie. It can also be programmed to work like a touch screen kiosk without the cost of the touch screen.

Touch screen presentations are gaining in popularity. They are fun to use and allow the user direct control over the information they receive. It operates unattended and can be updated with new information as needed. They make wonderful navigational guides also.

Sequential presentations are perfect for in-store windows displays, or in other areas where direct user access is either not available or not desired. At trade shows, where interaction with potential customers is preferred, a continuously playing sequential presentation can be used to capture attention and get viewers engaged in conversation with sales representatives about job particulars. A non-continuous sequential presentation has applications such as corporate training and initial product demonstration where you don't need to have the same information playing over and over again. This type operate just like a regular video.

✓***Knowledge Transfer*** : This kind of application involves transmission of a piece of information with the maximum impact, that is the transfer of information in such a fashion that it facilitates the retention. This application is meant for academic and business both.

In academies, the knowledge transfer is used as the building block, whereas, in business it is the effective transfer of information which might be essential for the survival of a business. Multimedia based teaching is gaining momentum as powerful teaching aids are quite common. Multimedia is one of the best ways to provide short-term training to the workers in a business houses. It gives lot of flexibility in providing training.

✓ ***Public Access*** **:** Public Access is an area of application where many multimedia applications will soon be available. One such application may be the tourist information system, where a person who wants to go for a sight seeing trip may have the glimpse of places he has selected for visiting. Using Multimedia. Many such applications may be developed providing a repository of information. For example, for a very simple public information, that is, the Railway Time table enquiry, a multimedia based system may not only display the trains and time but also the route map of the destination from the source you have desired.

Q2. Explain the role of multimedia in publishing industry.

Before discussing the role of multimedia in publications its very important to understand what does publication means. The publishing industry can be classified according to the market it caters for. One of the classifications is based on the information, which is presented in published text, for example; a publication may be for reference purposes or archival purposes or tutorials. It can also be grouped on the basis of the community for which a particular publication is meant, such as, for the family, or the school children or professional persons or the academics. The publication media for all above categories, traditionally, way printed texts.

But today publishing industry has changed drastically because of availability of Multimedia. The publications which are meant for family such as newspapers, family magazines etc. are readily available on-line, that is in multimedia form giving real life experiences.

For example, the on-line-news clippings are not only read but can also be experienced by seeing the video film associated with it. Examples in this category are: Microsoft Multimedia, the life and composition of Bethovan etc. where a rich mix of sound, visuals, and moving is provided for publication.

The publishing industry is being transformed through the use of multimedia and high speed networks. The market for media products is expanding rapidly as homes and businesses are connected to fibre networks. The publishing industry is divided into three major markets : education, entertainment and professional publishing.

Entertainment publishing can focus on the home or mobile system using all media professional publishing is probably the largest sector of the three and includes information whose value to companies ranges from the very short term such as stock prices, through the medium term such as company reports and world news to the long term such as directories of people and organizations. Publishers must commission and collect material, package it and distribute it to the target niche or broad markets. Given the volume of medium, the breadth of the market, and the value of the information to be published, fibre and wireless networks are two to routes for both the collection and distribution of material.

Publishing industry is very useful for multimedia. The largest amount of data, picture and graphics are captured through the help of multimedia software and putting on the required publishing materials.

Electronic publications consisting of user controlled education, interactive novels or stories, or educational/information based activity are eligible. School publishing materials are intended for class room use at the elementary through postgraduate level these are making interactive and intellectual for the user.

Thus, multimedia publishing has a great potential and will be the technology, which has tremendous potential. The multimedia technology also supports the process of collaborative development of documents for printing, thus, makes process of publishing faster and better.

The publishing meant for children has changed tremendously with the advent of multimedia. Today many encyclopedia and books providing a sort of edutainment are available. The advantages of using multimedia on these books are evident from the type of media rich experiences these CD-ROM based product provide. For example, an Atlas encyclopedia may not only allow you to pinpoint the location of Delhi in India but also shows you a Road map of Delhi showing several historical sites. A dictionary meant for children not only shows the meaning of the words but can also show its characteristics for example a tiger may be defined as a wild animal and along with that a movie in which tiger is shown in his natural habitat. Thus this kind of media rich experiences are much more entertaining and provide better learning environment for children.

In fact, we believe that for increasing general awareness of a child, multimedia is the best tool available us today. However, still the reading habits, listening habits, playing attention etc. are the capabilities on which the education will rely upon.

For professionals, today many a products are available in the market. For example, how to tackle many management-oriented issues, can be presented in multimedia form. Professionals, however, can use multimedia technology for on-line video-conferencing, on-line document editing etc. functions.

As far as academics are concerned multimedia publishing is a boon or get information from World Wide Web. Today, if a researcher wants to refer to conference proceedings, all he has to do buy a CD produced for it. This CD normally contains abstracts, paper presentations, reports presentation etc. The other advantage an Academician gets by having such a detail on CD is that his search through the material can be faster, as in general, several indexes are being provided in the CDs.

Thus, Multimedia publishing has a great potential and will be the technology, which has tremendous potential.

Q3. What is communication technology & multimedia services?
#What are the communication technology in the field of multimedia and what are their services?

The advances of computing, communication and creation of relevant standards have lead to the beginning of an era where people getting multimedia facilities at home. Many be in the form of an Interactive T.V or through the World Wide Web. Cable TV and telephone companies dot com companies, publishing industry etc.

are the main infrastructure providers for these facilities. The networking technology along with the improved compiling and compression technologies are delivering interactive services profitably. The entertainment cable, telephone, and internet passed industries companies are trying to design wide variety of such multimedia services.

These services may include:

✓ Basic Television Services

✓ Interactive entertainment

✓ Video on demand

✓ Home shopping through e-mail

✓ Financial transactions using e-commerce

✓ Interactive single and multimedia games

✓ Digital multimedia libraries

✓ Electronic versions of newspapers, magazines etc.

Today Personal Computers are the tool that promotes collaboration. They are essential to any multimedia workstations. Many high-speed networks are in place that allows multimedia conferencing, or electronic conferencing. Such facilities are even available today through Internet also. Today, we have to depend on our telephone to link us with others, whether it is a phone call or a group audio conference or dialup Internet connection. However, tomorrow it will be sort of based link that link us with other. A Computer-based multimedia conference allows us to exchange audio, text, image, and even video information. It also facilitates group development of documents and other information products. Let us discuss more about these concepts in greater details.

Q4. What is the use of multimedia in business?
#"Role of multimedia in business as the Global Team". Explain. How a multimedia is help full in business.

The multimedia technology along with communication technology has opened the door for formation of global work groups. Today, the team members may be working anywhere, and can work for various companies. These team members may:

✓ be in different cities or countries,

✓ speak different languages.

Thus, the work place will become global. If such is the future of a business then the multimedia network should support the following facilities.

🗀 ***Voice Mail* :** Voice mail is a tool, which communicates voice over a line. A recorded voice is better than having no voice. A, mail based system is not person dependent. The voice mail however, has the obvious limitation that it handle only audio information, however audio information is sufficient for quick and simple exchange of information.

Please note that voice mail is time-and location-independent. However, a voice mail system is non-interactive, that is if you want to get a ready then you have to wait however you can send and receive voice mail quickly.

🗀 **Electronic *Mail* :** Electronic mail is preferred than the voice mail to exchange information for the cases, which require wider distribution of complex information. In general the written word leaves less room for misinterpretation. In addition the word file are easier to store and retrieve.

The future electronic mail software must handle voice and video, FAX, and graphic information. In addition the user interface for e-mail should be very easy. Electronic mail is also time-and location-independent, however it is non-interactive.

🗀 **Multimedia *based FAX* :** FAX, in general, is better accepted than electronic mail because:

✓ it can be used to send detailed information

✓ is easier to use

✓ handles graphic information

✓ provides a printed copy of information.

FAX provides a non-interactive interface to the user. Today's multimedia PCs are equipped with FAX-modem card and the FAX message gets stored electronically in gradually become blurred and will gradually fade out.

🗀 **Office *Needs* :** The activities in an office such as meetings, group discussions, training are some areas where we need the concept such as brainstorming, sharing of idea, problem solving etc. for real-time meetings that involve geographically disperse group of people we can avail the choices as:

✓ Audio conferencing

✓ Video conferencing, or

✓ Document conferencing.

🗀 **Audio *Conferencing* :** This technology allows 'out-of-town' people to participate in a formal meeting. This technology can also be used by a group of people to meet frequently whatsoever is the physical distance among them. Audio conferencing is an effective means of communication for reporting about a project status. If can be used to solve problems quickly. One of the disadvantages of audio conferencing is that such conferences are restricted to only voice, so this conference can be preceded by sending email of documents that are to be used during the conference. The second disadvantage is that the person who is not proficient in spoken words cannot participate well in such conference.

Audio conferencing technology was first only in the conference room but is now available on desktop machines.

🗀 **Video *Conferencing* :** Video conferencing is being used successfully by several organization abroad. Video conferencing resembles an office meeting; thus, require setting of time, preparing rooms and place, agenda etc. However the biggest drawback is the cost of the equipment.

Video conferencing brings people together naturally and simulate a real life meeting environment. Today video conferencing has been brought to the computer however; it is not easy to use, as the participant has continuously look at the camera on the top of his machine.

🗀 **Document *Conferencing* :** Document conferencing, also called audio-graphic conferencing technology, allows people to meet using their PCs and telephone lines. The telephone lines connect the participants so they can share audio information and the data they have stored in their PC. In addition, it allows on line editing of a document by several participating people in the conference. This conferencing technology has been used in the education filed. It extends the boundaries of the classroom and reach out into the community. A document that can be used in the conference may consist of text, graphics, sound or even video clippings.

Q5. What are the E-Commerce based applications of multimedia?

Electronic commerce is an emerging model of new selling and merchandising tools in which buyers are able to participate in all phases of a purchase decision, while stepping through those processes electronically rather than in a physical store or by phone (with a physical catalog). The processes in electronic commerce include enabling a customer to access product information. Select items to purchase, items securely, and have the purchase setting financially. The multimedia technology may be used for presentation of information through the web for such systems. e.g. The products details can better be presented by use of multimedia like using animation, graphics and sound. A product's presentation can be made better which ease the consumer in understanding the product and make them comfortable with online purchase.

E-Commerce applications are available for Business-to-business transactions, Business-to-consumer transaction and for the Intra-Company (Enterprise) transactions

The basic requirements for an e-commerce based application are to develop an on-line catalog and handle transactions on-line. This can manage large product assortment and complete sales at lower costs.

Q6. What are the areas in education, except preparing a tutorial, where multimedia may be used? Describe one example for each identified area. [JUN01,Q4]

#: How can multimedia be used in education ? Describe an example of multimedia used in education ? Describe an example of multimedia used in education. How is it going to be advantageous in comparison to printed books ? [JAN01,Q2]

Apart from making use of multimedia in preparing tutorial in education field multimedia can also be used in developing Encyclopedia and Database production. e.g. an Encyclopedia production may provide Indexing by dates to create linear topics Multimedia source include unique sound still images, animations and video clips usually distributed on CD-ROM.

Multimedia with real time speed experience for printed books can be readily available online, that is the real time experience of multimedia. Solve question answer can be stored in CD-ROM. Printed books are not only read but you can seeing this printed books by video films through multimedia.

In these days Encyclopedia and books providing a sort of edutainment are available. Except preparing tutorial in the areas of education it (multimedia) can be used very rapidly as fastly in Encyclopedia and Database productions for example Encyclopedia Production is providing the indexing to create linear topics by dates.

Multimedia include verified (unique) sound, still images, video clips and animations usually distributed on CD-ROM.

Pedagogues are useful teaching aids only if they stimulate and motivate the students. The audio-visual support to a pedagogue can actually help in doing so. A multimedia tutor can provide multiple numbers of challenges to the student to stimulate his interest in a topic. The instructions provided by pedagogue have moved beyond providing only button level control to intelligent simulations, dynamic creation of links, composition and collaboration and system testing of the user interactions. Let us look at one of the examples of pedagogues:

🗁 **Simulations :** This is an important area of pedagogy where a student is engaged in situations of problem solving. Simulations are mainly categorized in two main form:

✓ Scenario based simulations

✓ Knowledge based simulations.

Scenario based simulations, which use video, graphics and sound to engage the student in a particular situation. However, these scenario-based tutors have limited answer and suggestions to offer.

Knowledge based simulations are more intelligent as far as behavior is concerned are adaptive to student needs, however, are difficult to design.

Q 7. Suggest suitable areas from your curriculum where multimedia can be used for teaching English (as per course CS610). Give details in the form of objectives, target audience, resource requirements and advantages of making multimedia for the area/application suggested. [DEC02,Q4]

Multimedia the type of technology that can express by their own. In school generally we use multimedia in form of games or computer or for giving any lecture to large number of students with the use of projector.

(A) Objective to Use:

Multimedia for teaching English in school are :

1. Class room : We can teach student with the help of multimedia CD of English speaking in which our main target will be object available in the classroom like

(i) Black Board / Check board

(ii) Communication with friends

A General communication with in a class with other student will be the main another objective to teach English.

2. Communication with senior students : The senior students who are well matured generally discourage the juniors is the main problems with the help of their English speaking ability the young or junior students can make or built their good impact. Their seniors can also help to improve their mental ability and patience to learn English.

3. Communication with teachers : With their daily routine students have to talk with their teachers depending on their problems which requires general permission, student should know how to take small permissions.

(B) Target Audience : Over target Audience will be student as well as teacher also and the parents of the student in their parents meeting.

(C) Recourse Requirement

1. English Story Book
2. Computer
3. Speakers
4. Projector
5. English Movie
6. Film Animated English Cartoon CD
7. Special Multimedia CD for Children for English Speaking Purpose

Besides the many technical considerations of hardware and software configuration for a multimedia project, the design process must also be separated into its various components. Although using a multimedia tool is in some ways similar to programming a computer, we saw in examining the development spectrum that it is also very different. In addition, these tools necessitate not only technical competence, but also a knowledge of the material to be conveyed and an idea of how that information can most effectively be displayed. This reveals three important areas to consider while developing a multimedia application in a teaching/learning environment:

(i) Content
(ii) Presentation
(iii) Programming

Advantage of multimedia in these areas:-

Content : The content is the important information which is being conveyed through the multimedia application. The gathering, refining and composing of this information is the most crucial task in creating a multimedia application. Often content which is included in an application is outside of the range of expertise of the actual developers of the applications. This is specially true for applications developed within an academic environment and it is important that someone with a degree of expertise in the subject matter. Contribute substantially to the project especially in the planning phase. It's the common mistake among people wishing to use multimedia that the responsibility for providing contents with the same individuals who create the application. An effective application is created when the strength of a application developer combines throughly with content expert.

Presentations : The aesthetic appearance of the multimedia application and the composition of the variety of media are very important in conveying the content of an application. The color scheme used in the user interface designed, and the integration of various media, are all elements of consideration in designing a professional quality multimedia presentation. This task requires that the developer has an artistic ability, or that someone with an artistic ability be specially designated to work on the application with a strong visual and audible presentation material which can be effectively communicated. When the choreography of an application is awkward, limited, or weak it will distract the user, making the information have less impact.

Programming : Generally the people who develop multimedia application have some degree of computer literacy, and as a result may be familiar with programming. Since, most applications are very related to programming. Either through a graphical flowchart of icons or the use of a scripting language, this technical competence is very important. Increasingly, however it is the case that multimedia tools are being designed are becoming easier to use. It is also necessary, as many tools besides the main development applications will be used which requires an understanding of different file formats and methods of data generation.

These three critical areas of application of multimedia development are very interrelated and are definitely not mutually exclusive. Teaching occurs best when the three areas can be understood and integrated, and when a balance exists between the areas of content, presentation and programming.

Q8. "Multimedia is stronger than multiple-media as it is interactive in nature." Comment on the above statement. [DEC02,Q1]

"Multimedia is stronger than multiple media as it is interactive in nature". Multimedia is an integration of various media, which convey the information with computing technology various media, such as text, graphics, animation, sound, audio, video etc. In practically, we can say that multimedia is a combination of both hardware and software. Another much used is multimedia in "hypermedia".

One of the key features of multimedia is "interactivity". Hypermedia and virtual reality applications are based on multimedia system. Hypermedia extends the media-oriented features of multimedia system by the concept of hyperlink. Virtual reality extends the interaction oriented features of multimedia system by the concept of cyberspace.

After, these all multimedia systems provide the facility of real time navigation.

In **multiple media** all the media are linked together. It also provides the facility of conferring the information with computing technology. Multiple-media doesn't provide the facility of hypermedia. Also it doesn't provide the facility of interactivity.

e.g.The Biomedical and multimedia information Technology (BMIT) group is an interdepartmental and interdisciplinary group of excellence. It has a strong research focus in the application of computer science and information technology in biomedicine and multimedia.

Through its research, this group seeks to gain a better understanding of information science and technology as applied to biomedical and multimedia problems and to facilitate the transfer of the knowledge gained for the benefit of our health care system and multimedia industry.

The medical application is MEDNET. Mednet provides the following services :

✓ *A* real time monitoring and multiparty consultation.

✓ Collaboration during brain surgery.

Mednet is being developed at University of Pittsburgh Medical Centre. The intra-operative monitoring places a real time control about the condition of the patient. Mednet is different from the other picture taking teleconferencing system as it provides real time monitoring and collaboration.

The term "collaboration" is one of the commonly used term in multimedia application. The verbal meaning of the collaboration is the actual meaning in the context of multimedia, that is collectively doing a particular work but for this collaborative work physical presence may not be required. How it can be achieved by mednet as in most of the surgeries the anesthesiologist, the system and other supporting staff

have to be present for patient.
After getting all the conclusion finally we can say that multimedia is stronger than multiple-media. Multimedia is interactive in nature.

Q9. Suggest various areas where multimedia can be used in a university. Take any one of the suggested area/application and define its objectives, prospective viewers, resource requirements and advantages/disadvantages. [JUN02,Q4]

The various areas where Multimedia is used in a University are :

(A) At Administrative level like
(i) Keeping records of students
(ii) Making Timetable
(B) Issue Certificates or Marksheets to students or receiving any others extra curricular Activities Certificates
(C) For teaching difficult subject
(D) For Entertainment
(E) For making different Projects
(F) For getting information outside the world
(G) Arrange competition at different level
(H) For decoration on different occasions

From the above mentioned areas we are taking administrative department of a University to define its objective, Prospective viewers resource requirement and advantages/disadvantages.

(1) Objectives
(i) Keeping records of students
(ii) Making Timetable
(iii) Issue Certificates or Marksheets to students or receiving any others extra curricular Activities Certificates

(2) Prospective viewers
(i) Students
(ii) Parents
(iii) Friends of Students
(iv) Board members of University

(3) Resource Requirements
(i) Records of grades / marks of students given by professors / teachers.
(ii) Appointment of new professor.
(iii) Admission of new students.
(iv) Proper use of donations.
(v) Keeping records of salary statement of all employees.

Advantages of Multimedia in administrative departments of University
(i) Fast work
(ii) Easy work
(iii) User friendly
(iv) Accuracy

Disadvantages of Multimedia in administrative departments of University
(i) Electricity failure can stop all work.
(ii) Only computer literate person can work on that multimedia software.

Multimedia applications in there diverse forms can be used in university campus with great advantage. Such use can help not only the student community, but also save time and energy of the teaching faculty and university administration while tackling problems of students.

And some of the other areas where it can be used are :-

(i) As teaching aid : Teachers can use multimedia presentations as an aid in their lectures to the students complex concepts in science and technology can be explained and illustrated to students with much more easier when multimedia presentations are available.

(ii) In science laboratories : Before performing difficult scientific experiments or medical operations (in a medical college or university) student can preview similar experiments on multimedia.

(iii) On University Website : Every university these days has its own website. Multimedia clips are an integral part of such website.

(iv) In university library : The university library can stock CDs and cassettes of multimedia presentation on various topics of student's interests. The library can provide facilities to let students view such CDs etc. in computer kiosks in library premises. Also a hypertext-based multimedia program can be prepared on various books the library has and the facilities it offers to its members. Hypertext can link various authors of same subject etc.

(v) Information about Courses offered at University : University can install a touch screen multimedia presentation. Using this a student can immediately seek information about any course he is interested in.

(vi) Multimedia in Distance Education : University is conducting distance education courses, it can use study material on multimedia and send it to study centres in remote places.

(vii) Declaring Results : Display of examination result can be made more interesting by incorporating pictures and clips of the top ranking students, the colleges they belong to etc. Such multimedia-based result displays can be used on the internet site.

(viii) For training the teachers : The biggest use university can make of multimedia is in training of its own teaching faculty. Such programs are available from leading publishers and can be used in training university lecturers on how to teach a particular subject.

(ix) In University Library : To help library members in finding any book immediately on their own by referring to title, author name, subject, accession number, publisher etc. Also to give details about availability of a title.

(x) Prospective viewers : Regular members and casual visitors of the library, staff member of the library.

Q10. Suggest various areas of applications, where multimedia may be used in Hospitals. Describe one of the areas in details giving the objectives, prospective viewers, approximate resource requirements for one of the applications.

[DEC01,Q4]

We are giving the example to suggest or understand the various areas of applications where multimedia may be used in hospitals. Just like any person can enquire on the hospital reception about the admission of patients. Doctor's haven't come in the hospital, a Person can enquire about the treatment given by the hospital. Then you must have the help of hypertext Presentation because hypertext Presentation can be made for a piece of information / questions (Query) asked by a Person. Communication should be Possible in any direction, Junior doctor can ask their senior doctor in case of any typical emergency.

Sometimes a Person is suffering from miscellaneous problems then the consulting doctor whose presence is not sure may remotely monitor and can listen to the responses of the patients on the screen (the achievement of Multimedia can be used during brain surgery / or for any other typical task).

Surgery scheduling centre which schedules operation, theatre surgeon enquiring that optimum use is made of the hospital facilities and the to also provide satisfaction to the patient. Another important activity of this unit is to publish schedule of surgeries for the next day so that the different departments involved and the surgeries can plan their work.

It is used to make up, send and receive Medical eXchange Folders (MXF) including nominative multimedia medical documents, doctors : GP and PCP, specialists surgeons.

The various areas where Multimedia is used in a Hospital are :

(A) At Administrative level like

(i) Keeping records of patient

(ii) Making Timetable of Operation Theatre (e.g. operation to be scheduled next day)

(B) Issue Test Reports or Birth Certificate / Death Certificate

(C) For providing details of various services provided by Hospital.

(D) Brief History of hospital.

And much more...

From the above mentioned areas we are taking administrative department of a Hospital to define its objective, Prospective viewers resource requirement.

(1) Objectives

(i) Keeping records of patient.

(ii) Making Operation Theatre schedule.

(iii) Issue Birth / Death Certificates

(2) Prospective viewers

(i) Patients

(ii) Doctors / Consultants

(iii) Relatives of Patient

(iv) Board members of Hospital

(3) Resource Requirements

(i) Records of disease / treatment given of patients by doctors.

(ii) Appointment of new Doctor.

(iii) Admission of new patient.

(iv) Proper use of donations.

(v) Keeping records of salary statement of all employees.

🗁 ***Mednet is a Multimedia based system which Provides Services are :***

✓ Collaborate brain surgery.

✓ Real time monitoring.

🗁 ***The approximate resource requirements for performing brain surgery follows:***

✓2 GB HDD to 80 GB

✓ Connection to an Internet Service Provider (ISP) or mobile connection will work better.

✓ Keyboard, Mouse, CD-ROM drive.

✓ Mednet diagnostic system

✓ Sound Card

✓ Micro Phone

✓A Modem with a speed of 28 thousand bps to 128 kbps

✓**Graphic** acclerator and pentium processor. (ranging from 550MHz to 2.8GHz)

Q11. A multimedia teaching aid is to be developed for teaching Binary Search Tree data structure. How will you design this multimedia? Give details on the objectives, target audience, resource requirements and advantages of making the above multimedia. Which of the multimedia components would you like to include in your above tutorial? Give reasons. [JUN03,Q5]

There are many search methods but the binary search tree method is very popular in professionals. The binary search tree is a binary tree which is either empty or contains a node whose keys satisfies the following conditions:

(a) The key in the left child of a node (if any) proceeds the key in the parent node.

(b) The key in the right child of a anode (if any) succeeds the key in the parent node.

(c) The left and right subtree of the root are again binary search trees.

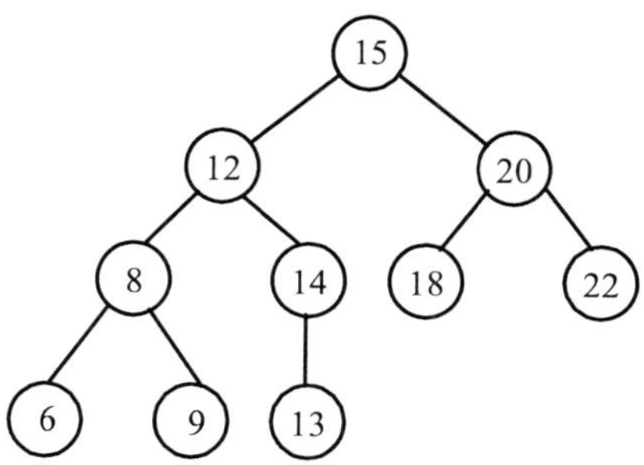

During the initial design phase all aspects of the multimedia projects are carefully planned before the production start. This is the phase or stage where director, the interface designer, the content designer and the main programmer have to take decision on key elements of the production.

1. Flow chart : This is the map that shows how all the elements in the titles are connected. They are the blueprint of the output.

2. Scripts : The script is just like a movie works in conjunction with the flowchart to provide a printed version of all the text.

🗁 **Objective :** To give demonstration on the topic binary search tree to the students, so that they would easily understand the concept of one of data structure element that is binary search tree.

🗁 **Target audience :** Our target audience are the students which has curriculum of studying the data structure like PGDCA/MCA/BCA/M.Tech(CS) students.

🗁 **Resource Requirements**

(a) Definition of BST, its objective and rules of designing the BST.

(b) Use of hyperlinks so that students can view the different aspects of BST in a better manner.

(c) Algorithm to design and search the element in BST can be linked with help of hyperlinks and any programming language.

(d) If LAN exists than every student should be able to view the topics.

(e) Proper FAQ should be designed so that students can ask for their problem.

🗁 **Advantages of Making this Multimedia**

(a) Data structure is one of the important topic for students because it helps a lot while designing programmes by designing multimedia software on this topic which also helps to those who cannot understand the things so easily.

(b) Students will have practical views on this topic.

Based upon the proceeded considerations, the following components of a Multi-media system that need to be designed :

Content : Specify the information needs and interaction requirements of the users in the different tasks, i.e. what kind and level of details of information do the users want to receive ? How do they want to select and access that information ? *

Structure : Specify the structure between different pieces or chunks of information and how the user might gain access to this information.

Access : Specify the information navigation and access techniques i.e. how will the user know the related information is available and how to access it ? Do users always know how to locate themselves in the information space and to find the way back to where they come from ? Is the user allowed to make new connection between arbitrary or selected pieces of information ?

Style : Specify the way each component of information will be presented to the user. In which modality will the information be presented (textually, verbally, graphically, by animation, by audio or video sequences, still images etc.) ? will be shown only once and disappear or remain for closer inspection or repeated presentation ? Can it be interrupted or hidden ? Can the user switch between different presentation modes depending upon preference or circumstances ?

Because any person can get easily this multimedia based teaching aids. Finally, this is fruitful for any person.

Q12. Describe how multimedia can be used in the following:

(1) Airline reservation system	**[DEC02,Q5(a)]**
(2) Railway enquiry system	**[DEC02,Q5(b)]**
(3) Railway station/bus station	**[DEC01,Q5(b)]**
(4) Bus stand	**[JUN02,Q5(c)]**
(5) An auditorium	**[DEC02,Q5(c)]**
(6) A hospital	**[JUN02,Q5(a)]**
#:Reception of a hospital	**[JUN01,Q5(a)]**
(7) Bank	**[JUN02,Q5(b)]**

(8) A departmental store. **[DEC01,Q5(c)]**
(9) Visitor Lounge of a company **[JUN01,Q5(b)]**
(10) Bookstore **[JUN01]**
(11) Web-based information portal **[JAN01,Q5(a)]**
(12) An interactive audio **[JAN01,Q5(b)]**
(13) A distributed learning platform **[JAN01,Q5(c)]**
(14) A Conference **[JUN03,Q5(a)]**
(15) A Library **[JUN03,Q5(b)]**
(16) A Museum **[JUN03,Q5(c)]**

(1) Airline reservation system

Use of multimedia can best be achieved here. It can be stated that the global computer reservation systems have reached a significantly high economic and technological level and travel agents would hardly be able to do their work without some tools which makes this task easier.

In airlines reservation multimedia is widely used. Multimedia is also compatible over the network. As airlines have offices all over the country or all over the world for that matter, multimedia plays on very important role. Multimedia can give detailed information like.

- Schedules of flights per day.
- Arrivals and departures of flights.
- Availability of seats & current position of the seats if waiting list is put.
- Rates of the tickets.
- Different schemes available if any for regular fliers.
- Information on connecting flights of domestic and international schedules.
- Multimedia can be used as an information kiosk for airlines reservation.

All this will increase productivity and increase the customer satisfaction level.

(2) Railway enquiry system

Use of multimedia can best be achieved here.India is a country with a population of 100 crores. The biggest network of public transport in India is Railways lakhs of people daily travel to their destination & for these lakhs of people thousands of trains are running daily. Thus it becomes very important to maintain a very accurate & efficient enquiring system. To do this multimedia has contributed a lot. Multimedia has the capability to work over the networks. A good network system can be well supported by a good multimedia.

Railways enquiry system with the help of multimedia can give the following data on a simple interaction.

- Train schedules & time table.
- Schedule departure and arrivals of trains.
- Ticket charges of different coaches attached in the train.
- Information of rescheduled time if any train is late or cancelled.
- Information regarding any new trains or special trains are available.
- Availability of seats & reservation status can be known.

- Refreshments, boarding & lodging & rest house info is also available.
- Information about lost & found articles.

(3) Railway station/bus station

Railway station/ bus station both are very posh area / or Hoch poch areas so much terrorism around these areas is observed. Through Multimedia in railway or bus station we can keep an eye on terrorist activities and providing a great help in case of an emergency. Railway station and Bus station are two places where people come to go to different places. As the population & commerce is increasing, the rush at these places have also increased. Now multimedia can be used here to :

- Give information & directions of places of departure e.g. platform no.
- Scheduled time of departures & arrivals.
- Rescheduled time of departures and arrivals if there is any delay.
- Before time information distribution if any changes made.
- Reservation status.
- Availability of seats.
- Rate charts & information of the place where to be the person travels.
- Tourist sports & information of business centers.
- Refreshment & resting places at Railway stations and bus stops.

Outfitting the railway stations with large-scale video screens enables updated customer information or advertising to be shown in television broadcasting quality. At the same time the connection can also be made for controlling escalators or automated ticketing machines.

ACCS-ATM is a dynamic passenger information system based on a ATM network that offers transport operators a modular, fully integrated system solution for customer information and operations monitoring. It acquires static timetable information and information on the current operating situation and evaluates these data for provision of information to travellers and for optimization of operations.

The system generates announcement texts with close approximation to a human speaker; it provides train and time controlled announcement output and, at the same time controls the text information for display on train, destination displays, information monitor and overview panels.

(4) Bus stand

The use of multimedia at bus stand is not applied till now in India. So we are giving the use of multimedia in bus stand in European country.

- Pre information of coming buses.
- Post information of coming buses.
- Exact location of the buses.
- Loading capacity of the buses.
- Traffic information on roads.
- Information display like the information of accidental areas and latest news of the country.

The multimedia system is able to manage complete bus stop / station information, to maintain real time information about arrivals and departures, to display publicity on the information panel to generate automatically a human voice that provides information on arrivals and departures, to print any kind of information from any terminal to be remotely controlled, to recognize the number plates of the vehicles. The information system is the centre of all this system. It is in-charge of gathering and providing all necessary information to the rest of modules of this system. The type of information like data of companies, buses, functional information on schedules, lines or complementary information such as generation of a human voice in real time, the transmission of advertising videos displayed on the information pannels of the bus station. The information pannels may be adapted to any video system and incorporates integrally, the possibility of showing advertising videos or entertainment in pannels thanks to the digital processing techniques. These systems may be seen on full screen or just on one side of it, with information of arrivals exists on the other side. This information can be sent through the habitual public address system. This is one of the most usual options for the workers of the station because they get this task done that requires constant attention, thus interrupting the workers. It is also possible to provide some information in different languages. This option is very interesting since it works with many foreign users, and it is essential for communities with more than one official language in which the information in all of them is required. A close circuit of video controls and monitors the arrivals and departures at/from the station as well as the security.

(5) An auditorium

Auditorium is a public place where many social, cultural and even political meetings and programs are held. It is not necessary that the meetings held everyday of the week. But its periodically held. Even stage shows are held here. Here too multimedia can be very handy and can be used in the following ways:

- To maintain a proper record of the scheduled programs.
- Directing the audience to their seats in a proper manner.
- Multimedia can be used for good sound quality and lights
- Multimedia projectors can be used for making presentations.

The Multimedia system is able to manage all the information, to maintain real time information about the auditorium, to display publicity on the information panel, to generate automatically a human voice that provides all the information which is related with auditorium.

The information system is the center of all this system. It is in charge of gathering and providing all the necessary information to the rest of modules of this system. It is also possible to provide some information in different languages. This option is very interesting since it works with many foreign users and it is essential for communities with more than one official language in which the information in all of them is required. A closed circuit of video controls and monitors at/from the exits are installed for security. A monitor in the information cabin has at least one camera at the entrance of the auditorium.

Finally, I would like to say that the Multimedia is able to manage all the functionality, which is related to an auditorium.

(6) Reception of a hospital

The basic use of multimedia is to provide easy information and user-friendly information too. Basically multimedia is greatly been used in public places. One of the public place is a reception of a hospital. Now if we just think that what information do we get when we go to a hospital reception. This information can be given through a person over the reception through a multimedia kiosk. Multimedia can be used in getting the following information :

- Details of different services provided by the hospital.
- Rates of the services.
- Brief history of the hospital.
- Details of patient.
- Patient ward number and their progress.
- Directions or road map of hospital.
- Information regarding visiting hours.
- FAQ (Frequently Asked Questions).
- Availability of doctors and their visiting hours etc.

(7) Bank

People go to bank to open saving/current accounts, deposit funds, withdraw money, know various financial schemes of the bank, obtain loan etc. Every bank has a lot of information which it wants to impart to its customers. For this purpose, it can use multimedia in many ways. To tell the people about its various loan schemes such as House loan, Car loan, Two-wheeler loan, Consumer durables loan, Education loan, Personal loan, Computer loan etc. a bank can use a touch screen system which does not require use of keyboard or mouse. Touch of fingers is enough. Bank can also display information about its various schemes on a PC monitor placed in the rest area for customers.

Customers can be informed about their status of withdrawal of money through display of token numbers. Today online and internet banking have become very popular. These use multimedia extensively. The ATM counters we see everywhere are nothing, but multimedia extensions of conventional counters.

Multimedia is thus helping banks give better service to their customers and also in educating them about banks attractive finance schemes.

In addition to the above following information can also be provided with the help of multimedia:-

- Brief history of the bank like time and year of establishment, address of main head office, different branches etc.
- The credit policy that banks follow can be displayed.
- Terms & conditions of the banks regarding savings and credits.
- Growth rate of the performance of bank over a period of time.
- Different services available like savings A/c, Current A/c, Locker facilities etc.
- Charges levied by the bank on various facilities like Demand Draft, Pay Order etc. provided to the Customers.

- Rate of interest paid by bank.
- Services regarding existing customers like balance in account, cheque status, overdraft facilities, request for new cheque book, statement etc.
- Procedure & documents required for opening a new A/c etc.
- E-banking, Internet Banking are the latest examples of use of multimedia in Bank.

(8) A departmental store.

Multimedia greatly facilitates interaction with customers.

A multimedia system is able to manage all the functionally of the departmental store. Product developers, vendors, systems integrators, value added resellers and service providers will find qualitative and quantitative information about their opportunity through multimedia. Analysis in end user organizations assessing the deployment costs and overhead associated with networked multimedia usage will also derive benefits from the detailed studies included.

A multimedia can be used for providing details of the commodities present in the departmental store, real-time monitoring on customer, terrorist activities etc.

The information system is the center of all this system. It is in charge of gathering and providing all the necessary information. The information pannels may be adapted to any video system and it incorporates integrally, the possibility of showing advertising videos or entertainment.

It is also to provide some information which is related with departmental store.

- Direction and roadmaps of different sections of the store.
- Information of the items to be purchased e.g. price, weights, brand etc.
- Information of different schemes available.,
- Information about discounts.
- Knowledge of introduction of new items in the store & their usage.
- Public feedback of different items available in the market.
- Availability of different services provided by the stores.

Contents kept for the customers etc.

In a departmental store a various types of customers come, faithful or sometimes unfaithful. By installing multimedia based cameras at sensitive corners we can monitor their activities. So the Multimedia helps in this field also because online product lists and their concern details can be given to the customers it will be a great help for the visitors (outsiders) if they do not have product knowledge.

(9) Visitor Lounge of a company

A visitors lounge is a place where an outsider who visits a company is made to sit and wait if the concern person is busy. This place has great importance as many thoughts come through the visiting person's mind. A multimedia info center at this place can give him all the information at the lounge itself.

Another sub technology of Multimedia is audio and video this technology can be used at visitors lounge of the company. A Boss can see through the monitor who is coming in the company or what is happening in the lounge from his cabin.

Multimedia is very useful in visitor lounge of a company.

One can access info like :

- Profile of the company.
- The history of the owner of the company.
- Areas of work in which the company deals.
- Infrastructure and management essentials of the company.
- Achievements and specialization of the company.
- Future projects and projections of the company.
- Other daily useful details regarding operating timings, holidays etc.

(10) Book Store

Book Store is the place where you can find your best friend. But in todays would you can gets books related to many topics written by different authors. Here too multimedia can be handy. With the help of multimedia a complete data base of books can be accessed. Thus multimedia can be used for the following ways:

- A complete database of the books can be maintained.
- Distribution of books as per the author.
- Complete reference of the availability of the books along with their authors.
- Preface of the books.
- List of best sellers.
- List of new arrivals etc.

(11) Web-based information portal

Multimedia is gaining popularity on the web with several technologies to support use of animation, video, and audio to supplement the traditional media of text and images. These new media provide more design options but also require design discipline. Unconstrained use of multimedia results in user interfaces that confuses users and make it harder for them to understand the information. Portals software should not only be capable of searching across multiple sources, it should also provide tools that enable the search results to be imported into the hub environment.

Some of these tools may be visible to end users to help them to manage their own search results. The portal system will use agreed mechanisms conforming to z39.50, LDAP, RSS, OAI protocols and standards. You can create your Web page portal using Microsoft personal web server 4.0 server. You can connect to a corporate network. You can share document with your co-workers from your own computers. You can also test your website before you upload it to an Internet Service Provider (ISP). To create a webpage programs such as Microsoft Front Page express, Dreamweaver can be used. And many other freeware are available on Internet which can be found by searching.

(12) An interactive audio

The main benefit of audio is that it provides a channel that is separate from that of the display. *An Interactive audio* especially for students and teachers is having a

great use is distributed learning. This system provides the real time communication. Speech can be used to offer commentary or help without obscuring information on the screen. Audio can also be used to provide a sense of place or mood as done to perfections. Mood setting audio should employ very quiet background sounds in order to match with the main information also to grab the user's attention.
Whenever you need to inform the user about a certain work of music, it makes much more sense to simply play it than to show the notes or to try to describes it in words. Speech is also perfect for teaching the pronunciation of words. Non-speech sound effects can be used as an extra dimension in the user interface to inform users about background events.

Good quality sound is used to enhance the user experience substantially so it will worth investing in professional quality sound production. The classic example is the video game study where user claimed that the graphics were better when the sound was improved, even though the exactly same earlier used graphics were used.

(13) A Distributed Learning Platform

One of the essential components of the learning process is social interaction. The informal peer learning is as important as formal teaching. The process of learning and motivation for learning are influenced by a variety of factors, which are not necessarily accessible to analysis. However, these factors are in the semiconscious or subconscious area of the human cognition.
Distributed learning means using a wide range of information technologies to provide learning opportunities beyond the bounds of the traditional class room. Some example of distributed learning technologies include the World Wide Web, e-mail, video conferencing, group ware, simulations, news groups, chat rooms. A distributed learning environment facilitates a learner-centered educational paradigm and promotes active learning. Distributed learning supports a "Pull" model of education in which a person engaged in learning activities at his or her own pace and at a self-selected time. This is in contrast to the traditional "Push" model of education in which the learners synchronize their needs and schedules to the delivery of the instructor.
The development of high performance computing and communications is creating new media such as the World Wide Web and virtual reality with the help of multimedia.
The innovative kind of pedagogy empowered by these emerging media, messages and experiences make possible a transformation of conventional distance education which replicates traditional class room teaching across barriers of distance and time into an alternative instructional paradigm distributed learning.

(14) A Conference : The activities in an office such as meetings, group discussions, training are some areas where we need the concept such as brainstorming, sharing of idea, problem solving etc. for real-time meetings that involve geographically dispersed group of people, we can avail the choices as:
✓ Audio conferencing

✓ Video conferencing, or

✓ Document conferencing.

🗁 **Audio conferencing :** This technology allows 'out-of-town' people to participate in a formal meeting. This technology can also be used by a group of people to meet frequently whatsoever is the physical distance among them. Audio conferencing is an effective means of communication for reporting about a project status. It can be used to solve problems quickly. One of the disadvantages of audio conferencing is such that conferences are restricted to only voice, so this conference can be preceeded by sending email of documents that are to be used during the conference. The second disadvantage is that the person who is not proficient in spoken words cannot participate well in such conferences.

🗁 **Video Conferencing :** Video conferencing is being used successfully by several organizations abroad. Video conferencing resembles an office meeting; thus, require setting of time, preparing rooms and place, agenda etc. However the biggest drawback is the cost of the equipment.

Video conferencing brings people together naturally and simulate a real life meeting environment. Today video conferencing has been brought to the computer however; it is not easy to use, as the participant is continuously looking at the camera on the top of his machine.

🗁 **Document Conferencing :** Document conferencing, also called audio-graphic conferencing technology, allows people to meet using their PCs and telephone lines. The telephone lines connect the participants so they can share audio information and the data they have stored in their PC. In addition, it allows online editing of a document by several participating people in the conference. This conferencing technology has been used in the education filed. It extends the boundaries of the classroom and reach out into the community. A document that can be used in the conference may consist of text, graphics, sound or even video clippings.

(i) Large screen display

(ii) Information of vacant seats.

(iii) Information of total strength.

(iv) Infirmation of unidentified objects.

(v) Emergency attention to all viewers.

A conference is a live connection between people in separate locations for the purpose of communication, usually involving audio and often text as well as video. At its simplest, conferencing provides transmission of static images and text between two locations. At its most sophisticated, it provides transmission of full motion video images and high-quality audio between multiple locations.

(15) A Library

Multimedia is very useful in library. The multimedia system is able to mange all the functionality of the library. It is used to maintain real time information about book, (topics, authors, title, availability) to display publicity on the information panel.

It easily integrates text, images, sound, music, animation, interactive controls, color and other graphical elements to create stunning multimedia productions. Neo Book can be used to produce electronic magazines (e-zines) that can be distributed over the Internet, interactive educational and training material, CD-ROM interfaces, electronic books, reference works, brochures, catalogs, entertainment titles and much more.

Multimedia CD-ROMs is a new learning method, which is not only user friendly but also saves storing space. Another additional advantage is the increased shelf life of the desired book in the CD. The multimedia is very useful in library system because the all information regarding books and catalogs are stored in CD-ROM in the way of video and audio form.

(16) A Museum

A museum is a place where art effects and ancient objects, paining is kept. Thus Museum becomes a huge place & this place is very useful for knowledge enhancement. Here also multimedia can have a very major role to play. As multimedia is used for distribution of knowledge and information & Museum is a place where one goes for knowledge and information. Multimedia can be used in just about any situation where computers are being used to deliver information. In the Museum it can be placed at the reception lounge various types of museum like Rail Museum, Doll Museum, Science Museum. These above museums guide every information to their own stream. It can provide various information and other relevant topics and one of the most important whether somebody damaging the museum things or not.

Multimedia here can be used for different ways.

- A complete road map of the museum.
- Proper distribution of different zones of the museum.
- Details regarding each ones.
- Complete details of the different things which are displayed i.e. the history of object.
- Value addition i.e. extra information regarding the topic.
- When & where did the object was found.
- What the object was made up of and how it was made.

CHAPTER 3

MULTIMEDIA AUTHORING TOOLS

In the previous two chapters we have discussed about the definition and components of multimedia and its applications. A multimedia production needs to be interactive. In this chapter we will try to answer the question how multimedia production can be made interactive. Several tools are used for developing interactive multimedia. These are:

- authoring systems
- authoring languages
- generic languages (e.g. C, C ++, JAVA)

The term authoring results from the fact that the person creating the learning material on the computer is often called the author.

Authoring systems are generally menu-driven systems intended to be easy to use by the multimedia developer. They do not require the trainer to get involved with program code. Such systems endeavour to provide a complete, comprehensive authoring environment where whatever multimedia developer wishes to do is either selected from a menu or entered into the computer in a straightforward, well-prompted way.

Authoring languages are specially designed programming languages, and have some distinct advantages over generic languages. They have been created specifically for the training/educational field, and provide appropriate commands and structures to cater for the types of presentation and interaction involved in CBT(Computer Based Tutorial).

In this chapter, our main focus shall be on the authoring systems.

In this chapter, you will be learning the need for multimedia authoring. (Why it is required), features of the authoring tools:

- Authorware
- Everest Authoring
- System Icon Author ImageQ
- Macromedia Director

Q1. What are the features that you may look for while selecting development tools for Animation using series of pictures, Video editing and Simulating a practical session in multimedia? [JUN03,Q3]

The features of development tools are as under :-

- Integrating multimedia elements.
- Script language programs.
- Icon-based programs.
- DLL'S for extending features.
- Supporting CD-ROM and laser disc sources.
- Supporting Video for windows.
- Hypertext.
- Cross platform capability.
- Run-time player for distribution

Now let us study each of the features in detail.

a) Integrating multimedia elements : As we all know important different media elements of a multimedia presentation. As there are many multimedia elements, a authoring software's has to support all the different media elements. Authoring programs provide developers with a great degree of control over each multimedia element than presentation programs. Authoring softwares are also geared towards education and training applications as well as business presentation.

b) Script language program : Authoring softwares has the feature to write scripts for software to build features that are not supported by the software itself. These type of commands linked together in a word processing typescript. The script language specifies multimedia elements, sequencing, hotspots, etc. nearly all the authoring softwares are backed up by powerful scripting programmes. This scripting program is object oriented. Here no editing of media elements can be done. They can only be used for handling the elements & increase interaction. Most of the scripting languages are interpreted instead of compiled. The runtime speed gains over other authoring methods are minimum. It also supports more & complete medias.

c) Icon based programs : Authoring a complete multimedia projects is very complex & this icon based programs are available where graphical icons are used to control the features. The main features of icon based programs are :

➢Icon-based programs are easier to learn than script programs.

➢Working on a icon based program is also easy as editing of anything can be done easily by just clicking on the icon.

Icon based authoring programs are also object oriented development programs where multimedia elements are represented by icons.

Icon based programs use less time for development. Many of these tools are also optimized for developing CBT's. The main part of such program are the icon palette, containing the possible functions/interactions of a program and the flow line, which shows the actual links between the icons. However, the high end packages, such as Authorware or icon author are extremely powerful and suffer least from runtime speed problems.

d) DLL's for extending features : With advance technologies developing authoring programs can call on special features available in the Windows is Dynamic Link Libraries (DLL's). These DLL's with special features are automatically installed with software itself. Programming languages like C, C++ allow the user to create their own DLL's.

e) Supporting CD-Rom & laser Disc sources : Saving the arrays of different media elements is often not practical to get the quality and speed. Authoring softwares allows full control of drives.

Authoring softwares supports MCI command language that helps direct control of CD-Rom drives. Multimedia presentation that depend on large amounts of sound or video clips require high end PC with great storage option & memory. This CD-Drive and DVD player as a video source. Authoring softwares provide seamless control on this hardware.

f) Supporting video for windows : Videos stored on the hard disk is sometimes the right media for your project. Authoring softwares has the capability to support most multimedia elements including video for windows latest softwares from Macromedia like Authorware and Director permits the loading of video clips from video for windows and animation clips from auto desk.

g) Hypertext : Hypertext is nothing but text working like a button. Hypertext capabilities can be used to link graphics, animation or frame and of course other text. Hypertext interfaces allows users to select individual hot words on a screen, which are then linked to other pages or layers or text etc. A perfect example of hypertext application is windows help.

Hypertext systems are useful when presenting large amount of textual information. Many hypertext authoring programs provide graphical links for animation, sound and video as well as text.

h) Cross platform capability : This is a very important feature. A multimedia project has to play on all different platforms. This is very important to expand your audience. A very important consideration with authoring programs is the capability of presenting on Macintosh or other hardware platforms. Now days all the authoring softwares are capable of work on different platforms.

i) Run-time player for distribution : Run-time software is often included in authoring software to explain the distribution of your final product. Advance authoring programs provide specialized packing and run time distribution for use with devices like CD-ROM & other hardware. While making professional presentation that all the DLL's & run time modules are packed with the presentation.

Q2. What is Hypertext? Explain.

Although the term "hypertext" is relatively new to many of us, it was actually coined in 1965 and article predicting hypertext was published in 1945.

Hypertext is nonlinear or non-sequential text: there is no single order that determines the sequence in which the text is to be read. That is, the text is organized so that one can easily jump around from topic to topic.

Although, hypertext is best brought to life on a computer, it can be found in simple paper documents too. A paperback novel and the for page of a newspaper are the two examples of text out of which the news paper page is hypertext because one can easily jump from topic to topic if one wants more depth on any one topic. While, the novel, on the flip side, does not encourage skipping around. The novelist assures he will be reading in a fixed sequence reading one page right after another. Figure below illustrates hypertext with an example.

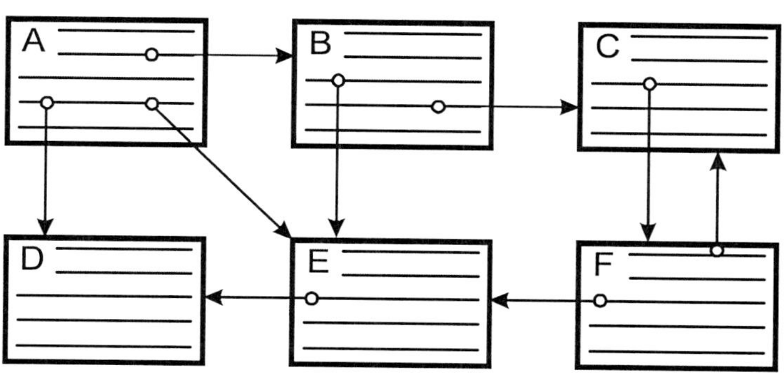

Hypertext Structure

Assumes that one starts reading the piece of text marked A. Instead of a single next place to go, this hypertext structure has three options for the reader: Go to B, D or E.

Assuming that one decides to go to B, then to E, C and from E, one can go to D. Since it is also possible to go directly from A to D, this example shows that there may be several different paths that connect two elements in a hypertext structure. Hypertext presents several different options to the readers, and the individual reader determines which of them to follow at the time of reading the text. This means that the author of the text has set up a number of alternatives for readers to explore rather than a single stream of information.

The same is true of footnotes in traditional printed texts, since readers have to determine upon reaching the footnote marker whether to continue reading the primary stream of text or to branch off to pursue the footnote. Therefore, hypertext is sometimes called the "generalized footnote".

When hypertext is implemented on a computer system there is potential for giving readers more flexibility jumping around from topic to topic. The text for each topic may be stored in a special area of computer memory and then easily be accessed. In the hypertext literature, these "areas of computer memory" are referred to as "notecards", "cards" or "nodes" whatever be the size of these nodes, each of them may have pointers to other units, and these pointers are called links. The number of links are normally not fixed in advance but depend upon the content of each node. Some nodes are related to many others and will therefore have many links, but have no outgoing links of there own. Sometimes, such nodes without further links are called leaf nodes.

Figure also shows that the entire hypertext structure forms a network of nodes and links. Readers move about this network in an activity that is often referred to as browsing or navigating rather than just "reading" to emphasize that users must actively determine the order in which they read the nodes.

A hypertext link connects two nodes and is normally directed in the sense that it points from one node (called the anchor node) to another (called the destination node).

In the early days of hypertext, nodes contained only textual data. Now nodes can contain various kinds of data: graphics, audio, video, computer-animated images, film clips of animated scenes, digital sound or other kind of information. The term hypermedia may be used, when referring to systems that include a wide variety of node types.

Hypertext is now being used in more and more areas. Educators are making good use of hypertext and making learning of difficult subjects more and more accessible. While reading some instructional material on a computer screen, the user may come across several technical terms on the screen that are highlighted (shown in a different color, say, yellow letters on a green background or black letters on a white background). Thus, a comfortable learning is achieved with a well designed hypertext system.

Q3. Explain the application of hypertext in different fields.

🗁 **Computer Applications :** Since hypertext is a medium, it is natural to use it in connection with computer-oriented applications. Hypertext can be used to prototype the user interface for almost any other computer program as most initial prototyping consists of linking together screen designs and presenting them to the user in an order determined by simple user actions.

(a) Online documentation : Online documentation may be the most natural of all hypertext applications. Hypertext is the obvious method for helping user in the situation when they require good access tool to help them retrieve the sections of the manual that are relevant to their current needs.

(b) User Assistance : hypertext provides a mechanism for integrating several forms of user assistance, including the online manual, an introductory tutorial, on online help system, and even the error messages. Because users only get massages when they are in some kind of trouble, the error messages are a print candidate for providing users with assistance.

In an integrated user assistance facility based on hypertext, it would be possible for the user to link an error message to the location in the help system that gives further assistance on the problem. Suppose if the user's difficult is not the error situation in general but a single incomprehensible word I the online message, it may become possible to link from that word to the location in the online manual where it is defined with the help of hypertext. Also if the user wanted further assistance than could be provided by the help system or the manual then it may become possible to link further, to the appropriate location in the tutorial component, to get a computer-aided instruction lesson.

This type of integrated user interface does not exist in current computer system and can be made possible with the hypertext facility.

(c) Software Engineering : The hypertext has a great potential for providing links among the large number of specification and implementation documents that are produced during the software development life cycle. For example, it would be possible to start from a requirements document and link to that part of the design specification that meets a given requirement. One could them link from the design specification to the actual code the use how that design is implement.

A development organisation would require to follow a software engineering methodology supported by an integrated set of computerized tools in a complete CASE (Computer Aided Software Engineering) environment, in order to derive full benefits from this form of hypertext links among the various documents in the software lifecycle.

It is also possible to use hypertext in a less lifecycle-oriented approach by including linking facilities in structure-oriented editors for program code. For example, it is possible to click on a variable to get to see its definition and associated comments, or to link from a procedure call to opening a window with the text of the procedure. The Smalltalk code browser links related pieces of code in somewhat this manner.

Q4. What are the applications of hypertext in the following areas :
(a) Dictionaries and Reference Books,
(b) Trade Shows, Product Catalogs and Advertising,
(c) Educational Applications,
(d) Foreign Languages,
(e) Entertainment and Leisure Applications,
(f) News, Newspapers, and Magazines,
(g) Legal application.

(a) Dictionaries and Reference Books : Several dictionaries and large reference books have been converted from a traditional paper from to a hypertext format. A hypertext dictionary from scratch has been generated for the children's dictionary. For pure environment the user can click on the picture of the dog to have it replaced

by another kind of dog. There are hypertext links to "dog words" and to other pats, as well as the links to other words from the definition. All features encourage the child to explore the dictionary and learn new words.
One of the biggest advantages of hypertext encyclopedias and dictionaries, compared to a printed work, is that they can show moving images and play sound. For example, Microsoft Bookshelf contains a dictionary with sound recordings of how the words are actually pronounced. Printed dictionaries for deaf users portray hand and facial gestures through line drawings with arrows to show movement, so multimedia dictionaries are clearly a superior format for communicating this dynamic language. Also, the computer format has added benefits such as the ability for less experienced users to view a sign at much slower speeds than normal conversation.

(b) Trade Shows, Product Catalogs and Advertising : Many kinds of advertising and communication to customers can be improve by hypertext. For example, one can attract attention at trade shows by having a computer with hypertext information about one's products.
Hypertext can also be used to provide information about an entire trade show and help people find those exhibitors that would interest them.
One of the intrinsic advantages of hypertext in an advertising context is the general ability of hypertext to provide access to large amounts of information but to show the user only those small parts that interest him or her. This property of hypertext is important for applications like product catalogs. A hypertext product catalog can reduce the complexity of choosing among a large number of options by showing only those that are relevant for the individual customer. It can also offer help in pacing the order and might even place it by an online connection to the vendor. A hypertext catalog could also include an option to remember what products the user ordered the previous time, thus making them especially easy to reorder.
Traditional types of advertising are certainly possible in hypertext, either by sending customers a disk or making promotional materials available on the Internet. Compared with paper publishing, where a majority of the pages in many newspapers consist of advertising, hypertext provides great potential for saving resources while making more advertising content available to those readers who express an interest in a certain ad and follow its link to the supplementary materials.

(c) Educational Applications : Many hypertext systems have been produced specifically for educational use. Hypertext is well suited for open learning applications where, the student is allowed freedom of action and encouraged to take the initiative. For example, the interactive *NOVA* hypertext allows the student to browse through a set of biology information and see those part that interest the student or make sense in the context of a current assignment. On the other hypertext may be less well suited for the drill-practice type learning that is still necessary in some situations.

(d) Foreign Languages : The linking abilities of hypertext are idea for the learning of foreign language. Hypertext can provide automatic access to dictionaries through implicit links from any text. A student who does not know English very well might still be able to understand material in Intermediate because if its ability to link to an explanation of any word. Hypertext also enables students to view two versions of the same text: An original version and a translation. The *video Linguist* is a hypermedia system that teaches a language by showing clips of television broadcasts from a country speaking that language. The advantage of this approach are that TV shows are fun and motivating and that they reach the culture of the county in addition to the language. One major problem with learning languages is that native speakers of many languages tend to speak in a very agitated and fast manner, which makes their utterances hard to understand for foreigners. But of course the goal of learning French is to understand the way the language is actually spoken in France and not the way a teacher may speak it in class. Therefore the Video Linguist initially plays the original sound track from the broadcast version of the show.

If there is a part of sound track that students do not understand they can utilize the hypertext facilities and link to a version where the same words are spoken more slowly. If they still don't understand it, they can follow a link to a version where each word is spoken v-e-r-y s-l-o-w-l-y and clearly. A final hypertext feature in the Video, Linguist allows the student to click on any word in the subtitles and dictionary definition.

(e) Entertainment and Leisure Applications : Hypertext provides several opportunities for pure enjoyment. Although, there has been very little research conducted in this area, but still there has been some pioneering research as well as the first few commercial examples.

(f) News, Newspapers, and Magazines : News delivery is an obvious candidate for online services since events can be reported as they occur instead of having to wait for the scheduled publication time of a newspaper of magazine. Online versions of large newspapers help the articles to be accessed around the clock. Some added value derives from search capabilities where one can find, for example, all news stories about a certain company over the last month before deciding whether to invest in it or how to solicit it as a customer. Also information filtering can be used to design personalized electronic newspapers with exactly those news-stories that are of interest to the individual reader.

The ability to link between articles from several magazines is a value-added feature of the hypertext versions of the magazines. Even the discussions between readers is a value-added feature for the hypermedia versions of the magazines: if somebody is reading, say an article about an upgrade to a spreadsheet application, that person is likely to be interested in the experience other readers have had when installing the upgrade.

(g) Law : Hypertext has two main applications in the legal field. The first is to support legal research and is mainly used by professional lawyers. The second is support of legal document creation and management and is used by both lawyers and people who wish to avoid paying legal fees. Legal texts are filled with cross-references and are therefore well suited for hypertext support. Typically, a lawyer's brief might refer to several count rulings, each of which would refer to further rulings and to the applicable statutes. Having each of these references available online saves the lawyer much time in ruling in researching the law. A special aspect of law is the new statutes or higher court ruling may invalidate earlier decisions, meaning that something may be legal one day but illegal the next.

This time varying nature of the law two consequences for legal hypertext systems. The first is that a lawyer who accesses one overruled cases would better be informed that it is no longer a valid law. Legal information services achieve this purpose by inserting bi-directional links from the new law to any earlier nodes referring to the same issue. Lawyers can then follow the links in the opposite direction in a process know as Shepardizing after the printed books that originally supplied these inverse links. The second implication is that layers will sometimes need temporal scrolling of the law to discover what the rules were at some earlier point in time when the action under consideration took place. For example, if a client is taken to count over an old income tax return, the defense should be based on the tax rules for the year question.

Another legal application is the use of multimedia visualizations by trial. Lawyers to illustrate this version during a trial. Since visualizations are so compelling, hurries can often be convinced that something has really happened because they saw it on the computer.

Q5. What are the elements of hypertext? Describe each of the element with the help of an example?

Following are the basic elements of hypertext :

1. Nodes

2. Links

3. Annotations

4. Buttons

5. Editors

6. Browsers

7. Trails

8. Built-in programming languages

1. Nodes : Hypertext is a network of nodes. A node is a collection of data organized around a specific topic and related or linked to another body of information. In a network, each node is linked to some other node. In different hypertext systems, different terms are used for nodes. In HyperCard, a card is a node. In HyperPAD, the node is a PAD.

In many hypertext systems, a node is a screenful of data. Nodes can be categorized in different ways and there can be different kinds of nodes.

The Figure illustrates the node reference within the screens.

This first node reference is {Advertisement Notes} in Figure 4A. It is called the top-level control text because it contains only references and pointers to other node and it is always enclosed in braces. That is, each item in braces is a pointer to another node. By moving the cursor to an opening brace and pressing F10, the user can instantly branch to the corresponding node in the network as shown in Figure 4B. The second level node in this figure also contains reference to other nodes rather than the content information. So, in this case, it is also a control node-it only allows the users to control their navigation through the network

Placing the cursor on a backslash and pressing F10 instantly displays the contents of that node as shown in Figure 4C. Here each node is shown as a separate text file.

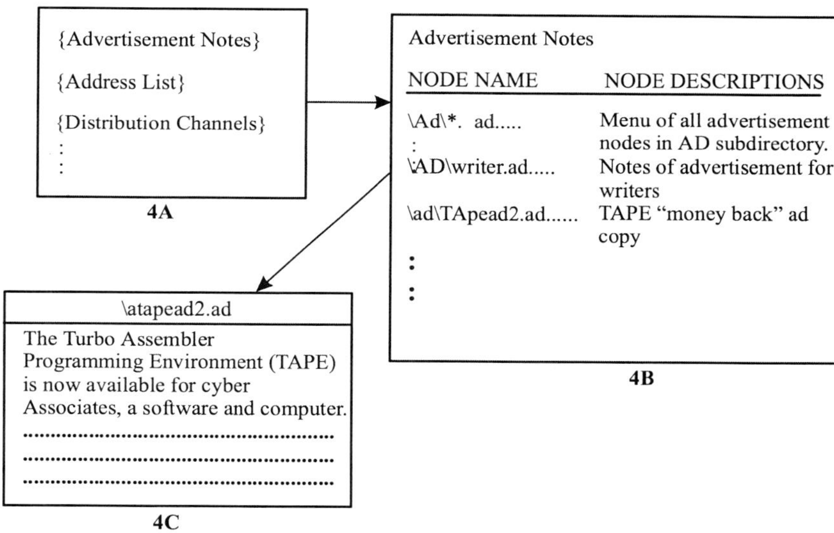

Network of Nodes

2. Links : Links are the other fundamental unit of hypertext besides nodes. A link is information embedded in a node that connects it in some way to another node. Links are almost always anchored at their departure point to provide the user with some explicit object to activate in order to follow the link. The result of activating the anchor is to follow the link to its destination node.

Most links are explicit in the sense that they have been defined by somebody as connecting the departure node with the destination node. Some systems also provide implicit links, which are not defined as such but follow from various properties of the information.

A hypertext link has two ends. Even if a link is not bi-directional, there may still be a need to anchor it explicitly at the destination node. Hypertext systems also have plain links, which are just connections between nodes. The advantage of the approach is of course the simplicity of both authoring and reading. There is nothing to do with links except to follow them, and that one action can be achieved by a click of the mouse.

In addition to the standard links connection two nodes, hypertext systems also have "super-links" to connect a larger number of nodes. There are several possibilities for dealing with a single anchor connected to several destinations. The two simplest options are either to show a menu of the links or to go to all the destinations at the same time.

3. Annotations : A special link type is the annotation link to a small, additional information. The reading of an annotation typically takes the form of a temporary excursion from the primary material to which the reader typically takes the form after having finished with the annotation. Annotations are quite similar to footnotes in traditional text and can be implemented, as Guide pop-up windows that disappear as soon as the user releases the mouse button. Annotations can be accessed through an icon.

Hypertext writers can use annotations in the same way they would use footnotes in traditional text with the exception that hypertext annotations are less intrusive because they are not shown unless the research asks for them. Many hypertext systems allow readers to add new links to the primary material even they do not always allow the reader to change the original nodes.

4. Button : A *button* is a visual clue in a node that alerts a user that a link exists. In other words, a button is a visual representation of a link in a node. By pressing a mouse button, or appropriate function key user can cause the system to activate link to display a different node. Some literature describes a button as a "hot spot" on the screen-a spot that is sensitive. If the cursor (or pointer) is moved over a "hot spot", it will change shape indicating the type of button presented.

In this discussion, the button includes the diamonds and text in between the diamonds. When you move the cursor is moved on to a diamond (or on to a text delimited by the diamonds) and F1 is a note node appears in a small window in the upper right corner of the screen.

5. Editors : An editor is the part of the hypertext systems that enables user to create a node and link it into the network. Some hypertext systems are net distributed with the editors because they are intended as "presentation-only system".

6. Browsers : A hypertext *browser* is a program or subprogram that can display a diagram of a network of nodes. Few hypertext systems for personal computers currently have browsers.

A *hierarchical browser* has some nodes that are regarded as "parent" nodes, which are at higher level than nodes beneath them. They are sometimes regarded as "child" nodes.

In a hierarchical browser, each of the child nodes are linked to each parent node. That is, one can see what child nodes spring from any given node. If the same child node is connected to two different parent nodes, the child node is repeated under each parent node. In a hypertext network, however, there may not be a hierarchical relationship among nodes. Nodes may be equal and just linked together. In such a case a network browser might be more appropriate. In a network browser each node would be designated only once and lines would be drawn to show all of the links between all of the nodes.

7. Trails : A *trail* is a record of the nodes that a user has accessed in viewing a hypertext network. Ideally the trail would include "note nodes" created by the user in the process. It might be enjoyable for example, to follow a trail made by others (famous or otherwise) and read their comments on various stories, illustrations, new items and so on.

Trail recording can be a useful tool for refining hypertext networks. If one can study the trails that users take in searching for information or in studying an instructional network, he can spot problems and refine the network.

8. Built-in programming languages : Some hypertext systems have built-in programming language, so one can customize the system to fit one's specific needs. A good example of a program that has a built-in programming language is KnowledgePro. KnowledgePro enables to build *expert system,* systems that can emulate the behavior of human experts within a limited subject area. KnowledgePro allows store number of rules in a file called a *knowledge base* using special Knowledge-Pro commands. One can program KnowledgePro to present information and ask questions to help users solve complex problems. KnowledgePro differs from many expert systems in that any word in question or response can serve as a hypertext button. One can program KnowledgePro so that when the user selects a hypertext button, a built-in subprogram is activated. The subprogram may go off on its own tangent-ask questions, branch to other subprogram and so on. Eventually, though, when the user finishes the subprogram, control will return to the node that contained the hypertext button.

Q6. Describe the features of any one of the following multimedia development platforms:

(i) Flash **[DEC02,Q1(d)]**

Flash : Macromedia's Flash is aimed at reducing file download times on the Web, and may contain both bitmaps and drawn art.

Flash is a software which supports vector based animation. It is a product of Macromedia. Flash is a software which is generally used for web animation, but as the field of multimedia expanding the work area of Flash has also increased.

Following are the features of Flash :-

- It is a very light i.e. less sized animation software.
- It supports vector based animation.
- It is very easy to learn.
- It is less complex & user friendly.
- Its interface is attractive.
- It supports different layer animation.
- It supports masking.
- It has option related timed animation and frames can be controlled.
- It has facility to make attractive and interactive buttons.
- It comes with effects like alpha, tint & motion path etc.
- Different scenes can be added.
- It has a very strong feature of action script.
- It is compatible to authoring tools like director & authorware.
- Creation of different objects are very easy.
- Objects can be saved in library for reuse again and again & thus saves time and energy.

- With the help of generator a plug in of Flash, it can be connected to a database also.
- Now it support scripting language, which provide much flexibility in creating interactive animations.

(ii) Authorware **[JUN03,Q1(d)][DEC02,Q1(d)]**

#: Authorware Professional **[JUN02,Q1(d)]**

Macromedia's Authorware is a dependable industrial-strength environment that allows multiple people to contribute to an application. Artists can load a library with media, programmers can provide templates for complex interactions, and interface designers can put everything together. And one non-programming designer can even do the entire job alone.

Authorware allows authoring of programs in identical environments on either the PC or the Macintosh and produce runtimes for either. Authorware's icons hold a wealth of programming information that never requires the user to think like a programmer.

Some icons in Authorware can manipulate media on the screen. They can display and erase graphics, move or animate objects. Play AVI and Quick Time digital movies as well as WAV sound files, and access videodisk and videotape players. The new framework icon automates hypermedia interactions and provides a default navigation structure. With a 10-page document in rich text format (RTF), it is easy to import it into the first "page" of framework using Authorware. Authorware can create a new display page for each hard page break in RTF (Rich Text Format) file. Eight buttons are used to move between pages, pop up a pick list of pages, search documents and exit the framework.

Authorware 3 has added text styles that you can apply to any text (labels, menu, options, scrolling text boxes).

Designing in Authorware is also allowed. Authorware elegantly provides full data integrity for it's naming of icons and variables. Change a variable name and it changes everywhere it's used.

(iii) Macromedia Director **[JUN03,Q1(d)] [JUN02,Q1(d)]**

Now the latest version for macromedia Director is Director MX. It is most powerful tool for multimedia presentations and kiosk application than CBT or interactive catalogs that require more database work. The features of their product are as under:

- Precise time control due to central scoring component.
- Cross-platform compatibility.s
- Strong animation features.
- Extensive architecture to add functionality.

The interface of director includes a stage or movie, a playback screen and all elements imported as cast members. The animation done in director consists of frame comprising individual channels. It can hold sound, custom palette, text, etc. An ultimate time-based control can be achieved as all sprites can be accessed during each frame of movies sprites are only copies of the cast member so that they can be transformed in each frame. Each channel number represents a stage layer so the sprites can be moved between layers by simply shuffling them up. The strongest feature of director is its cross-platform compatibility. It is compatible for windows as well as Macintosh platforms. A Broad range of file formats. From graphics, sound, movies etc. Each time a object is imported the object becomes a last member with a specific number on it. In director one can have 32000 cast members now much more in current versions. Director allows a non-programmer to arrange cast members frequently and put them in motion, but interactive movies need some coding. This coding is known as Lingo. Though Director can create complex multimedia events such as CBT, a bit of programming knowledge is still required.

Director is extremely useful tool that exports the logical metaphor to achieve spectacular results.

Q7. What do you mean by hypertext? Describe its applications. [JUN01,Q1(iii)]

When a hypermedia project includes large amounts of text of symbolic content, this content can be indexed and its elements then liked together to afford rapid electronic retrieval of the associated information. When words are keyed in or indexed to other words, you have *hypertext system;* the "text" part of this term represents the project's content and meaning, rather than the graphical presentation of text. Hypertext is what the World Wide Web is all about.

When text lives in a computer instead of printed pages, the computer's powerful processing capabilities can be applied to make the text more accessible and meaningful. The text can then be called *hypertext;* because it can be accessed in nonlinear way, quickly and intuitively.

🗀 **Applications of Hypertext :** Since hypertext is a medium, it is natural to use it in connection with computer-oriented applications. Hypertext can be used to prototype the user interface for almost any other computer program as most initial prototyping consists of linking together screen designs and presenting them to the user in an order determined by simple user actions.

(a) Online Documentation : Online documentation may be the most natural of all hypertext applications. Hypertext is the obvious method for helping user in the situation when they require good access tool to help them retrieve the sections of the manual that are relevant to their current needs.

(b) User Assistance : Hypertext provides a mechanism for integrating several forms of user assistance, including the online manual, an introductory tutorial, online help system, and even the error messages. Because users only get massages when they are in some kind of trouble, the error messages are a print candidate for providing users with assistance.

In an integrated user assistance facility based on hypertext, it would be possible for the user to link an error message to the location in the help system that gives further assistance on the problem. Also if the user wants further assistance than it could be provided by the help system then it may become possible to link it further, to the appropriate location in the tutorial component, to get a computer-aided instruction lesson.

This type of integrated user interface does not exist in current computer system and can be made possible with the hypertext facility.

(c) Software Engineering: The hypertext has a great potential for providing links among the large number of specification and implementing documents that are produced during the software development life cycle. For example, it would be possible to start from a required document and link to that part of the design specification that meets a given requirement. One can then link from the design specification to the actual code. A developed organisation would require to follow a software engineering methodology supported by an integrated set of computerized tools in a complete CASE (Computer Aided Software Engineering) environment, in order to derive full benefits from this form of hypertext links among the various documents in the software lifecycle.

It is also possible to use hypertext in a lifecycle-oriented approach by including linking facilities in structure-oriented editors for program code. For example, it is possible to click on a variable to see its definition and associated comments, or to link from a procedure call to open a window with the text of the procedure.

Q8. For making a digital multimedia one has to use many different types of packages in addition to authoring tools. Describe features of the packages (other than authoring tools) that might be needed for development of multimedia.

[JUN02,Q3]

 # What are the other multimedia software prevalent in current market? Write a brief explanation of them.

Authoring tools or softwares are generally used only for the final presentation. Following are the some of the packages with their features :

(i) Photoshop : Photoshop is a software which is a product of Adobe. Adobe Photoshop is an image editing software. It can be used to make layouts, editing images and creating visual effect too. Photoshop is a bitmap image software. It has great options related to masking. One can get different colour modes to work with. One can also create outwork in vector based software like illustrator & edit it out in Photoshop. Another software for graphic creation and manipulation is CorelDraw.

(ii) Sound Forge : Sound forge is a software which is used for digital sound recording and digital sound effects. This software works with sound card and one can have all the features which facilitates in manipulating sound.

(iii) 3DS Max : 3DS Max can be used extensively for 3D animation and special effects. Thus this software can be used to create 3D animation as per our story board. One can apply state of the art effects like camera, light, textures. These effects look very realistic.

(iv) Flash : Flash is a product of Macromedia. It is a vector shape animation product. It is used basically for web animation. But due to its good interactive option and compatibility it is also used in authoring. It also supports action script that gives enhance output as per requirement.

These are the softwares used apart from Authoring Softwares.

Q9. What is the purpose of Multimedia authoring tools? Does Multimedia development starts with multimedia authoring? Describe one of the tools that may be used for multimedia authoring. **[DEC01,Q1(c)]**

The purpose of multimedia authoring tools is to create highly interactive applications in which the information can flow from application to user and from user to application. It helps in creating higher quality, audio and video applications with very little expertise.

Yes, multimedia development starts with multimedia authoring because Authoring systems are generally menu-driven systems intended to be easy to use by multimedia developer and authoring programs could be grouped into two different types:

- Those relied on point and click
- Those requires simple scripting

🗁**ImageQ:** ImageQ is another multimedia authoring software package. Although, it is a windows 3.1 application but it can also play back on windows 95, create slide show presentations well and provides a way to distribute them easily. It lacks the intuitive programming language and strong interface necessary for truly productive multimedia applications development.

ImageQ presentations comprise a series of background image and associated control scripts that add user interface controls, overlay images, and underlying programming to each slide. It uses a multiple-document interface to manage one or more presentations simultaneously.

The slide strip window for each presentation contains either thumb nails or file information for each slide image and provide the means of navigating through the presentation at design time. Although the image in the slide strip are, miniature versions of the background image they do not show any of the users interface element that the user has added such as button and list boxes. The user must create these through code, which ImageQ will interpret only at runtime-a major deficiency that other authoring system (such as Icon Author and Director) avoid by offering design tools to arrange interface controls visually without code.

While ImageQ does not provide the robust slide design tool that competing products include, it does import a wide variety of graphics formats. Once the images have been imported into an ImageQ presentation, they can be kept in their native formats or saved as .BMP or .HKF files.

Whenever images are imported into an ImageQ presentation, it involves only creation of thumb nails slide references, the image themselves remain as separate files. The list of filenames and the control and transition setting are stored with an IMQ extension, which serves as the main file for the presentation.

ImageQ's programming language is awkward to work with, because it uses unconventional syntax and event handlers. For example, ImageQ uses lines like "and X to Y", put 150 into X for adding the two values in a single statement and assigning the value to 150 to X, respectively.

Though ImageQ lacks and programming tools, it does well with distribution. It is easy to build portable presentations as alone .EXE files that includes the ImageQ runtime. ImageQ is really a presentation package in an authoring system's clothing. Its real strength lies in ability to create traditional slide shows with prebuilt images and distribute them with no royalty. Yet the product's lack of interactive design tools and its clumsy programming languages ultimately make it a poor choice for robust multimedia applications development.

Q10. What is Quick Time? How it does work? What is the importance of Quick Time?

Quick time is a software developed by apple that supports time-based multimedia on the Macintosh. It has also been ported for windows environment. The given figure describes how the different development environment relate to one another.

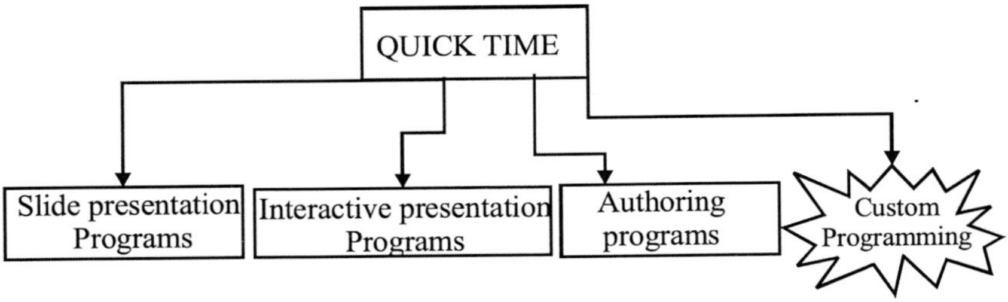

Importance of Quick Time: Quick time adds support for time-based media to the basic Macintosh system architecture. The most common media that require this kind of support are video, animation and sound. It is important that quick time supports sound because quick time can synchronize round tracks with video track. Quick time provides synchronization between the animations that would otherwise play at different speeds when played on different machines.

Quick time stores video digitally i.e. it converts the frames of video to digital images that are stored in the computer's hard disk.

The advantage of storing video this way is that computer can very quickly and easily access other information on a hard disk.

Another advantage is that once the frames are stored on the hard disk they can be manipulated using a number of difficult editing applications.

The disadvantage of storing video this way is that the computer has to do a lot of work to display the video sequences.

To achieve digital video, the computer needs two things :

- The computer must be capable of handling video's large amount of data. This is accomplished by streaming in which the computer displays one frame as it read the following frame from the disk.
- The computer needs kind of timing mechanism that keeps video and sound synchronized. Timing is particularly important when the people are displayed speaking on the screen, as without synchronization their lips won't move in synch with the sound. Quick time fulfills both needs.

Quick time has many features but the two most important are its compressors and its timing mechanism. The compressors enables the program to reduce the frames to a manageable size, so the computer can stream the information from the disk. The timing mechanism ensures that multiple tracks maintain synchronization.

CHAPTER 4

MULTIMEDIA DEVELOPMENT ISSUES AND SUGGESTIONS

☞**Introduction**
☞**Objectives**
☞**Learning interface design**
✓*Interface design and the psychology of learning*
✓*Working with learning style*
✓*Considering interface design*
☞**Planning the Multimedia Programme/application**
✓*Defining the Goal*
✓*Outlining*
✓*Logic Flowchart*
✓*Program Storyboard*
✓*Planning for Creation of Multimedia Building Blocks*
✓*Copyright issue and its management*
☞**Development TIPS of multimedia building blocks**
✓*Text*
✓*Graphics in Multimedia*
✓*Sound and video in multimedia applications*
☞**Multimedia Authoring**

Multimedia design and development involves lot of creative activities. While developing multimedia many a times you are provided with many unrelated multimedia elements. Even in the developed multimedia many a times difficulties such as navigation through large amount of text, non-existent of online help, poor documentation, and non-coordinated video and audio sequences exists. Therefore, for creation of good multimedia one must try to follow the process of multimedia development. In addition, one must also be exposed to basic principles of learning as that contributes in having a good presentable academic session through multimedia. In this chapter, we will be discussing about these types of concepts relating to multimedia development.

In this chapter, we have presented brief outlines of the process of multimedia development we have covered aspects relating to planning, which is the most important activity of multimedia development. We have also presented many tips for creations of multimedia elements and authoring tools. You may explore any tool for multimedia for application development, but to begin with it is always advisable to start with the tools available in windows operating system. Please note that to create a good multimedia a proper plan and design is essential and you should pay more attention to such areas.

Q1. What is learning interface design? Explain.

The term multimedia interface design refers to the means through which a user interacts with application content or information. Through the interface you may be provided with navigation buttons, text fields, instruction, graphics, animation, audio recourses and other means of help users achieve the goals of application. Since one of the main use of multimedia is in education and training, therefore, the basic concepts of how learning takes place is helpful and even necessary in designing a meaningful and useful multimedia application interface. In the following subsection let us explore the basic principles of the psychology learning and its application to interface design.

🗁**Interface design and the psychology of learning :** Multimedia involves multi-sensory experiences. Multimedia content reaches users in many different forms, therefore, providing an enhanced learning environment. But how does we learn in a learning situation?

The first step in the cyclic process of learning is attention to information. The human brain obtains information through senses, fundamentally through our eyes and ears. However, the information is accepted only if one is paying attention. The information so gathered is transferred to the local working memory. This local memory is to be continuously refreshed: otherwise the information so gained may be lost. This process is called rehearsal. The rehearsal process may cause transfer of information to short term memory to the long-term memory of the human. This process is termed as encoding. For using encoded information it must be retrieved from the long-term memory and delivered to the working memory for the processing, thus completing the cycle of learning. The following figure shows the learning cycle.

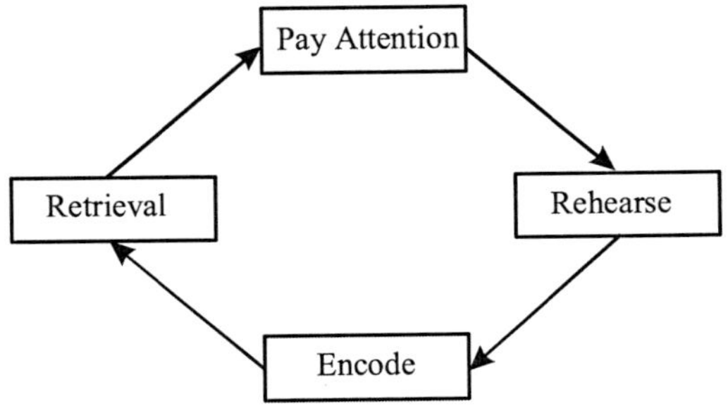

A well-designed multimedia programme demands the simultaneous attention of several senses through process of appealing to more than one sense simultaneously, facilitating the rehearsal process. Even the process of retrieval is facilitated for the concept being presented by the power of multiple media. Thus, multimedia enhances the retention of knowledge.

Another important issue for multimedia application design is the amount of information that can be assimilated at given time: this is referred to as the cognitive load. Too much information in a multimedia presentation may overload users cognitive abilities, thus, making learning less effective. This will defeat the basic design objectives.

Q2. Explain the working with learning styles.

The individual style of learning has got different dimension. Some people learn by graphic learning while others learning primarily by reading, seeing, or visualizing. Some of the learner learns more effectively through physical movement or touching, these are called kinesthetic learners. To get a general feeling the of learning style of the users, you may ask the following question to the intended audience of the multimedia: "How do you learn? What kinds of books do you prefer? Do you like the Books with tots pictures and diagrams? Do you learn better by watching video? etc.

You will discover that the intended audience of your multimedia package follows a variety of learning styles, that is, they learn and prefer to learn in different ways. The design of your application must incorporate different multimedia building blocks that in turn appeal to different learning styles. Therefore, you must use effectively text, audio, graphics, animation, and digital video such that your multimedia application is more meaningful to the people having different learning styles.

Q3. What are the fundamental rules for designing the computer based instruction?

Designing the computer-based instructions required the fundamental rules:

✓ Keep low cognitive load. Keep a simple, consistent screen design

✓ Do not divide the learner's attention; you must use various media elements such as text, graphics, and sound to reinforce a concept rather than introducing different types of concepts.

✓ You may use color, special effects, and sound to direct the learner's attention to important areas of the presentation. However, use them only if it is essential.

✓ The information, which a learner may need to undertake an activity must be available on the screen, for example, the reference information for answering a feedback form must be available.

✓ Encourage frequent revision/rehearsals by the learner.

✓ Encourage reinforcement of learning by using concrete words and different media to repetition the message.

✓ Avoid repetition in interactions.

✓ For imparting procedural skills simulation can be used. Simulation should be as close as possible to the actual job environment.

Q4. What are the plan to design a multimedia programme or application?

A multimedia development team consists of many different skills oriented people, who include a producer, education consultant, media consultant, media designers, media specialists, webmaster etc. However, the whole team works for a single objective that is creation of an effective multimedia application. Therefore, one of the major issues for multimedia production is to plan an application. Let us discuss it in grater details in this section.

To start the authoring process of multimedia application development without planning all the components of the project is a major mistake as it may lead to an insufficient application being developed. A multimedia project should be planned through following stepwise process:

✓ Develop the Multimedia programme/application concept.
✓ Outline your programme.
✓ Development of flowchart.
✓ Develop programme storyboard.
✓ Consider copyright issue.
✓ Plan the production of text, graphic, animation, auto, and video,
✓ Prepare the project budget and time schedule.

This planning process is also presented in figure given below.

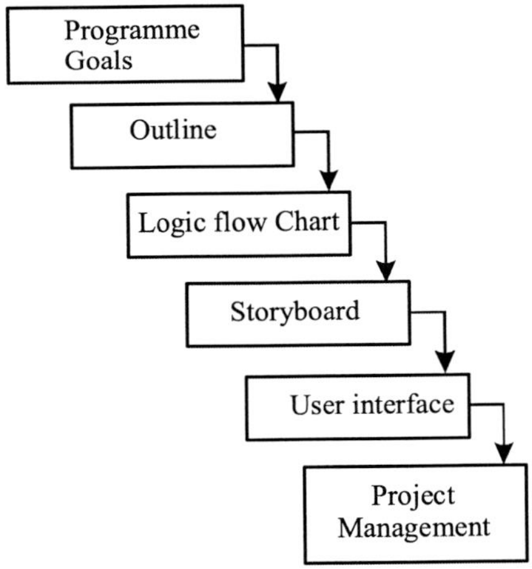

Q5. Define the goal of multimedia for an application.

The goal of a multimedia application is defined by the scope of work, which is a written description of the proposed multimedia project. The scope of work clarifies your ideas and goals regarding the proposed project. It also helps the development team members to visualize the basic objectives of the programme.

The following example illustrates the scope of an application, which may be designed to teach a Programming Language at Graduate level.

"The textbooks and instruction materials of the programming emphasis mainly the basic components and syntax of a programming language. However, one of the skills where students are facing difficulties is the problem solving skill, which is essential in order to solve various problems. Science the goals of the this course is bot only to development know how of a programming language but also to enable student to solve problems using the programming language, we expect that a multimedia based tutorial which helps the student to solve problems using data structures and programming language may be extremely useful. We except that making a direct correlation between the general principles of problem solving using data structure, and the concepts of a programming language, the student will be able to develop better problems solving skills that will develop his confidence in computing. This will also result in better student motivation, and will help in reducing the dropout rate."

🗁**Project outcomes :** "The objective of this project is to developed one experimental module referring to problem solving using a Programming Language. This experimental module will mainly focus on the concepts of pointers and related data structures. This module will be used buy the instructor in a classroom. Integration of multimedia in teaching of programming language will allow the instructor to reach student with a diversity of learning style; this module will be tested in the classroom, and evaluate. It will be revised on the basis of evaluation of faculties and students."

🗁**Outlining :** Once the goal and the objectives of the programme are clear, the next step is to create outline of the project., an interactive multimedia presentation may not necessary be linear presentation like a slide show or a video programme. It has the capacity f branching. The outline of a programme represents branching in a multimedia programme. The content specialist does the outlining.

Development an outline for an interactive multimedia project is almost the same as that of development an outline for a chapter in the book. However, the outlining of multimedia structure is translated into branches or points of decision on the screen. Even the main outlining headings may become options available to the user in the main menu of the multimedia presentation program with sub-heading becoming the sub-menu entries.

To continues the examples, the outline of this program is:

🗁**Problem solving using Pointer**

1. Pointer Basics

✓ Introduction

✓ Pointers and Addresses

✓ Pointers and Function Arguments

2. Pointers and Simple Arrays

✓ Address arithmetic

✓ Character Strings

✓ Pointer arrays

1. Definition
2. Features
3. Implementation issues
4. Usage examples and situations

3. Multi-dimensional Array using Pointers

✓ Definition of Multidimensional

✓ Initialization Issues

✓ Implementation using Pointers

✓ Command line arguments

4. **Pointers and Self Referential Structures**

✓ Basic of Structures

✓ Pointers to structures

✓ Self-referential structure

✓ Implementation of binary tree using pointers

An outline is further developed to include some details of the information to be provided to
the intended audience on each screen, which may have multiple media forms in it.

Q6. What is logic flow chart?

The logic flow chart is an important component of an interactive multimedia programme. A flow chart is a graphical road map of the proposed application. The authoring team takes the help of this flowchart to produce the final multimedia application. A flow chart represents the choices available from each topic to other topics. The complexity of these flow charts is dependent on the applications being developed. The flowcharts, which illustrate games, are among the most complex flowcharts. The flow chart shown below extends the example project about programming language.

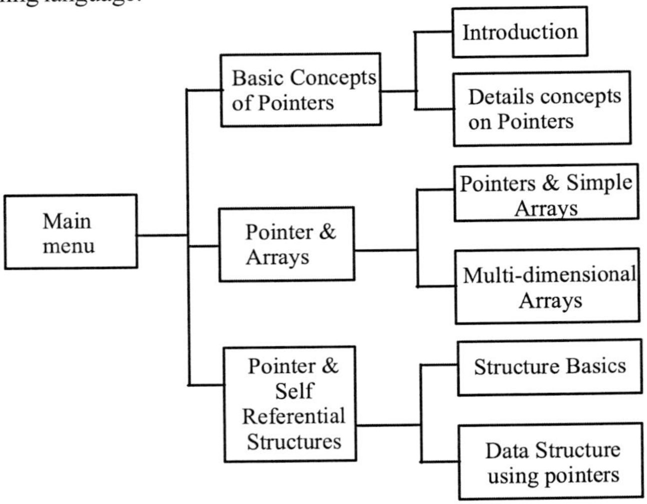

Q7. Define the program story board.

The storyboard is a graphical representation of the proposed multimedia project. The storyboard is an extension of ideas presented in the programme script. It is presented with a series of temples used for various purposes. Some of the common templates, which are required to represent a complex application, are:

✓ Logic flow and branching sequence templates

✓ The storyboard template

✓ Animation sequence templates
✓ Button details template
✓ Audio/ video scripting templates

We are including few sample templates here. Please note that these are not standard templates, the format of such template changes as per the requirements and practices at various multimedia organisations.

These templates are very useful information and help the developer to keep a production log or history of the work. They also help in keeping track of the production design and help in identifying the design parameters for the application development. Throughout the authoring process, the development team should discuss progress on the multimedia development project with the client or with the members of application target group.

Multimedia Application Development Template
Logic Flow and Branching sequence.

Project Name: ______________________

Intended Audience: ______________________

Prepared By: ______________________

Script No: ______________________

Moderation Date: ______________
Moderated by: ______________
Received for Authoring on: ______________

Page No. __________

Audio Script

Branching in Application

Example Branching Sequence

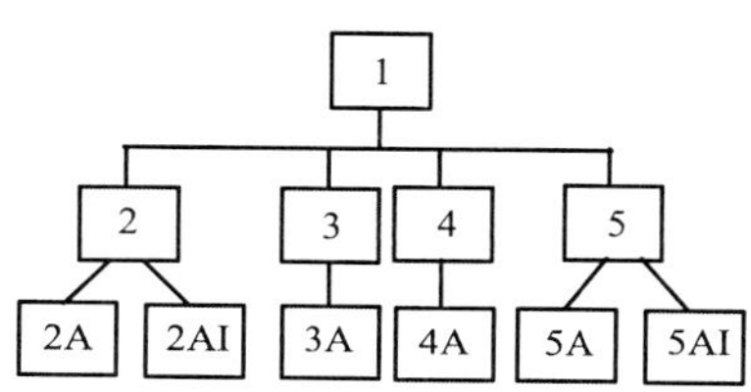

Multimedia Application Development Template
Audio Description Template

Project Name: ____________________

Intended Audience: ____________________

Prepared By: ____________________

Moderation Date: ____________________
Moderated by: ____________________
Received for Authoring on: ____________________

Script No: ____________________ Page No. __________

Audio Script

Audio Sources if already exist

Audio CD ____________________

MIDI: ____________________

Computer Sound File: ____________________

Video Sound File: ____________________

Copyright ownerships of the resources: ____________________

When to play audio: ____________________

Multimedia Application Development Template
Storyboard Templete

Project Name: ____________________

Intended Audience: ____________________

Prepared By: ____________________

Script No: ____________________

Moderation Date: ____________
Moderated by: ____________
Received for Authoring on: ____________

Page No. ________

STAGE

🗁Planning For Creation Of Multimedia Building Blocks

The development building block is an extensive process and requires number of production steps. In the planning phase of it, the basic script or content of this element is defined. For examples, a proposed script for the Programming Language Project may be:

"Pointers is a variable in a programming language which contains the address of a variable. They are used because:

✓ They usually help in development of more compact program code.
✓ They result in development of more efficient program code.
✓ They sometimes are the only way to express a computation.
✓ They allow implementation of call by reference.

🗁*Pointers and Address*

A pointer is a variable location, which holds the address of a memory location. For example, if c is a character type and p is a pointer type and if we say that p points to c it means that the pointer named p is holding the address of memory location which is also referred to as variable name c. (A graphics in this respect can be shown) ……………"

Please note that in various situations the details given through textual component may be different. For example, since this multimedia package is to be used for classroom presentations the text is presented in short phrases or bullets.

Even the basic formats for graphics and video scripts may be planned at this juncture. The content specialist may be requested to provide such information. Availability of already available resource should also be indicated at this level.

Q8. What are the copyright laws in designing multimedia application?

while designing multimedia application, copyright issue plays a crucial role because of two fundamental reasons.

✓ Multimedia involves use of multiple media each of that media element may be protected under the copyright laws.

✓ Original multimedia works are also protected by copyrights.

The copyright laws protect the following types of works:

✓ Printed or Electronic text of the form of prose, poetry, news paper articles, magazine articles, books, computer software, etc.

✓ Musical works such as songs, advertisements recording of music, sounds, or words etc.

✓ Dramatic works such as plays, sits etc.

✓ Dances and mime works.

✓ Pictorial, drawings, graphics, and sculptural works such as photographs, posters, maps, paintings, drawings, graphic arts, display ads, works of fine arts etc.

✓ Motion pictures and others audiovisual works including multimedia.

Therefore, it is important that during the planning phase you sort the copyright issues relating to getting permissions of using copyright material from its owner. Please make sure that you have the licensed copies of all the software that are required for the development of multimedia.

Q9. What are the building blocks in multimedia? Explain.

Once the planning phase is over, the multimedia building blocks are to be developed. In the subsequence subsections we will discuss about the important issues relating to various multimedia components.

🗁 **Text :** Text is one of the primary mediums of communication of information. Text can also be used for reinforcing a concept. Text for multimedia can be produced using a number of word processing software. Many newer authoring packages also allow most of the word processing facilities. While developing text for multimedia application please make sure that the text format, which you have developed, is compatible to the authoring tool text format.

Some of the tips for creation of textual information are:

✓ The amount of text put in a multimedia application may be limited to short paragraphs or point wise lists.

✓ The font size should be large enough to be read easily by the multimedia user. For examples, the application, which is to be used for the training of a group the minimum point size, should be 20 points so that it is visible from a distance.

✓ The text styling and formatting should be consistent over the complete application.

✓ The special effects on text should be used to highlight important concepts or messages, but do not overdo them.

✓ Use font types (bitmapped or outlined fonts) and point sizes, which are commonly available. This will make sure that the text looks the same as it was designed.

🗁 **Graphics in Multimedia :** Graphics is the most predominant component of a multimedia. Graphics may be used in many form such as photos, charts for illustration and summarization numerical data, environments simulation, logos, and colors that illustrate the content of the application. The content specialist provides content in the application.

Graphics help people to learn and retain more information from other forms of information. There are many kinds of graphics that are integrated into multimedia application. These are:

- ✓ Background
- ✓ Pictures, photographs and 3d pictures
- ✓ Charts, flow charts and organizational charts
- ✓ Buttons.

🗁**Background :** Background of an application may establish the tone and the theme of an application. The background of various applications may vary from solid colors to highly complex graphics, incorporating photographs, maps and logos. Following are some tips for designing background of an application:

- ✓ It should not be too complex to leave strain on eyes on continuous use.
- ✓ It should in some way reflect the theme of the application
- ✓ It should not involve high storage capacity, for applications, which the download time.
- ✓ It should not exceed the display capabilities of display devices.
- ✓ It should to be packed with the text.

🗁**Pictures, photographs, and 3d graphics :**

- ✓ Commercially available Clip Art's which are a collection of drawings, usually available as back-and-white or 4-bit (16 color) images in ESP (Encapsulated formats), PIC (Macintosh Picture), and BMP (Bitmapped Graphics) formats and are classified in categories.
- ✓ Photo CDs consists of professional quality photos, which are normally classified by topics.
- ✓ Online web based resources, which are available in many different types format.
- ✓ Digital still photographs are the user created resource. The photographs can be obtained either from the digital cameras or captured from video still images. Portable, small digital cameras of companies like apple, Casio, and Kodak etc. are available in the market at affordable prices. This camera can be connected to one of the serial port of the computer and software can be used to get an image file.

In addition, many application software are available to create and edit images in different formats. One such very simple utility available is paintbrush in Windows.

🗁**Charts, Flow-charts and organizational charts : Charts** are an appealing way of resenting numerical information visually. Charts can be developed using electronic spreadsheets, statistical programs, or integrated applications. One important consideration while placing the chart in your multimedia application is its contrast with the screen background. You have to ensure the visibility and readability on the charts.

Figures given below show the pie chart and bar chart.

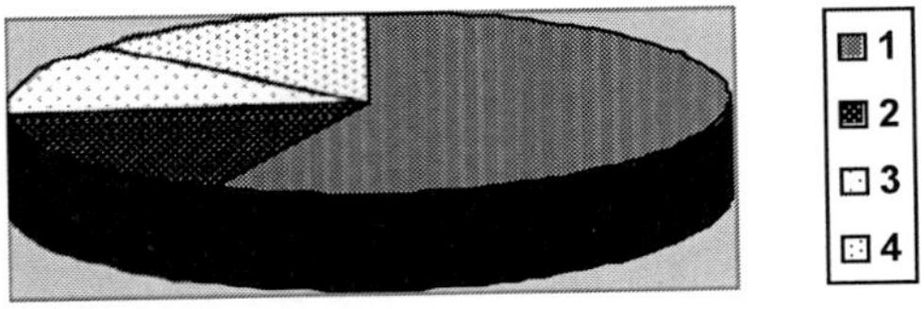

✓ **Flow charts** are graphical stepwise representation of a logical process. The concept of flowchart is not new for you. You may keep simple flowcharts making the details available once a user needs more details on a typical step of the process. Do not try to put all the information on a single screen.

✓**An organization chart** provides information on the hierarchical structure of the organisation. A simple organisation chart is shown in the following :

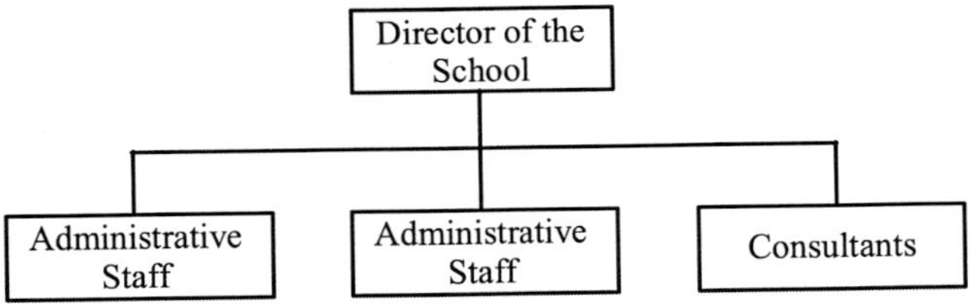

These charts can also be created using the integrated packages, which are available with most of the presentation programs.

Graphics

✓ Do not overburden your graphics screens with too much of simultaneous information.

✓ Keep the graphics on the screen simple, clear, user-friendly, and elegant as possible.

✓ Keep a check on screen resolution. Sometimes on reducing the resolution or number of colors used in a graphics may result in loss of sharpness of original picture.

Q10. Explain the role of Sound and video in multimedia applications.

Video and sound help in communicating a lot of information in a small time. Sound is a very exciting part of multimedia application. You multimedia should be equipped with good supportive sound, however, please do not use excessive sound in your application. It may be annoying to the user. Video enhances the impact of multimedia application, especially in area involving difficult concepts. However, please note that good quality digital video clips can be displayed only if there exist good hardware and software configurations in the client machine.

Some of the usage of audio and video in multimedia may be for:

✓ The background sound

✓ Sound/video recordings of an eminent person.

✓ Narration of historical facts

✓ Narration of an industrial process preferably through video

✓ A welcome message showing a walk through a building museum, historical place etc.

🗁The Digital video

The digital video is represented as a sequence of frames having a rectangular screen with each pixel being represented by 8 bits (black and while video) or 24 bits (colored video). Digital video can be acquired from either digital recording or by converting analog video footage of high quality into digital video. Adding a number of other interactive elements such as interactive glossary, graphics overlays, text bullets, or animation can further enhance the converted digital video. It also allows and incorporation of transition effect. There are many digital video formats available. The most common of those are quick time, MPG and AVI.

🗁Video Compression : A full screen video clip having a screen resolution of 800×600, having 24 bit color at about 30 frames per second require about many MB of space. Even the disk transfer rates are to sufficient to support such kind of data rates. Thus, without using data compression algorithms such motion pictures cannot be used in digital systems. Common data compression standards are **MPEG, JPEG, DVI** etc.

The JPEG (joint photographic expert group) standard is for compressing continuous still pictures. It is normally used to encode 24-bit RGB video images and will leave out some of the minor picture details for the sake of simplicity. It produces a compression ration of 20:1 for still images without any appreciable degradation of pictures. This is a popular standard on Macintosh and Amiga platforms.

MPEG (Moving Picture Expert Group) is compression standard for compressing video since 1993. MPEG was developed specifically for motion images. MPEG can compress both audio and video. It produces a compression ration of 50:1 before the degradation in picture quality occurs. MPEG standard allows fast video and audio compression, and real time decompression. MPEG allows a decompression data rate of 1.2 to 1.5 M per second, thus, allowing full motion, full screen video.

🗁Video in Multimedia Application : Some of the basic considerations, which need to addressed for integrating video in a multimedia application are:

✓ Data transfer rate and capacity of the storage device

✓ Size of the Windows to be used for display

✓ Frame rate and image resolution.

In a multimedia system one need a high data transfer rate and capacity to sustain full motion video capabilities. The size of display window can be controlled to lower sizes to reduce the transfer rate requirements. A lower frame rate or resolution may reduce the data-handling rate but will result in poor quality of video.

🗁Sound in multimedia : In a multimedia application text, images, animation can be greatly complemented by the use of sound. Sound is an integral part of video also. Sound can be used in a number of a ways in a multimedia application such as:

✓ Sound of the surrounding a multimedia environment can be recorded, for example, while showing a photograph of jungle the associated sound track can leave a lasting impression.

✓ Sound helps the users to receive and retain the multimedia message in a better way.

✓ Sound can also be used for catching attention in a boring graphics oriented presentation.

✓ Sound may also break the monotony of multimedia base tutors and enhance the learning process.

Q11. What is the need of authoring software? What are the basic features needed in an authoring software ? Compare the features of any two authoring software in the context of "creation of games multimedia".

One all the components of multimedia have developed, one has to use authoring tool to stitch the multimedia application, which also involves interactivity.

🗁**There are four basic function provided by almost all authoring software:**

✓ **Importing:** it should be able to import carious media elements, which may have been developed using other software package.

✓ **Creating:** it should allow some basic features for creation of text, graphics and may be sound if not video.

✓ **Integrating:** it should allow you to define sequences and provide linkages

✓ **Delivering:** it should allow developing self-running application and encryption of application data.

ImageQ is multimedia authoring software package. Although, it is a windows 3.1 application but it can also play back on windows 95, create slide show presentations well and provides a way to distribute them easily. It lacks the intuitive programming language and strong interface necessary for truly productive multimedia applications development.

ImageQ presentations comprise a series of background image and associated control scripts that add user interface controls, overlay images, and underlying programming to each slide. It user a multiple-document interface to manage one or more presentations simultaneously.

Q12. Compare and contrast the features of various authoring tools available. Indicate which type of application a given authoring tool is more suitable for. Give justification in support of your answer.

#: Suppose you are developing a multimedia which requires lot of animation and interaction. Compare and contrast the features of various authoring software for suitability for the above application. Choose one software for final development and describe reasons of your selection. [JUN01,Q3]

Let us briefly clearly the type of authoring tools available in the market.

✓ **Time-based authoring :** They use time scale to decide duration of message on the screen. Some of the authoring tools in this category are macromedia action, animation works interactive etc.

✓ **Card-based or Page based Authoring Tools :** These tools allow information to be put in as stack of cards can further be linked with each other in predefined sequences. Even the cross linkages along with branching facility is also possible in such packages. Examples in this category are hyper card by Apple, asymmetric tool book and many presentation softwares.

✓ **con-base Authoring Tools :** These tools allow creation of an Icon based flow script, which is then converted to an application. Examples in the category are macromedia authoring professional, icon Author etc.

✓ **Theatrical Authoring Tools :** These types of tools refer to media elements as independent cast members, which are assembled using score which is a sequencer in terms of time, linking and animation. Complex visual effects can be applied on these scores to create powerful presentations. Macromedia director is one such package.

Now the question is which authoring software is most suitable for what applications? There are no standard guidelines, however, the following are some suggested usage.

Business applications	:	Time based authoring tools Icon based authoring tools
Education	:	Icon based authoring tools Theatrical based authoring
Games / Multimedia which	:	***Requires lot of Animation Preferably Theatrical based authoring software is better suited. As it provides better support for the development of highly animated and interactive applications.***

Interactivity in an Application:

Most of the authoring tools of multimedia allow the following type of navigational structures:

✓ Linear or sequential mainly used in business and educational applications.
✓ Hierarchical, like a tree structure, used in educational and business applications
✓ Non-linear, like a graph, users select the path of its own, used in various encyclopedia development
✓ A combination of the above tools.

In most of the system interactivity is built by creating menu-based options through questions and their feedback.

Q13. A multimedia tutorial is to be developed for delivery through Internet. How will you plan and develop the application? [JUN02,Q2]

Internet has become a popular means to spread knowledge. When a multimedia tutorial is to be developed for delivery through Internet, planning has to be done first.

Developing a Multimedia Presentation

1. Index (Contents) of the Presentation
2. Developing the audience for which presentation is targeted to.
3. Tools used to create presentation.
4. Media used for Presentation.

MULTIMEDIA DELIVERED THROUGH INTERNET

1. The audience is similar to student who can access the Internet to reach to tutorial. He also uses the downloading system to capture the study Material.
2. The contents of the tutorial will have to be written to suit the Web Page format, links to related sites, icons, images etc.
3. Tools to be used in the context of the content and the media to be used.
4. Tutorial has the format of Internet access therefore it is to be used in designing coming the way from browser like Netscape Navigator or Internet Explorer.

🗁The whole Project will be planned and executed in the following steps:

1. The contents of Tutorial firstly specify through out and put on paper.
2. The specimen of audience i.e. those students who use Internet is always remembered while designing the contents of Presentation.
3. The structure in a Web Page format.
4. Providing the E-mail feedback facility and online question in the tutorial Web format.
5. Check and verify the access.

Before delivering (releasing) to public it must be extensively sampled and tested.

Q14. Suppose you are asked to develop a multimedia tutor for the topics of "Introduction of Computer". Describe the process of multimedia development for the above tutor. Give description on each step of development in the context of above application. [JUN01,Q2]

#: Describe the process of planning and development of a mathematics tutorial through multimedia. [DEC02,Q2]

#: Suppose you are asked to develop a multimedia presentation that is to be used for presentation of Information through Internet. The speciality of the application is that the tutorial information is dispersed on many sites and these tools present the information as a single source with search facility. How will you plan and develop the suggested application? [DEC01,Q2]

The following are the points to develop a Multimedia tutor for the topics of "Introduction to Computer" or "Mathematics Tutorial" or "Information through Internet" or "Computer Fundamentals".

(i) First of all you have to plan a structure in your Mind to develop the project.

(ii) The specimen of audience (what you say and how you say will depend on the type and age group of student).

(iii) Outlining the Programme.

(iv) Develop a flow chart.

(v) Making a dynamic Question, answer sessions so the students question can be justified.

(vi) Plan the production of text, graphics, animation, audio and video.

(vii) Preparing the time schedule and the budget of project.

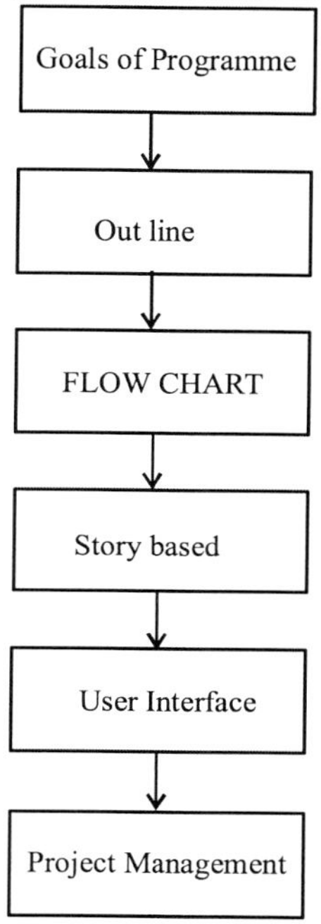

Multimedia is very useful in any development of the tutorial. When we develop any tutorial then planning is the necessary thing. Firstly it provides the analysis of the tutorial.

At the analysis phase of a development, all the members of the team gradually construct a set of assumptions about the interactive product you are developing. It is sound practice to confirm those assumptions before undertaking the bulk of the design work of the product. The assumption should be confirmed with your client and with any vendors that may be collaborating on the project. The "Assumption check list" is a tool that can help you confirm the assumptions underlaying your multimedia development effort.

The assumption check list presumes that time has passed between the initial estimate of project scope and the approval to begin the project.

There are various steps involved in this assumption which are :

Step 1 : Meet with the client and determine :

- Are the goals and objectives still on target ?
- Is the audience still the same ?
- Is the review of each proposed element same ?
- Are the plans for marketing the product same ?
- Are implementation plans same ?

Step 2 : Review your estimates of project scope, including :

- Materials required
- Time needed
- Project cost

Step 3 : If required, rethink the project goals :

If serious questions about project scope or other assumption arise, don't hesitate to raise a red flag. **It is better to rethink the multimedia development project now than to cancel it later.**

After getting all things we think about Assessment Matrix.

The assessment matrix is designed to help you assume that each of the goals or objectives you've defined for your multimedia product is assessed by one or more reliable and valid outcome measures. Often development teams wait until a product is almost complete before making up a test intended to measure its outcomes. By planning for assessment early in the design stage of your product, your will've a much greater chance of designing a program that is actually capable of achieving its objectives.

After completing all these steps we specify the objectives specification tools.

A key element in the instructional development process is to specify the objectives for your program as clearly as possible. Poorly stated objective often result in instruction that is inappropriate. This tool is designed to help you write more specific objectives by providing you with a list of observable verbs. The tool includes verbs for both the cognitive domain and affective domain.

After completing all these things finally we check the user characteristics checklist :

(i) Cognitive characteristics :

- General aptitudes
- Specific aptitudes
- Functional literacy
- Computer literacy
- Learning style
- Prerequisite content knowledge

(ii) Social characteristics :

- Attitudes toward
- Relationships with poor
- Attitude toward authority
- Ethnic background
- Education level

(iii) Personality characteristics :

- Motivation to use this program
- Motivation to learn
- Attitude toward learning
- Attitude toward technology
- Self esteem

(iv) Physical characteristics :

- Visual abilities
- Auditory abilities
- Tectile abilities

Whenever you write objectives, review the verbs to select the ones most appropriate to your job or content. This is by no means a complete list of all the possible verbs and its primary value may be in spurring your imagination in writing better objectives.

Q15. Assume that you have been assigned the job of creation of Windows tutor. Design the multimedia tutor for the above case. Explain each step of the process of development by giving suitable details. [JAN01]

Firstly we will be starting in Multimedia Projects with the following points which are as follows:

1. Create Multimedia Programme.
2. Outline the Programme.
3. Create flowchart.
4. Create Program Storyboard.
5. User interface must be planned.
6. Plan the production of text, graphics and video.
7. Finally project object and time schedule.

Then next to be used authoring tool e.g. in education generally we use theatrical authoring tool which refer to media elements as independent members, complex visual effects can be applied on these scores to create powerful presentation.

The first step in the cyclic process of learning is attention to information. The information so gathered is transferred to the local working memory. This local memory is to be continuously refreshed; otherwise the information so gathered may be lost. This process is called Rehearsal. The rehearsal process may cause transfer of information to short term memory to the long term memory of the human. This process is called encoding. For using encoded information it must be retrieved from the long term memory and delivered to the working memory for the processing.

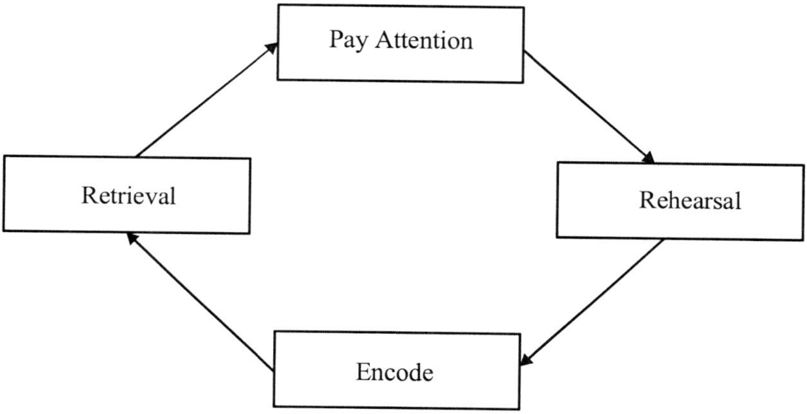

A well-designed multimedia program demands the simultaneous attention of several senses through process of appealing to more than one sense simultaneously, facilitating the rehearsal process. Even the process of retrieval is facilitated for the concept being presented by the power of multiple media.

Another important issue for multimedia application design is the amount of information that can be assimilated at a given time. This is referred to as the Cognitive load. Too much of information in multimedia presentation may overload users cognitive abilities, thus making learning less effective. This will defeat the basic design objectives.

When we are assigning the job of creation of windows tutor that time we consider the interface design :

- Keep low cognitive load.
- Keep a simple, consistent screen design.
- Don't divide the leaner's attention.
- Encourage frequent revision/rehearsal by the learner.
- Avoid repetition in interactions.
- Encourage reinforcement of learning by using concrete words and different media to reinforce the message.

SOLVED PAPERS

GUESS PAPERS

Q1(a). What is morphing? How is it similar to/different from Warping?

(b)What is hypertext? Describe its applications.

(c)Describe the basic feature of any one of the following authoring tools:
(i)Macromedia Director
(ii)Authorware Professional

Q2. What are the various hardware components needed for multimedia display and development? Describe the usage of these components.

Q3. Describe how multimedia can be used in the following :
(a) Airline reservation system
(b) Railway enquiry system
(c) A departmental store

Q4. What is the purpose of Multimedia authoring tools? Does Multimedia development starts with multimedia authoring? Describe one of the tools that may be used for multimedia authoring.

Q5. Compare and contrast the following :
(a) Analog audio and Digital Audio
(b) Analog video and Digital video
(c) Analog image and Digital image
(d) JPEG and MPEG

CS-66 : MULTIMEDIA
JAN 2001

Note : *There are* ***five*** *questions in this paper. Question no. 1 is* ***compulsory*** *and carries 30 marks. Attempt any* ***three*** *from the rest.*

Q1. (i) Compare and contrast the following : **[20]**
(a) Analog audio and Digital audio
(b) Analog video and Digital video
(c) Analog image and Digital image
(d) JPEG and MPEG

Ans.

	Analog audio		Digital audio
1.	When we hold a microphone up in the air & screen, the microphone connects the changes in the air & connects into electric voltage, This is known as analog signal.	1.	Digital audio is a technological process whereby an analog audio is first converted into a continuous stream of numbers. This is known as digital audio.
2.	Analog audio when plotted on a paper it would look like a graph.	2.	But where as digital audio give the output in series of 0 & 1.
3.	The recording is done on a magnetic tape for further play modes.	3.	The recording done on a hard disk or any media which supports digital format.
4.	The output device for an analog sound is a simple speakers.	4.	The output device of a digitized audio is amplified speakers which are built in.
5.	The quality of the sound output is less.	5.	Here the sound quality is excellent.
6.	Editing analog audio piece is quite difficult & time consuming & less accurate.	6.	Digital audio editing gives high quality output with less complexity & less time consuming. Accuracy level is high.

	Analog video		Digital video
1.	Analog video can be classified as interlaced.	1.	Digital video can be classified as non-interlaced.
2.	Video programs like SECAM(broad casting standards) are interlaced where each frame consisting two fields displayed in two passes.	2.	Most PC displays uses progressive slams in which all lines in a frame are displayed in one pass from top to bottom before next frame.
3.	A frame of an interlaced video is divided into fields. Each field contains every horizontal line.	3.	While for the digital video frame, the whole frame is read from top to bottom then to the next.
4.	Due to the analog we see a flicker affect (horizontal line moving down.	4.	Due to the digital format the flicker effect is eliminated.
5.	Due to our T.V. being analog devices all the broadcasting is done on analog video.	5.	Computer related work & post production work is done using digital videos.
6.	VHS are examples of analog videos.	6.	VCD, DVD,are examples of digital video.
7.	Analog cameras are used to capture the shots.	7.	Now we get digital cameras to capture the shot.

(c) Analog image and Digital image

	Analog Image		Digital Image
1.	A normal image which is sketched or even has been printed is a Analog Image	1.	When any image created on a computer or scanned into the PC becomes a Digital Image.
2.	Analog images are in one format only	2.	Digital images are in many formats like TIFF, JPEG,etc.
3.	Analog images are only of one type	3.	While there are two types of Digital Images. Bitmap & Vector image.
4.	Examples of Analog Image are paintings , Sketches, Cartoons etc.	4.	Examples of Digital Images are all images which are in computers.

(g) JPEG and MPEG

The JPEG (joint photographic expert group) standard is for compressing continuous still pictures. It is normally used to encode 24-bit RGB video images and will leave out some of the minor picture details for the sake of simplicity. It produces a compression ration of 20:1 for still images without any appreciable degradation of pictures. This is a popular standard on Macintosh and Amiga platforms.

MPEG (Moving Picture Expert Group) is compression standard for compressing video since 1993. MPEG was developed specifically for motion images. MPEG can compress both audio and video. It produces a compression ration of 50:1 before the degradation in picture quality occurs. MPEG standard allows fast video and audio compression, and real time decompression. MPEG allows a decompression data rate of 1.2 to 1.5 M per second, thus, allowing full motion, full screen video.

	JPEG		MPEG
1.	JPEG-joint people exprt group.	1.	MPEG-motion picture expert group.
2.	Digital format for an image.	2.	Digital format for a movie chip.
3.	Compressed format for a digital image.	3.	Compressed format for a digital video.
4.	High compression rate but the quality is same for image.	4.	Quality does not reduce a seven then compression is done.
5.	Used for image on web & multimedia presentation.	5.	Used for movies on the web & of course for multimedia presentation.

(ii) Give various input/output devices for multimedia applications. [5]

Refer to DEC2003,Q2,Page NO.-110

(iii) Give various storage devices for multimedia. [5]

Refer to Study Material, Chapter-1, Page no. - 7, Q8

Q2. How can multimedia be used in education ? Describe an example of multimedia use in education ? Describe an example of multimedia use in education. How is it going to be advantageous in comparison to printed books ? [15]

Apart from making use of multimedia in preparing tutorial in education field multimedia can also be used in developing Encyclopedia and database production. e.g. an Encyclopedia production may provide Indexing by dates to create linear topics Multimedia source include unique sound still images animations and video clips usually distributed on CD-ROM.

Multimedia real time speed experience for printed books can be readily available online, that is the real time experience of multimedia. Solve question answer can be stored in CD-ROM. Printed books are not only read but you can seeing this printed books by video films through multimedia.

In these day Encyclopedia and books providing a sort of edutainment are available. Except preparing are tutorial in the areas of education it (multimedia) can be used very rapidly an fastly in Encyclopedia and database productions for examples Encyclopedia Production to providing the indexing to create linear topics by dates. Multimedia include verified (unique) sound, still images, video clips and animations usually distributed on CD-ROM.

Pedagogues are useful teaching aids only if they stimulate and motivate the students. The audio-visual support to a pedagogue can actually help in doing so. A multimedia tutor can provide multiple numbers of challenges to the student to stimulate his interest in a topic. The instructions provided by pedagogue have moved beyond providing only button level control to intelligent simulations, dynamic creation of links, composition and collaboration and system testing of the user interactions. Let us look into some of the examples of pedagogues:

Simulations : This is an important area of pedagogy where a student is engaged in situations of problem solving. Simulations are mainly categorized in two main form:

✓ Scenarios based simulations

✓ Knowledge based simulations.

Scenario based simulations, which are multimedia based use video, graphics and sound to engage the student in a particular problem situation. However, these scenario-based tutors have limited answer and suggestions to offer.

Knowledge based simulations are more intelligent as far as behavior is concerned are adaptive to student needs, however, are difficult to design. Let us discuss about some good examples in this area.

Q3. What is the need of authoring software ? What are the basic features needed in an authoring software ? Compare the features of any two authoring software in the context of "creation of games multimedia". [15]

Let us briefly clearly the type of authoring tools available in the market.

✓**Time-based authoring :** They use time scale to decide duration of message on the screen. Some of the authoring tools in this category are macromedia action, animation works interactive etc.

✓**Card-based or page based authoring tools :** These tools allow information to be put in as stack of cards can further be linked with each other in predefined sequences. Even the cross linkages along with branching facility are also possible in such packages. Examples in this category are hyper card by Apple, asymmetric tool book and many presentation software.

✓**Icon-base authoring tools :** These tools allow creation of an Icon based flow script, which is then converted to an application. Examples in the category are macromedia authoring professional, icon Author etc.

✓**Theatrical authoring tools :** These types of tools refers to media elements as independent cast members, which are assembled using score which is a sequencer in terms of time, linking and animation. Complex visual effects can be applied on these scores to create powerful presentations. Macromedia director is one such package.

Now the question is which authoring software is most suitable for what applications? There are no standard guidelines, however, the following are some suggested usage.

Business applications	:	Time based authoring tools Icon based authoring tools
Education	:	Icon based authoring tools Theatrical based authoring

Games / Multimedia which requires lot of Animation	:	Preferably Theatrical based authoring

🗁Interactivity in an Application :

Most of the authoring tools of multimedia allow the following type of navigational structures:

✓ Linear or sequential mainly used in business and educational applications.

✓ Hierarchical, like a tree structure, used in educational and business applications

✓ Non-linear, like a graph, users select the path of its own, used in various encyclopedia development

✓ A combination of the above tools.

In most of the system interactivity is built by creating menu-based options through questions and their feedback.

Q4. Assume that you have been assigned the job of creation of Windows tutor. Design the multimedia tutor for the above case. Explain each step of the process of development by giving suitable details. [15]

Firstly we will be starting in Multimedia Projects with the following points which are as follows:

1. Create Multimedia Programme.
2. Outline the Programme.
3. Create flowchart.
4. Create Program Storyboard.
5. User interface must be planned.
6. Plan the production of text, graphics and video.
7. Finally project object and time schedule.

Then next to be used authoring tool e.g. in education generally we use theoretical authoring tool which refer to media elements as independent members complex visual effects can be applied on these scores to create powerful presentation.

The first step in the cyclic process of learning is attention to information. The information so gathered is transferred to the local working memory. This local memory is to be continuously refreshed; otherwise the information so gathered may be lost. This process is called Rehearsal. The rehearsal process may cause transfer of information to short term memory to the long term memory of the human. This process is called encoding. For using encoded information it must be retrieved from the long term memory and delivered to the working memory for the processing. A well-designed multimedia program demands the simultaneous attention of several senses through process of appealing to more than one sense simultaneously, facilitating the rehearsal process. Even the process of retrieval is facilitated for the concept being presented by the power of multiple media.

Another important issue for multimedia application design is the amount of information that can be assimilated at a given time. This is referred to as the Cognitive load. Too much of information in multimedia presentation may overload users cognitive abilities, thus making learning less effective. This will defeat the basic design objectives.

When we are assigning the job of creation of windows tutor that time we consider the interface design :

- Keep low cognitive load.
- Keep a simple, consistent screen design.
- Don't divide the leaner's attention.
- Encourage frequent revision/rehearsal by the learner.
- Avoid repetition in interactions.
- Encourage reinforcement of learning by using concrete words and different media to reinforce the message.

Q5. Describe the usage of multimedia in the following applications: [15]

(a) web-based information portal

Refer to Study Material, Chapter-2, Page no. - 44, Q12(11)

(b) An interactive audio

Refer to Study Material, Chapter-2, Page no. - 44, Q12(12)

(c) A distributed learning platform

Refer to Study Material, Chapter-2, Page no. - 44, Q12(13)

CS-66 : MULTIMEDIA
JUNE -2001

Note : *There are **five** questions in this paper. Question no. **1** is **compulsory** and carries 30 marks. Attempt any **three** from the rest.*

Q1 (i). Compare and contrast the following in the context of Multimedia: [20]
(a) CD-ROM and DVD
(b) Analog Audio and Digital Audio
(c) Analog Video and Digital Video
(d) Icon based and time based multimedia authoring softwares.

(a) CD-ROM and DVD

🗁 **CD-ROM :** CDROM is widely used for multimedia storage as it has an amazing amount of flexibility and potential as multimedia storage and distribution medium. One CD-ROM can hold up to one and half hour of digital audio or around 700 to 750 MS of computer data for that matter.

To install a CD-ROM drive, there must be a free bay and the computer system also have a sound card installed or a square slot into either a card or CD-ROM drive can be placed. Before installation all the jumper setting should be properly done according to the specification. Once the CD-ROM drive is fitted in the drive bay with proper jumper setting, necessary software can be installed to make the CD-ROM drive work.

🗁 **DVD :** DVD is the short for Digital Video Disc now it is more commonly referred to as "digital Versatile Disc" as it has many potential applications than video. DVD is the cohesion of multimedia and digital video player, movies and interactivity. By employing the latest advances in digital technology, DVD can hold up 25 times more digital info than a CD-ROM and DVD can be used to create innovative cutting edge video-discs with all sorts of data including director's cuts, photo galleries, interview with actors in fact practically anything today's video producers can imagine. Using DVD technology. Besides multilingual capabilities of DVD the producers can create a limitless range of interactive titles, instead of watching a video in the linear fashion as with traditional videotape.

(b) Analog Audio and Digital Audio

1) In digital audio, multimedia can be used in its full potential whereas in analog, this is not the case.

2) In analog sound is a repeated pattern of pressure in the air and a microphone converts a sound wave into an electrical whereas digital signal a are in the form of 0s and 1s.

3) In digital sound can be recorded and reproduced using digital signals and the error can be reduced very much.

4) In digital the storage space required for storing digital audio is used e.g. 1 MB for one minute of audio.

In Analog audio, physical sound pressure waves are converted to corresponding electrical waves are converted to corresponding electrical signals by an acoustic transducer such as microphone or phonegraph cartridge. The electrical output of transducer is called an analog signal because electrical signal is analogous to the pressure patterns of the sound waves.

(c) Analog Video and Digital Video

	Analog video		Digital video
1.	Analog video can be classified as interlaced.	1.	Digital video can be classified as non-interlaced.
2.	Video programs like SECAM(broad casting standards) are interlaced where each frame consisting two fields displayed in two passes.	2.	Most PC displays uses progressive slams in which all lines in a frame are displayed in one pass from top to bottom before next frame.
3.	A frame of an interlaced video is divided into fields. Each field contains every horizontal line.	3	While for the digital video frame, the whole frame is read from top to bottom then to the next.
4.	Due to the analog we see a flicker affect (horizontal line moving down.	4.	Due to the digital format the flicker effect is eliminated.
5.	Due to our T.V. being analog devices all the broadcasting is done on analog video.	5.	Computer related work & post production work is done using digital videos.
6.	VHS are examples of analog videos.	6.	VCD, DVD,are examples of digital video.
7.	Analog cameras are used to capture the shots.	7.	Now we get digital cameras to capture the shot.

(d) Icon based and Time based multimedia authoring softwares.

With **icon-based** authoring tools, non-technical multimedia authors can build sophisticated applications without scripting. By placing icons on a flow line, you can quickly sequence events and activities, including decisions and user interactions. These tools are useful for story boarding, as you can change sequences, add options, and restructure interactions by simply dragging and dropping icons. You can print out your navigation map or flowchart, an annotated project index with or without associated icons, design and presentation windows, and a cross-reference table of variables.

Time-based systems are popular multimedia authoring tools. Each uses its own distinctive approach and user interface for managing events over time. Many use a visual timeline for sequencing the events of a multimedia presentation, often displaying layers of various media elements or events alongside the scale in increments as precise as one second. Others arrange long sequences of graphic frames and add the time component by adjusting each frame's duration of play.

(ii) What do you mean by animation ? Describe two applications of animation.[5]

🗁 **Animation :** The word animation comes from a latin word Anima meaning to breath. If anything breaths means it has life & thus animation means to bring life i.e. to make or give moments to any object or thing. This can be any object created on computer. An animation is just a continuous series of still images that are displayed in a sequence. There are mainly two types of animation used in multimedia, namely, 2D and 3D animation. 2D animation also known as cell (pixel based) animation, is the most common kind of animation, where flat images are drawn one frame at a time. This process is very time consuming but result obtained is spectacular in nature. Computer animation has increased the efficiency, and enhanced the results of cell animation with introduction of wide ranges of colour and speed. In 3-D animation mathematical model of 3-D object is created to realistically portray with depth. Now it has become a common media element in film, video and multimedia packages. 3-D animations follow mainly three steps; modelling, animation and rendering.

There are endless examples of the applications of animation. Two examples where it is used are following :

In Analysis and Understanding

British Telecom for example uses a sophisticated program that plots on a map of the U.K. the density of telephone fault reports using different colours. When a storm was plotted on top of this map, and the whole system was animated it could be seen that the density of the faults increased at areas from which the storm had just passed. It would have been very difficult to visualise this in a different way.

Astronomers also rely on computers to do animations of high speed jets penetrating different gases in order to determine why a few galaxies flare dramatically. This research has given out valuable information about why some galaxies flare into broad plumes and why some others remain extremely straight and narrow.

In Teaching

On of the most difficult things in teaching, is communicating ideas effectively. This might be very difficult in complex situations, and here is where animation might help to convey information. For example there are many programs that show the planetary system in action in three dimensions - an idea that would be very difficult to grasp otherwise.

(iii) What do you mean by hypertext? Describe its applications. [5]

Refer to DEC2003,Q1(c),Page NO.-108

Q2. Suppose you are asked to develope a multimedia tutor for the topics of "Introduction of Computer". Describe the process of multimedia development for the above tutor. Give description on each step of development in the context of above application. [15]

Refer to DEC2002,Q2,Page NO.-134

Q3. Suppose you are developing a multimedia which requires lot of animation and interaction. Compare and contrast the features of various authoring software for suitability for the above application. Choose one software for final development and describe reasons of your selection. [15]

Once all the components of multimedia have developed, one has to use authoring tool to stitch the multimedia application, which also involves interactivity.

There are four basic function provided by almost all authoring software:

✓ **Importing:** it should be able to import carious media elements, which may have been developed using other software package.

✓ **Creating:** it should allow some basic features for creation of text, graphics and may be sound if not video.

✓ **Integrating:** it should allow you to define sequences and provide linkages

✓ **Delivering:** it should allow developing self-running application and encryption of application data.

ImageQ is multimedia authoring software package. Although, it is a windows 3.1 application but it can also play back on windows 95, create slide show presentations well and provides a way to distribute them easily. It lacks the intuitive programming language and strong interface necessary for truly productive multimedia applications development.

ImageQ presentations comprise a series of background image and associated control scripts that add user interface controls, overlay images, and underlying programming to each slide. It user a multiple-document interface to manage one or more presentations simultaneously.

Q4. What are the areas in education, except preparing a tutorial, where multimedia may be used? Describe one example for each identified area. [15]

Apart from making use of multimedia in preparing tutorial in education field multimedia can also be used in developing Encyclopedia and database production. e.g. an Encyclopedia production may provide Indexing by dates to create linear topics Multimedia source include unique sound still images animations and video clips usually distributed on CD-ROM.

Multimedia real time speed experience for printed books can be readily available online, that is the real time experience of multimedia. Solve question answer can be stored in CD-ROM. Printed books are not only read but you can seeing this printed books by video films through multimedia.

In these day Encyclopedia and books providing a sort of edutainment are available. Except preparing are tutorial in the areas of education it (multimedia) can be used very rapidly an fastly in Encyclopedia and database productions for examples Encyclopedia Production to providing the indexing to create linear topics by dates. Multimedia include verified (unique) sound, still images, video clips and animations usually distributed on CD-ROM.

Pedagogues are useful teaching aids only if they stimulate and motivate the students. The audio-visual support to a pedagogue can actually help in doing so. A multimedia tutor can provide multiple numbers of challenges to the student to stimulate his interest in a topic. The instructions provided by pedagogue have moved beyond providing only button level control to intelligent simulations, dynamic creation of links, composition and collaboration and system testing of the user interactions. Let us look into some of the examples of pedagogues :

🗁 **Simulations :** This is an important area of pedagogy where a student is engaged in situations of problem solving. Simulations are mainly categorized in two main form :

✓ Scenarios based simulations

✓ Knowledge based simulations.

Scenario based simulations, which are multimedia based use video, graphics and sound to engage the student in a particular problem situation. However, these scenario-based tutors have limited answer and suggestions to offer.

Knowledge based simulations are more intelligent as far as behavior is concerned are adaptive to student needs, however, are difficult to design. Let us discuss about some good examples in this area.

Q5. Describe how multimedia can be used in the following: [15]
(a) Reception of a hospital
(b) Visitor Lounge of a company
(c) Bookstore

(a) Reception of a hospital

The basic use of multimedia is to provide easy information and user-friendly information too. Basically multimedia is greatly been used in public places. One of the public place is a reception of a hospital. Now if we just think that what information do we get when we go to a hospital reception. This information can be given through a person over the reception through a multimedia kiosk. The following information can be obtained :

- ➢ Details of different services provided by the hospital.
- ➢ Rates of the services.
- ➢ Brief history of the hospital.
- ➢ Details of patient.
- ➢ Patient ward number and their progress.
- ➢ Directions or road map of hospital.
- ➢ Information regarding visiting hours.
- ➢ FAQ (Frequently asked questions).
- ➢ Availability of doctors and their visiting hours etc.

(b) Visitor Lounge of a company

A visitors lounge is a place where an outsider who visits a place is made to sit and wait if the concern person is busy. This place has great importance as many thoughts come through the visiting person's mind. A multimedia info center at this place can give him all the information at the lounge itself.

Another sub technology of Multimedia is audio and video this technology can be used at visitors lounge of the company. A Boss can see the monitor who is coming in the company or what is happening in the lounge from his cabin.

Multimedia is very useful in visitor lounge of a company.

One can access info like :

- ➢ Profile of the company.
- ➢ The history of the owner of the country.
- ➢ Areas of work in which the company deals with.

- Infrastructure and management essentials of the company.
- Achievements and specialization of the company.
- Future projects and projections of the company.

(c) Bookstore

One can check that whether a put is available in the books store or not. One can keep on the customers.

Multimedia allows you to produce royalty free, professional quality, electronic publications. It easily integrates text images, sound, music, animation, interactive controls, colors and other graphical elements to create stunning multimedia productions. NeoBook can be used to produce electronic magazines (e-Zines) that can be distributed over the internet, interactive educational and training materials. CD-ROM interfaces, electronic books, reference works, brochures, catalogs, entertainment titles and much more.

Marketing on the internet is your introduction to the new and powerful multimedia part of the internet called the world wide web. It shows you how to get access to the web and how to build multimedia web pages that gives internet users access to your marketing and sales information.

Multimedia CD-ROMs is a new learning methods. Which is not only user friendly but also saves storing space. Another additional advantage is the increased shelf life of the desired book. The multimedia is very useful in bookstore because the all information regarding books and catalog are stored in CD-ROM in the way of audio and video form.

CS-66 : MULTIMEDIA
DEC- 2001

Note : *There are **five** questions in this paper. Question no. **1** is **compulsory** and carries 30 marks. Attempt any **three** from the rest.*

Q1(a). What is Multimedia? What are its advantages? Where can one use Multimedia? [5]

The term multimedia is often associated with the information superhighway, or with interactive TV that can produce videos (information on demand) or with hypermedia. However, multimedia can be considered as text, graphics, images video and audio in computer. One of the key features of multimedia is Interactivity. It may, convey enriched interactive information to its users.

Multimedia system support the physical and logical coexistance and interactive use of heterogeneous media classes such as print, audio and video in specific application environments.

About the above definitions the question is whether multimedia is a computer itself or a computer software product. In practical sense it is the combination of both. The fact remains that it has best potential to be one of the most powerful form of communicating ideas, searching for information and experiencing new concept of common media ever developed.

Advantage of Multimedia :

The basic advantage of multimedia over the conventional from of media, which uses sound graphics and text for example, TV, audio etc. is the interactive feature of multimedia. For example, a multimedia version of news bulletin would be the situation where you can request the broadcaster the type of news you are interested in, when you want to hear it, and with the press of a button or click of the mouse you can hear the news.

Multimedia can be used in various fields :

- Education
- Corporate Training
- Medical and health care
- Entertainment
- Marketing
- Publishing
- Web etc.

(b) What are the various hardware components needed for Multimedia display and development ? Describe the usage of these components. [10]

Refer to Study Material, Chapter-1, Page no. - 7, Q8

(c) What is the purpose of Multimedia authoring tools? Does Multimedia development starts with multimedia authoring? Describe one of the tools that may be used for multimedia authoring. [10]

Refer to Study Material, Chapter-3, Page no. - 68, Q9

(d) What is Morphing? How is it similar/different to that of warping? [5]

Refer to DEC2003,Q1(a),Page NO.-106

Q2. Suppose you are asked to develop a multimedia presentation that is to be used for presentation of Information through Internet. The speciality of the application is that the tutorial information is dispersed on many sites and these tools present the information as a single source with search facility. How will you plan and develop the suggested application? [15]

The following points to develop a Multimedia tutor for the topics of "Introduction to Computer" or "Mathematics Tutorial" or "Information through Internet".

(i) First of all you have to plan a structure in your Mind to develop the project.

(ii) The specimen of audience (what you say and how you say will depend on the type and age group of student).

(iii) Outlining the Programme.

(iv) Develop a flow chart.

(v) Making a dynamic Question, answer sessions so the students question can be justified.

(vi) Plan the production of text, graphics, animation, audio and video.

(vii) Preparing the time schedule and the budget of project.

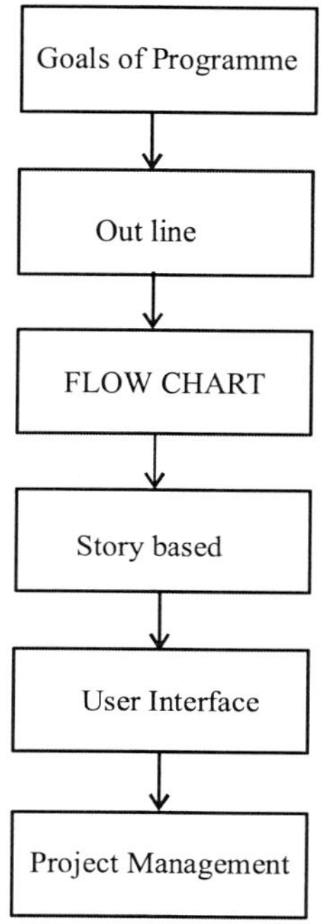

Multimedia is very useful in any development of the tutorial. When we develop any tutorial then planning is the necessary thing. Firstly it provides the analysis of the tutorial.

During the analysis phase of a development effort, all the member of the team gradually constructed a set of assumptions about the interactive product you are developing. It is sound practice to confirm those assumptions before undertaking the bulk of the design work of the product. The assumption should be confirmed with your client and with any vendors that may be collaborating on the project. The "Assumption check list" is a tool that can help you confirm the assumptions underlaying your multimedia development effort.

The assumption check list presumes that time has passed between the initial estimate of project scope and the approval to begin the project.

There are various steps involved in this assumption which are :

Step 1 : Meet with the client and determine :

- Are the goals and objectives still on target ?
- Is the audience still the same ?
- Is the review of each proposed element same ?
- Are the plans for marketing the product same ?
- Are implementation plans same ?

Step 2 : Review your estimates of project scope, including :

- Materials required
- Time needed
- Project cost

Step 3 : If required, rethink the project goals :

If serious questions about project scope or other assumption arise, don't hesitate to raise a red flag. It is better to rethink the multimedia development project now than to cancel it later.

After getting all things we think about Assessment Matrix.

The assessment matrix is designed to help you assume that each of the goals or objectives you've defined for your multimedia product is assessed by one or more reliable and valid outcome measures. Often development teams wait until a product is almost complete before making up a test intended to measure its outcomes. By planning for assessment early in the design stage of your product, your will've a much greater chance of designing a program that is actually capable of achieving its objectives.

After completing all these steps we specify the objectives specification tools.

A key element in the instructional development process is to specify the objectives for your program as clearly as possible. Poorly stated objective often result in instruction that is inappropriate. This tool is designed to help you write more specific objectives by providing you with a list of observable verbs. The tool includes verbs for both the cognitive domain and affective domain.

After completing all these things finally we check the user characteristics checklist :

(i) Cognitive characteristics :
- General aptitudes
- Specific aptitudes
- Functional literacy
- Computer literacy
- Learning style
- Prerequisite content knowledge

(ii) Social characteristics :
- Attitudes toward
- Relationships with poor
- Attitude toward authority
- Ethnic background
- Education level

(iii) Personality characteristics :
- Motivation to use this program
- Motivation to learn
- Attitude toward learning
- Attitude toward technology
- Self esteem

(iv) Physical characteristics :
- Visual abilities
- Auditory abilities
- Tectile abilities

Whenever you write objectives, review the verbs to select the ones most appropriate to your job or content. This is by no means a complete list of all the possible verbs and its primary value may be in spurring your imagination in writing better objectives.

Q3. Compare and contrast the features of various authoring tools available. Indicate which type of application a given authoring tool is more suitable for. Give justification in support of your answer. [15]

Refer to DEC2003,Q5,Page NO.-118

Q4. Suggest various areas of applications, where multimedia may be used in Hospitals. Describe one of the areas in details giving the objectives, prospective viewers, approximate resource requirements for one of the applications. [15]

We are giving the example to suggest or understand the various areas of applications where multimedia may be used in hospitals. Just like any person can enquire on the hospital reception about the admission of patients. Doctor's haven't come in the hospital, a Person can concert about the treatment given by the hospital. Then you must have the help of hypertext Presentation because hypertext Presentation can be made for a piece of information / questions (Query) asked by a Person. Communication should be Possible in any direction, Junior doctor can ask their senior doctor in case of any typical emergency.

Sometimes a Person is suffering from miscellaneous Problems then the consulting doctor whose presence is not sure may remotely monitor then be listen to the responses of the patients on the screen (The achievement of Multimedia can be used in during brain surgery)

Multimedia is very useful for the reception of a hospital. The reception used main reception is the department, which provides quality service to people who come from various places throughtout the day by attending to their requirements efficiently and effectively.

Secretaries are posted to provide medical records of the patients, incorporating necessary information to the workup staff owing by helping in time saving for patients and to help in productivity of consultant.

Surgery scheduling centre in yet and thus vital unit which schedules operation in terms of data, theatre surgeon enquiring that optimum use is made of the hospital facilities and the convince of the patient is also met. Another important activity of this unit is to publish schedule of surgeries for the next day so that the different departments involved and the surgeries can plan their work.

It is used to make up, send and receive Medical eXchange Folders (MXF) including nominative multimedia medical documents, doctors : GP and PCP, specialists surgeons.

🗀 ***Mednet is a Multimedia based system which Provides services are :***

✓ Collaborate brain surgery

✓ Real time monitoring

🗀 ***The approximate resource requirements for performing brain surgery follows:***

✓ 2 GB HDD to 80 GB

✓ Connection to an Internet Service Provider (ISP) or mobile connection will work better.
✓ Keyboard, Mouse, CD-rom drive.
✓ Mednet diagnostic system
✓ Sound Card
✓ Micro Phone
✓A Modem with a speed of 28 thousand bps to 128 kbps
✓**Graphic** acclerator and pentium processor. (ranging from 550MHz to 2.8GHz)

Q5. Describe how multimedia can be used in the following : [15]
(a) A Museum
(b) Railway station/bus station
(c) A departmental store.

(a) A Museum
In the Museum it can be place in the reception lounge various types of museum like Rail Museum, Doll Museum, Science Museum. These above museum guide every information to their own stream. It can guide various information an other relevant topics and one of the most important whether somebody damaging the museum things or not.
Multimedia can be used in just about any situation where computers are being used to deliver information, and a number where they are not traditionally used.
The multimedia system is able to manage all the information, to maintain real time and information about museum, to display publicity on the information panel, to generate automatically a human voice that provides all the information which is related with museum.
The information system is the centre of all this system. It is in change of gathering and providing all the necessary information to the rest of modules of this system. The type of information that include this module is very diverse : administrative information like data of museum, old things, functional information or complementary information such as generation of human voice in real time.
Multimedia can be used in the museum for real time monitoring of the objects :
• Can guide tourist with the details of the respective area, objects, history of the objects.
• Real time control over objects presents in the museum etc.

(b) Railway station/bus station
Railway station/ bus station both are very posh area / or Hoch poch areas so much terrorism around this area is observed. Through Multimedia in railway or bus station we can keep an eye on terrorists activities and providing a great help in case of an emergency. In the opinion of simple Public Multimedia can provide information such as Railway station and Bus station are two places where people come to go to different places. As the population & commerce is increasing, the rush at these places have also increased with this a perfect distribution of information to different travellers is also important. Now multimedia can be used here for the following ways.

- Give information & directions of places of departure e.g. platform no.
- Scheduled time of departures & arrivals.
- Rescheduled time of departures and arrivals if there is any delay.
- Before time information distribution if any changes made.
- Reservation status.
- Availability of seats.
- Rate charts & information of the place where to be the person travels.
- Tourist sports & information of business centers.
- Refreshment & resting places at Railway stations and bus stops.

Outfitting the railway stations with large-scale video screens enables updated customer information or advertising to be shown in television broadcasting quality. At the same time the connection can also be made for controlling escalators or automated ticketing machines.

(c) A departmental store

Multimedia greatly facilitates interaction with customers.

A multimedia system is able to manage all the functionally of the departmental store. Product developers, vendors, systems integrators, value added resellers and service providers will find qualitative and quantitative information about their opportunity in networked multimedia in this report. Analysis in end user organizations assessing the deployment costs and overhead associated with networked multimedia usage will also derive benefits from the detailed studies included.

A multimedia can be used for providing details of the commodities present in the departmental store, real-time monitoring on customer, terrorist activities etc.

The information system is the center of all this system. It is in charge of gathering and providing all the necessary information. The information pannels may be adapted to any video system and it incorporates integrally, the possibility of showing advertising videos or entertainment.

It is also to provide some information which is related with departmental store.

- Direction and roadmaps of different sections of the store.
- Information of the items to be purchased e.g. price, weights, brand etc.
- Information of different schemes available.
- Information about discounts.
- Knowledge of introduction of new items in the store & their usage.
- Public feedback of different items available in the market.
- Availability of different services provided by the stores.

Contents kept for the customers etc.

In a department store a various types of customers come faithful or sometimes unfaithful. By installing multimedia based cameras at sensitive corners. So the Multimedia help in this field also because online product lists and their concern details can be given to the customers it will be a great help for the visitors (outsiders) if they do not have product knowledge.

CS-66 : MULTIMEDIA
JUNE -2002

Note : *There are* ***five*** *questions in this paper. Question no.* ***1*** *is* ***compulsory*** *and carries 30 marks. Attempt any* ***three*** *from the rest.*

Q1(a). "Multimedia is not just Hardware but also Software". Comment on the above statement. [5]

In practical sense it is the combination of both. The fact remains that it has best potential to be one of the most powerful form of communicating ideas, searching for information and experiencing new concept of common media ever developed.

(b) What are the various multimedia hardware components? What additional components of hardware will be needed in case you want to download multimedia contents from the Internet? [10]

Refer to Study Material, Chapter-1, Page no. - 7, Q8

(c) What is MIDI in the context of multimedia? Describe one application of it. [5]

Through the MIDI interface, a computer can control output of individual instruments. On the other hand, the computer can receive, store or process coded musical data through the same interface. The data are generated with a keyboard and reproduced through a sound generator. A *sequencer* can store data. Further, it may also modify the musical data. In a multimedia system, the sequencer is a computer application. The heart of any MIDI system is the MIDI *Synthesizer* device. Atypical synthesizer looks like a simple piano keyboard with a panel full of buttons, but it is far more. Most synthesizers have the following common components:

✓ **Sound Generators :** Sound generators do the work of synthesizing sound; the purpose of the rest of the synthesizer is to control the sound generators. The principal purpose of the generator is to produce an audio signal that becomes sound when fed into a loudspeaker. By varying the voltage oscillation of the audio signal, a sound generator changes the quality of the sound- its pitch, loudness and tone color –to create a wide variety of sounds and notes.

Internally, sound generation can be done in different ways. One way is to store the acoustic signals as MIDI data in advance. Afterwards, the stored MIDI data are transformed with a digital-analog adapter into acoustic signals. Individual notes are composed in a timely fashion. Another method is to create acoustic signals synthetically.

✓ **Keyboard :** The keyboard affords the musician's direct control of the synthesizer. Pressing keys on the keyboard signals the microprocessor what notes to play and how long to play them. Some synthesizer keyboards can also signal to the microprocessor how loud to play the notes and whether to add vibrato or other effects to the notes. The sound intensity of tone depends on the speed and acceleration of the key pressure. The keyboard should have at least five octaves with 61 keys.

✓ **Control Panel :** The control panel controls those functions that are not directly concerned with notes and durations (controlled by the keyboard). Panel controls include: a slider that sets the overall volume of the synthesizer, a button that turns the synthesizer on and off, and a menu that calls up different patches for the sound generators o play.

✓ **Auxiliary Controllers :** Auxiliary controllers are available to give more control over the notes played on the keyboard. Two very common variables on a synthesizer are *pitch bend* and *modulation.* Pitch bend controllers can bend pitch up and down, adding *portamento* (a smooth, uninterrupted glide in passing from one tone to another) to notes; modulation controllers can increase or decrease effects such as *vibrato.*

✓ **Memory :** Synthesizer memory is used to store patches for the sound generators and settings on the control panel. Many synthesizers also have a slot for *external memory cartridges.* By using several memory cartridges, the musician can plug in a different cartridge each time s/he wants a set of new sounds for the synthesizer.

There are many other MIDI devices that augment the standard synthesizer in a MIDI system. Examples are drum machines which specialize in percussion sounds and rhythms, the master keyboard which increases the quality of the synthesizer keyboard, guitar controllers, guitar synthesizers, drum pad controllers and so on.

An important MIDI device is *sequencer*, which can be a drum machine, computer or dedicated sequencer. An sequencer was used originally as a storage server for generated MIDI data. Today, a sequencer, being a computer, becomes additionally a music editor. Data can be modified in a proper way because of their digital data representation. There are several possibilities to represent musical data. The most common representation and manipulation of data are musical notes. The musical piece appears on the screen in the form of a sheet of music. The sequencer transforms the notes into MIDI messages. Another representation is a direct input of MIDI messages. Here, the user specifies required musical events per channel with time dependencies. This input depends on the keyboard type.

There are endless examples of the applications of animation. Two examples where it is used are following :

In Analysis and Understanding

British Telecom for example uses a sophisticated program that plots on a map of the U.K. the density of telephone fault reports using different colours. When a storm was plotted on top of this map, and the whole system was animated it could be seen that the density of the faults increased at areas from which the storm had just passed. It would have been very difficult to visualise this in a different way.

Astronomers also rely on computers to do animations of high speed jets penetrating different gases in order to determine why a few galaxies flare dramatically. This research has given out valuable information about why some galaxies flare into broad plumes and why some others remain extremely straight and narrow.

In Teaching

On of the most difficult things in teaching, is communicating ideas effectively. This might be very difficult in complex situations, and here is where animation might help to convey information. For example there are many programs that show the planetary system in action in three dimensions - an idea that would be very difficult to grasp otherwise.

(d) Describe the basic feature of any one of the following authoring tools: [10]

(i) Macromedia Director

Refer to Study Material, Chapter-3, Page no. - 65, Q6(iii)

(ii) Authoware Professional

Refer to Study Material, Chapter-3, Page no. - 65, Q6(ii)

Q2. A multimedia tutorial is to be developed for delivery through Internet. How will you plan and develop the application? [15]

Internet has become a popular means to spread knowledge. When a multimedia tutorial is to be developed for delivery through Internet, planning has to be done first.

🗁Developing a Multimedia Presentations are :

1. Index (Contents) of the Presentation
2. Developing the audience for which presentation is targeted to.
3. Tools used to create presentation.
4. Media used for Presentation.

🗁MULTIMEDIA DELIVERED THROUGH INTERNET

1. The audience is similar to student who can access the Internet to reach to tutorial. He also uses the downloading system to capture the study Material.
2. The contents of the tutorial will have to be written to suit the Web Page format links to related sites, icons, images etc.
3. Tools to be used in the context of the content and the media to be used.
4. Tutorial has the format of Internet access therefore it is to be used in designing coming the way from browser like Netscape Navigator or Internet Explorer.

🗁The whole Project will be planned and executed in the following steps:

1. The contents of Tutorial firstly specify through out and put on paper.
2. The specimen of audience i.e. those students who use internet is always remembered while designing the contents of Presentation.
3. The structure in a Web Page format.
4. Providing the E-mail feedback facility and online question in the tutorial Web format.
5. Check and verify the access.

Before delivering (releasing) to public it must be extensively sampled and tested.

Q3. For making a digital multimedia one has to use many different types of packages in addition to authoring tools. Describe features of the packages (other than authoring tools) that might be needed for development of multimedia. [15]

Authoring tools or softwares are generally used for only the final presentation. Following are the some of the packages with there features :

(i) Photoshop : Photoshop is a software which is a product of Adobe. Adobe photoshop is an image editing software. It can be used to make layouts, editing images and creating visual effect too. Photoshop is a bitmap image software. It has great options related to masking. One can get different colour modes to work with. One can also create outwork in vector based software like illustrator & edit it out in Photoshop. Another software for graphic creation and manipulation is CorelDraw.

(ii) Sound Forge : Sound forge is a software which is used for digital sound recording and digital sound effects. This software works with sound card and one can have all the features which facilitates in manipulating sound.

(iii) 3DS Max : 3DS Max can be used extensively for 3D animation and special effects. Thus this software can be used to create 3D animation as per our story board. One can apply state of the art effects like camera, light, textures. These effects look very realistic.

(iv) Flash : Flash is a product of Macromedia. It is a vector shape animation product. It is used basically for web animation. But due to its good interactive option and compatibility it is also used in authoring. It also supports action script of Flash that gives enhance output as per requirement.

These are the softwares used apart from Authoring Softwares.

Q4. Suggest various areas where multimedia can be used in a university. Take any one of the suggested area/application and define its objectives, prospective viewers, resource requirements and advantages/disadvantages. [15]

The various areas where Multimedia is used in a University used

(A) At Administrative level like

(i) Keeping records of students

(ii) Making Timetable

(B) Issue Certificates or Marksheets to students for receiving any others extra curricular Activities Certificates

(C) For teaching difficult subject

(D) For Entertainment

(E) For making different Projects

(F) For getting information outside the world

(G) Arrange competition in different level

(H) For decoration on different occasions

From the above Mentions areas we are taking administrative department of a University to define its objective, Prospective viewers resource requirement and advantages/disadvantages

(A) Objectives

(i) Keeping records of students

(ii) Making Timetable

(iii) Issue Certificates or Marksheets to students for receiving any others extra curricular Activities Certificates

(B) Prospective viewers

(i) Students
(ii) Parents
(iii) Friends of Students
(iv) Boards members of University

(C) Resource Requirements

(i) Records of grades / marks of students given by professors / teachers.
(ii) Appointment of new professor.
(iii) Admission of new students.
(iv) Proper use of donations.
(v) Keeping records of salary statement of all employees.

Advantages of Multimedia in administrative departments of University

(i) Fast work
(ii) Easy work
(iii) User friendly
(iv) Accuracy

Disadvantages of Multimedia in administrative departments of University

(i) Electricity failure can stop all work
(ii) Only computer literate person can work on that multimedia software.

Multimedia applications in there diverse forms can be used in university campus with great advantage. Such use can help not only the student community, but also save time and energy of the teaching faculty and university administration while tackling problems of problems of students.

And some of the other areas where it can be used are :-

(i) As teaching aid :- Teachers can use multimedia presentations as an aid in their lectures to the students complex concepts in science and technology can be explained and illustrated to students with much more easier when multimedia presentations are available.

(ii) In science laboratories :- Before performing difficult scientific experiments or medical operations (in a medical college or university) student can preview similar experiments on multimedia.

(iii) On university website :- Every university these days has its own website. Multimedia clips are an integral part of such website.

(iv) In university library :- The university library can stock CDs and cassettes of multimedia presentation on various topics of student's interests. The library can provide facilities to let students view such CDs etc. in computer kiosks in library premises. Also a hypertext-based multimedia program can be prepared on various books the library has and the facilities it offers to its members. Hypertext can link various authors at same subject etc.

(v) Information about courses offered at university :- University can install a touch screen multimedia presentation. Using thus a student can immediately seek information about any course he is interested in.

(vi) Multimedia in distance education :- Of the university is conducting distance education courses, it can use study material on multimedia and send it to study centres in remote places.

(vii) Declaring results :- Display of examination result can be made more interesting by incorporating pictures and clips of the top ranking students, the colleges they belong to etc. Such multimedia-based result displays can be used on the internet site.

(viii) <u>For training the teachers</u> :- The biggest use university can make of multimedia is in training of its own teaching faculty. Such programs are available from leading publishers and can be used in training university lecturers on how to teach a particular subjects.

(ix) <u>In university library</u> :- To help library members find any book immediately on their own by referring to title, author name, subject, accession number, publisher etc. Also to give details about availability of a title.

(x) <u>Prospective viewers</u> :- Regular members and casual visitors of the library, staff member of the library.

Q5. Describe how multimedia can be used in the following: [15]

(a) A hospital

(b) Bank

(c) Bus stand

(a) A hospital : The basic use of multimedia is to provide easy information and user-friendly information too. Basically multimedia is greatly been used in public places. One of the public place is a reception of a hospital. Now if we just think that what information do we get when we go to a hospital reception. This information can be given through a person over the reception through a multimedia kiosk. The following information can be obtained :

- Details of different services provided by the hospital.
- Rates of the services.
- Brief history of the hospital.
- Details of patient.
- Patient ward number and their progress.
- Directions or road map of hospital.
- Information regarding visiting hours.
- FAQ (Frequently asked questions).
- Availability of doctors and their visiting hours etc.

(b) Bank : People goes to bank to open saving/current accounts, deposit funds, withdraw money, know various financial schemes of the bank, obtain loan etc. Every bank has a lot of information which it wants to impart to its customers. For this purpose, it can use multimedia in many ways. To tell the people about its various loan schemes such as House loan, Car loan, Two-wheeler loan, Consumer durables loan, Education loan, Personal loan, Computer loan etc. a bank can use a touch screen system which does not require use of keyboard or mouse. Touch of fingers is enough. Bank can also display information about its various schemes on a PC monitor placed in the rest area for customers.

Customers can be informed about their status of withdrawal of money through display of token numbers. Today online and internet banking have become very popular. These use multimedia extensively. The ATM counters we see everywhere are nothing, but multimedia extensions of conventional counters.

Multimedia is thus helping banks give better service to their customers and also in educating them about banks attractive finance schemes.

In addition to the above following information can also be provided with the help of multimedia :

- Brief history of the bank like time and year of establishment, address of main head office, different branches etc.
- The credit policy that banks follow can be displayed.
- Terms & conditions of the banks regarding savings and credits.
- Growth rate of the performance of bank over a period of time.
- Different services available like savings A/c, Current A/c, Locker facilities etc.
- Charges levied by the bank on various facilities like Demand Draft, Pay Order etc. provided to the Customers.
- Rate of interest paid by bank.
- Services regarding existing customers like balance in account, cheque status, overdraft facilities, request for new cheque book, statement etc.
- Procedure & documents required for opening a new A/c etc.
- E-banking, Internet Banking are the latest examples of use of multimedia in Bank.

(c) Bus stand : The use of multimedia at bus stand is not applied till now in India. So we are giving the use of multimedia in bus stand in European country.

- Pre information of coming buses.
- Post information of coming buses.
- Exact location of the buses.
- Loading capacity of the buses.
- Traffic information on roads.
- Information display the information of accidental areas and latest news of the country.

The multimedia system is able to manage all the station information, to maintain real time information about arrivals and departures, to display publicity on the information panel to generate automatically a human voice that provides information on arrivals and departures, to print any kind of information from any terminal, to be remotely controlled, to recognize the number plates of the vehicles.

The information system is the centre of all this system. It is in-charge of gathering and providing all necessary information to the rest modules of this system. The type of information like data of companies, buses, functional information on schedules, lines or complementary information such as generation of a human voice in real time, the transmission of advertising videos displayed on the information pannels of the bus station. The information pannels may be adapted to any video system and incorporates integrally, the possibility of showing advertising videos or entertainment in pannels thanks to the digital processing techniques. These systems may be seen on full screen or just on one side of it, with information of arrivals exists on the other side. This information can be sent through the habitual public address system. This is one of the most usual options for the workers of the station because they get this task done that requires constant attention, thus interrupting the workers. It is also possible to provide some information in different languages. This option is very interesting since it works with many foreign users, and it is essential for communities with more than one official language in which the information in all of them is required. A close circuit of video controls and monitors the arrivals and departures at/from the station as well as the security. A monitor in the information cabin has at least one camera at the entrance of the station.

CS-66 : MULTIMEDIA
DEC-2002

Note : *There are* ***five*** *questions in this paper. Question no.* ***1*** *is* ***compulsory*** *and carries 30 marks. Attempt any* ***three*** *from the rest.*

Q1(a). "Multimedia is stronger than multiple-media as it is interactive in nature." Comment on the above statement. **[5]**

"Multimedia is stronger than multiple media as it is interactive in nature". Multimedia is an integration of various media, which convey the information with computing technology various media, such as text, graphics, animation, sound, audio, video etc. In practically, we can say that multimedia is a combination of both hardware and software. Another much used is multimedia in "hypermedia".

One of the key features of multimedia is "interactivity". Hypermedia and virtual reality applications are based on multimedia system. Hypermedia extends the media-oriented features of multimedia system by the concept of hyperlink. Virtual reality extends the interaction oriented features of multimedia system by the concept of cyberspace.

After, these all multimedia systems provide the facility of real time navigation.

Now, the **multiple-media** is the collection of multiple media. In multiple media all the media are linked together. It also provides the facility of conferring the information with computing technology. Multiple-media doesn't provide the facility of hypermedia. Also it doesn't provide the facility of interactivity.

e.g.The Biomedical and multimedia information Technology (BMIT) group is an interdepartmental and interdisciplinary group of excellence. It has a strong research focus in the application of computer science and information technology in biomedicine and multimedia.

Through its research, this group seeks to gain a better understanding of information science and technology as applied to biomedical and multimedia problems and to facilitate the transfer of the knowledge gained for the benefit of our health care system and multimedia industry.

The medical application is MEDNET. Mednet provides the following services :

- A real time monitoring and multiparty consultation.
- Collaboration during brain surgery.

Mednet is being developed at University of Pittsburgh Medical Centre. The intra-operative monitoring places a real time control about the condition of the patient. Mednet is different from the other picture taking teleconferencing system as it provides real time monitoring and collaboration.

The term "collaboration" is one of the commonly used term in multimedia application. The verbal meaning of the collaboration is the actual meaning in the context of multimedia, that is collectively doing a particular work but for this collaborative work physical presence may not be required. How it can be achieved by mednet as in most of the surgeries the anesthesiologist, the system and other supporting staff have to be present for patient.

After getting all the conclusion finally we can say that multimedia is stronger than multiple-media. Multimedia is interactive in nature.

(b) What are the hardware components needed for professional multimedia development platforms? Define the purpose of each of the hardware components. [10]

Refer to Study Material, Chapter-1, Page no. - 7, Q8

(c) What is morphing? Describe a situation where it can be used. [5]

Refer to Study Material, Chapter-1, Page no. - 19, Q14

(d) Describe the features of any one of the following multimedia development platforms: [10]

(i) Flash

(ii) Authorware

(i) Flash

Flash :- Macromedia's Flash is aimed at reducing file download times on the Web, and may contain both bitmaps and drawn art. The anti-aliased character shown in the bitmap of Color Plate 5 is an example of the fine touches that improve the look of an image.

🗁**Look for these features in a drawing or painting package :**

✓ An intuitive graphical user interface with pull-down menus, status bars, palette control, and dialog boxes for quick, logical selection

✓ Scalable dimensions, so you can resize, stretch, and distort both large and small bitmaps

✓ Paint tools to create geometric shapes, from squares to circles and from curves to complex polygons

✓ Ability to pour a color, pattern, gradient into any area

✓ Ability to paint with patterns and clips art

✓ Customizable pen and brush shapes and sizes

✓ Eyedropper tool that samples colors

✓ Auto trace tool that turns bitmap shapes into vector-based outlines

✓ Support for scalable text fonts and drops shadows

✓ Multiple Undo capabilities, to let you try again

✓ Painting features such as smoothing coarse-edged objects into the background with anti-aliasing (see Color Plate 5); airbrushing in variable sizes, shapes, densities, and patterns; washing colors, in gradients; blending; and masking

✓ Support for third-party special effect plug-ins

✓ Object and layering capabilities that allow you to treat separate elements independently

✓ Zooming, for magnifies pixel editing

✓ All common color depths: 1-, 4-, 8-, and 16-, 24-, or 32-bit color, and gray-scale

✓ Good color management and dithering capability among color depths using various color models such as RGB, HSB, and CMYK

✓ Good palette management when in 8-bit mode

✓ Good file importing and exporting capability for image formats such as PIC, GIF, TGA, TIF, WHF, JPG, PCX, EPS, PTN, and BMP

(ii) Authorware

Macromedia's Authorware is a dependable industrial-strength environment that allows multiple people to contribute to an application. Artists can load a library with media, programmers can provide templates for complex interactions, and interface designers can put everything together. And one non-programming designer can even do the entire job alone.

Authorware 3 allows authoring of programs in identical environments on either the PC or the Macintosh and produce runtimes for either. Authorware's icons hold a wealth of programming information that never requires the user to think like a programmer.

Some icons in Authorware can manipulate media on the screen. They can display and erase graphics, move or animate objects. Play AVI and Quick Time digital movies as well as WAV sound files, and access videodisk and videotape players. The new framework icon automates hypermedia interactions and provides a default navigation structure. With a 10-page document in rich text format (RTF), it is easy to import it into the first "page" of framework using Authorware. Authorware can create a new display page for each hard page break in RTF (Rich Text Format) file. Eight buttons are used to move between pages, pop up a pick list of pages, search documents and exit the framework.

Authorware 3 has added text styles that you can apply to any text (labels, menu, options, scrolling text boxes).

Designing in Authorware is also allowed. Authorware elegantly provides full data integrity for it's naming of icons and variables. Change a variable name and it changes everywhere it's used.

Q2. Describe the process of planning and development of a mathematics tutorial through multimedia. [15]

The following points to develop a Multimedia tutor for the topics of "Introduction to Computer" or "Mathematics Tutorial" or "Information through Internet".

(i) First of all you have to plan a structure in your Mind to develop the project.

(ii) The specimen of audience (what you say and how you say will depend on the type and age group of student).

(iii) Outlining the Programme.

(iv) Develop a flow chart.

(v) Making a dynamic Question, answer sessions so the students question can be justified.

(vi) Plan the production of text, graphics, animation, audio and video.

(vii) Preparing the time schedule and the budget of project.

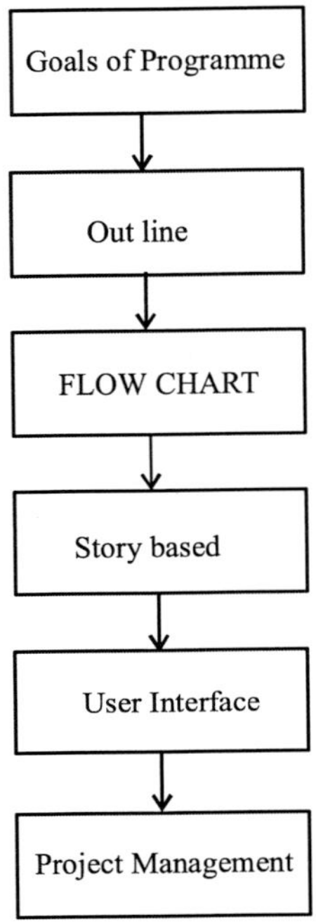

Multimedia is very useful in any development of the tutorial. When we develop any tutorial then planning is the necessary thing. Firstly it provides the analysis of the tutorial.

During the analysis phase of a development effort, all the member of the team gradually constructed a set of assumptions about the interactive product you are developing. It is sound practice to confirm those assumptions before undertaking the bulk of the design work of the product. The assumption should be confirmed with your client and with any vendors that may be collaborating on the project. The "Assumption check list" is a tool that can help you confirm the assumptions underlaying your multimedia development effort.

The assumption check list presumes that time has passed between the initial estimate of project scope and the approval to begin the project.

There are various steps involved in this assumption which are :

Step 1 : Meet with the client and determine :

- Are the goals and objectives still on target ?
- Is the audience still the same ?
- Is the review of each proposed element same ?
- Are the plans for marketing the product same ?
- Are implementation plans same ?

Step 2 : Review your estimates of project scope, including :

- Materials required
- Time needed
- Project cost

Step 3 : If required, rethink the project goals :

If serious questions about project scope or other assumption arise, don't hesitate to raise a red flag. It is better to rethink the multimedia development project now than to cancel it later.

After getting all things we think about Assessment Matrix.

The assessment matrix is designed to help you assume that each of the goals or objectives you've defined for your multimedia product is assessed by one or more reliable and valid outcome measures. Often development teams wait until a product is almost complete before making up a test intended to measure its outcomes. By planning for assessment early in the design stage of your product, your will've a much greater chance of designing a program that is actually capable of achieving its objectives.

After completing all these steps we specify the objectives specification tools.

A key element in the instructional development process is to specify the objectives for your program as clearly as possible. Poorly stated objective often result in instruction that is inappropriate. This tool is designed to help you write more specific objectives by providing you with a list of observable verbs. The tool includes verbs for both the cognitive domain and affective domain.

After completing all these things finally we check the user characteristics checklist :

(i) <u>Cognitive characteristics :</u>

- General aptitudes
- Specific aptitudes
- Functional literacy
- Computer literacy
- Learning style
- Prerequisite content knowledge

(ii) <u>Social characteristics :</u>

- Attitudes toward
- Relationships with poor
- Attitude toward authority
- Ethnic background
- Education level

(iii) <u>Personality characteristics :</u>

- Motivation to use this program
- Motivation to learn
- Attitude toward learning
- Attitude toward technology
- Self esteem

(iv) <u>Physical characteristics :</u>

- Visual abilities
- Auditory abilities
- Tectile abilities

Whenever you write objectives, review the verbs to select the ones most appropriate to your job or content. This is by no means a complete list of all the possible verbs and its primary value may be in spurring your imagination in writing better objectives.

Q3. Describe the features that you will consider while selecting a development tool for the following multimedia components: [15]
(a) Sound/Audio
(b) Graphics
(c) Animation

Refer to Study Material, Chapter-1, Page no. - 28, Q21

Q4. Suggest suitable areas from your curriculum where multimedia can be used for teaching English (as per course CS610). Give details in the form of objectives, target audience, resource requirements and advantages of making multimedia for the area/application suggested. [15]

Multimedia the type of technology that can express by their own. In school generally we use multimedia in form of games or computer or giving any lecture to large number of students with the use of projector.

(A) Objective to Use:

Multimedia for teaching English in school are :

1. Class room : We can teach student with the help of multimedia CD of English speaking in which our main target will be object available in the classroom like

(i) Black Board correct is Check board

(ii) Communication with friends

a. General communication with in a class with other student will be the main another objective to teach English

3. Communication with senior student : The senior student who are well matured generally discourage the juniors is the main problems with the help of their English speaking ability the young or junior student can make or built their good impact on their seniors it also helps to improve their mental and patience for the juniors.

4. Communication with teachers : With their daily routine student have to talk with their teachers depending on their problems help an for general permission student should know how to take small permissions.

(B) Target Audience : Over target Audience will be student as well as teacher also the parents of the student in their parents meeting.

(C) Recourse Requirement

1. English Story Book
2. Computer
3. Speakers
4. Projector
5. English Movie
6. Film Animated English Cartoon CD
7. Special Multimedia CD for Children for English Speaking Purpose

Besides the many technical considerations of hardware and software configuration for a multimedia project, the design process must also be separated into its various components. Although using a multimedia tool is in some ways similar to programming a computer, we saw in examining the development spectrum that it is also very different. In addition, these tools necessitate not only technical competence, but also a knowledge of the material to be conveyed and an idea of how that information can most effectively be displayed. This reveals three important areas to consider when developing a multimedia application in a teaching/learning environment:

(i) Content

(ii) Presentation

(iii) Programming

Advantage of multimedia in these areas:

Content : The content is the important information which is being conveyed through the multimedia application. The gathering, refining and composing of this information is the most crucial task in creating a multimedia application. Often content which is included in an application is outside of the range of expertise of the actual developers of the applications. This is specially true for applications developed within an academic environment and it is important that someone with a degree of expertise in the subject matter. Contribute substantially to the project especially in the planning phase. It's the common mistake among people wishing to use multimedia that the responsibility for providing content rets with the same individuals who create the application. An effective application is created when the strength of a effective application is created when the strength of a content expert are effectively communicated.

Presentations : The aesthetic appearance of the multimedia application and the composition of the variety of media are very important in conveying the content of an application. The color scheme used the user interface which is designed, and the integration of various media, are all elements of consideration in designing a professional quality multimedia presentation. This task requires that the developer have an artistic ability, or that someone with an artistic ability be specially designated to work on the application with a strong visual and audible presentation material can be effectively communicated, when the choreography of an application is awkward, limited, or weak it will distract the user, making the information have less of an impact. It should bot be assumed that a developer possesses skills in the artistic presentation.

Programming : Generally the people who develop multimedia application have some degree of computer literacy, and as a result may be familiar with programming. Since, most applications are very related to programming. Either through a graphical flowchart of icons or the use of a scripting language, this technical competence is very important. Increasingly, however it is the case that multimedia tools are being designed with the developer in mind and as a result are becoming easier to use. It is also necessary, as many tools besides the main development applications will be used which requires an understanding of different file formats and methods of data generation.

These three critical areas of application of multimedia development are very interrelated and are definitely not mutually exclusive. Teaching occurs best when the three areas can be understood and integrated, and when a balance exists between the areas of content, presentation and programming.

Q5. Describe how multimedia can be used in the following: [15]

(a) Airline reservation system

(b) Railway enquiry system

(c) An auditorium

(a) Airline reservation system

It can be stated that the global computer reservation systems have reached a significantly high economic and technological level and travel agents would hardly be able to do their work without some tools which makes this task easier.

In airlines reservation multimedia is widely used. Multimedia is also compatible over the network. As airlines have offices all over the country or all over the world for that matter, multimedia plays on very important role. Multimedia can give detailed information like.

(i) Schedules of flights per day.

(ii) Arrivals and departures of flights.

(iii) Availability of seats & current position of the seats if waiting list is put.

(iv) Rates of the tickets.

(v) Different schemes available if any for regular fliers.

(vi) Information on connecting flights of domestic and international schedules.

(vii) Thus multimedia can be used as an information kiosk for airlines reservation.

(b) Railway enquiry system

(i) Arrival time

(ii) Departure time

(iii) Vacant seats

(iv) Possibility seats

(v) Cancellation of any train

(vi) Latest change in fair

(vii) Latest schemes

(c) An auditorium

Auditorium is a public place where many social, cultural and even political meetings and programs are held. It is not necessary that the meetings held everyday of the week. But its periodically held. Even stage shows are held here. Here too multimedia can be very handy and can be used in the following ways:

- To maintain a proper record of the scheduled programs.
- Directing the audience to their seats in a proper manner.
- Multimedia can be used for good sound quality and lights
- Multimedia projectors can be used for making presentations.

The Multimedia system is able to manage all the information, to maintain real time information about the auditorium, to display publicity on the information panel, to generate automatically a human voice that provides all the information which is related with auditorium.

The information system is the center of all this system. It is in charge of gathering and providing all the necessary information to the rest of modules of this system. It is also possible to provide some information in different languages. This option is very interesting since it works with many foreign users and it is essential for communities with more than one official language in which the information in all of them is required. A closed circuit of video controls and monitors at/from the exists as well as the security. A monitor in the information cabin has at least one camera at the entrance of the auditorium.

Finally, I would like to say that the Multimedia is able to manage all the functionality, which is related to an auditorium.

CS-66 : MULTIMEDIA
JUNE-2003

Note : *There are **five** questions in this paper. Question no. 1 is **compulsory** and carries 30 marks. Attempt any **three** from the rest.*

Q1(a). "Multimedia is the tool for teaching tomorrow." Comment on the above statement. **[5]**

Another critical application of multimedia is educational sector. Multimedia enhances the quality of education. It provides new way for teachers to encourage one of the most rare and important elements of learning i.e., curiosity to know and explore. Topics can be linked with other related information. Linking is possible with graphics, text and sound (may be a lecture session from the subject teacher and so on).

With a large screen projector and a multimedia playback system, teachers can use multimedia as a way to enhance their standard lesson plan and stimulate questions. On the other hand students will be able to further explore the topics using standard multimedia platform. The assignments, which require students to make their own interpretation of facts, can be represented in the multimedia topics, there are several applications possible in this area of education using multimedia. The use of multimedia in education would go a long way.

In a complete sense pictures, graphics, text and sound is the essence of multimedia and it provides the user friendly environment with most flexible interactive facilities. Multimedia is very important in all the field but from education point of view it has done wonders. Education with the help of entertainment is provided by multimedia. This is also known as edutainment, i.e. fun with education. Now let us understand the whole process of education & see where multimedia is useful. For teaching books are required & thus the use of multimedia also begins here. Right from the designing of books to the content & the outer look multimedia is used. To enhance the learning experience proper text highlights, graphics are used. Apart from the books now a days. One gets the facility of learning through CBT. To develop this CBT different elements of multimedia like text, graphics, animation etc. are used. This CBIT is useful for the students and also to the tutors. With latest technology of distributed computing multimedia education can also be helpful over the network.

Thus we can see that multimedia definately helps the fun of education.

The use of multimedia in education are many ways. Lets take one example of an encyclopedia. Now we all know that encyclopedia is used for all round education. Encyclopedia has all the information of everything. They come in the sets of 5 to 10 books. Now just imagine that if these books were boring black & white text only. Naturally the interest automatically goes. But the books now being more graphical and colourful becomes very simple to learn & fun to read also. You can get the whole book on an interactive CD. This is very exciting & great fun as its like playing game when you are learning. This has many advantage as compared to a text book as per the following ways:

- Very interactive
- Very colourful & attractive.
- Made more powerful by adding sound & video where needed.
- Easy to browse through the content.
- Its fun and easy just like game.
- Visual presentation helps to remember more.
- Entertains you even when you are learning that is edutainment.

Thus we can see that multimedia definitely helps in education.

(b) A multimedia hardware platform is to be used for delivering multimedia based tutorials available on the CD. What will be the configuration of such multimedia computers. Describe the purpose of each component in your selection. [10]

Refer to DEC2003,Q2,Page NO.-110

(c) What are the various sound formats that may be allowed in multimedia? Describe in detail any one of them. [5]

The various sound formats that may be allowed in multimedia are :

- ✓ CDA
- ✓ RAM
- ✓ MIDI
- ✓ MJF
- ✓ XM
- ✓ S3M
- ✓ STM
- ✓ MOD
- ✓ DSM
- ✓ WAV
- ✓ WMA
- ✓ M3U
- ✓ DAT
- ✓ MP3

MIDI Description:

MIDI : MIDI or musical system interface is the second most popular type of PC sound. MIDI was not designed for the PC; it was created for the Musicians, to allow them to create, store and play a broad cross Section of instruments, including those invented on synthesizers. A MIDI file can be best described as " electronic sheet music".

Role and Subsystems : The sound card is part of the multimedia subsystem. It plays music and sound from digital files within the PC, and also plays audio from audio CDs played on an optical drive. The speakers connect to the sound card to actually play the music.

Related Components : The sound card is most closely related to the optical drive and the motherboard.

Key Compatibility Selection Criteria : Here are the key criteria to consider in selecting a sound card and speakers.

Interface: Sound cards can connect to the system using either an ISA slot or a PCI slot. ISA slots are more commonly found on older machines PCI is the trend for the future. If you are planning to reuse an older ISA card in a new system, be sure there is an available ISA slot in the motherboard.

Resource Availability : Sound cards are notorious for using a large number of system resources interrupt request lines (IRQs), direct memory access channels (DMAs) and I/ O addresses. On a new system the PC maker will take care of these issues, but if you are upgrading or adding a card to a system, be sure to check for availability of resources. The fancier the card, the more likely it will require a lot of resources.

SoundBlaster Compatibility : The SoundBlaster was one of the first sound cards and became a virtual standard in the PC world. Virtually all cards are compatible with at least one version of the SoundBlaster family, and this is something you want to make sure you have, especially for games.

Performance and Capacity Selection Criteria : Generally speaking, the more you spend on the card, the more performance you get from it, but it's debatable as to how important this really is. You want to be sure to look for a card that supports wave table playback, not just FM synthesis, as this will give you much better sound. Beyond that, you are paying for support for more simultaneous "voices", faster processing and so on. As I have mentioned, these are really of primary interest if you are heavily into gaming, otherwise virtually any sound card will do the job.

Speakers are pretty much the same story : paying more gets you more power (volume) and better quality. Virtually any speakers will work for occasional gaming, but if you want the full gaming experience you need to use either good speakers or a home stereo system.

Quality Selection Criteria : Name-brand cards are all fairly reliable and quality problems are not great. Sound cards usually come down to a comparison of features, and just avoiding the "really cheap" ones that can be of poor quality.

As for speakers, this is one place where you really do get only what you pay for. Cheap speakers generally sound like junk; if all you can afford is $20 for a couple of teeny speakers then you will be able to hear what sounds and music your software is producing, but that's about it. If you can, consider using a patch cord from the sound card to the auxiliary input of a stereo system; the sound produced by even an economy portable stereo will be much better than what you get from most inexpensive computer speakers. If you can't do this and you are on a budget, I personally would spend more on the speakers and less on sound card features.

To test if a PC's sound system sounds good or bad due to its sound card or its speakers, try using a good pair of headphones in the output jack of the sound card. Or better, try different sets of speakers with the same sound card on the same system.

(d) Describe the features of any *one* of the following multimedia S/W: [10]
(i) Macromedia Director
(ii) Authorware

Refer to Study Material, Chapter-3, Page no. - 65, Q6

Q2. Describe the process of development of advertising capsule of small duration through multimedia. [15]

Advertising through Multimedia Multimedia is a natural for advertising - natural images, special effects, animation, 3-D. There are three main areas of current opportunity: CD-ROM, the Internet, and customer point-of-contact use of multimedia. As manufacturers seek to gain greater competitive advantage through the application of Information Technology there will need to be increasing use of Multimedia and high networks.

The publishing industry is being transformed through the use of Multimedia and high speed networks. The market for Media products is expanding rapidly as homes and businesses are connected to the fibre major markets : education, entertainment and professional publishing. Educational publishing is aimed at schools. Entertainment publishing can focus on the home or mobile system using all Media. Professional publishing is probably the largest sector of these three and includes information whose value to companies ranges from the very short term such as stock prices through the Medium term such as company reports and world news to the long term such as directories of people and organization.

A Multimedia development team consists of many different skills oriented people, who include a producer, educational consultant, media consultant, media designers, media specialist, web master etc.

However, the whole team works for a single objective that is creation of an effective multimedia application. Therefore, one of the major issues for Multimedia production is to plan an application.

To start the authoring process of Multimedia application development without planning all the components of the project is a major mistake as it may lead to an insufficient application being developed. A Multimedia advertising project should be planned through following stepwise process :-

✓ Develop the Multimedia program/application concept.
✓ Outline of the program.
✓ Develop a flow chart.
✓ Develop program story board.
✓ Plan the user interface.
✓ Consider copyright issue.
✓ Plan the production of text, graphics, animation, audio and video.
✓ Prepare the project budget and time schedule.

CD-ROM offers the opportunity to make a sophisticated sales pitch to a potential customer without a sales rep's having to call. Toyota is typical. It offers a free CD-ROM, advertised in magazines. These ads in themselves save money. The following is almost all the text for a one-eighth page black-and-white ad in *Scientific American,* (September1995), which is, of course, much cheaper than a full-page color ad or a four-page insert "Imagine live footage of every Toyota Car, Truck, SUV and Van in any COLOR or from any ANGLE, right in front of your EYES. With all the information of every brochure right at your fingertips. All in full STEREO." The CD-ROM meets most of Toyota's promises. It takes a few minutes to install and contains a lot of sheer hype before you can get to the content. Like most of today's CD-ROMs, it is slower than it could and should be. You have to sit for several seconds watching the screen change the menu, and you can't quickly cancel and skip over an item. (It is much like being a captive of a television information.)

That said, once you locate the information you want to look at, the CD-ROM is easy to use, instructive, and attractive. One of its most useful features is the ability to rotate the car, which goes well beyond looking at a color photograph. You can also change its color and see it move in video clips. In 1996, GM introduced an on-line equivalent of the Toyota CD-ROM on the Internet. It contained 16,000 pages on GM cars and also includes the rotation of images. The Internet is at present much slower than CD-ROM, if you are using standard dial-up phone lines.

The low cost of reproduction for CD-ROMs, around 60 cents, as well as the growing number of home PCs with drives, makes them almost throwaways; they are regularly given away with magazines that offer demo versions of software, for instance. Until either interactive TV, the Internet, or other on-line information services combine very fast and almost free telecommunications, CD-ROM seems likely to be the main vehicle for advertising that meets the four criteria for effective use of multimedia identified in the Introduction:

- **Knowledge management :** They provide the storage and retrieval tools to manage large volumes of complex data. The Toyota disk would be a many-hundred-page series of printed brochures that could not be easily explored and assimilated.
- **Customer interaction :** You can't interact with a TV ad or a brochure. The Toyota CD-ROM is like having a somewhat gabby car salesperson at your shoulder who gives you answers to your questions and points you to the topics you might want to explore in more depth.
- **Natural decision input :** Obviously, the value of visual information and motion depends on the specific type of product or service being advertised. It's not surprising that car makers are among the leaders in the use of multimedia for advertising. The more they can show images of the cars, close-ups of features, and the car in motion, the more easily you can visualize the real thing.
- **Shared understanding :** When you go to the nearest Toyota dealer (identified for you by the disk), you are a more informed buyer than you would have been otherwise. Whatever he or she has to show you, you have already seen. You have a shared context that should make it faster and easier for you to choose and for the sales rep to work with you.

CD-ROM is the primary off-line medium for digital advertising. On-line advertising can reach a wider audience, just as broadcast television reaches more of the population than individual newspapers and magazines. There are many on-line information services, including America Online, CompuServe, and the Microsoft Network, but it is the Internet that is the fastest-growing target for advertising in many forms. Some companies use vivid World Wide Web pages with graphics, video, and music as a sort of giant billboard that will, they hope, immediately attract the attention of the estimated (or, rather, guessed-at) 30 million people who surf the Internet and the hundreds of millions they believe will be doing so within a few years.

Companies that place ads and information on the Internet often pay less attention to how to lead the surfers to them in the first place than to catchy design. The Net is not organized in any way. There are no tidy product or market categories, only sites where pages are joined to each other in a very tenuous way through "hot links," words or phrases that you click on to move to other pages on the relevant topic. There is no comprehensive classified directory. It's very hard to browse the Internet efficiently.

Browsers are also not yet likely to be buyers. Many are "lurkers," who view a site and move on quickly. The only information advertisers get that tells them how successful their ads have been is the number of "hits" on their site. This is the equivalent of a Nielsen rating, which estimates how many television sets were tuned to a particular TV program, without reliably indicating what proportion were actively watching it rather than keeping it on in the background while they ate dinner. Page hits are simply a count of the number of times a single page is accessed. It may not even be read, only skimmed and abandoned. A Web "page" can be as long as a book - it's really a computer file. If a Web page has 10 pages of text and graphics and all ten are retrieved, this counts as ten hits. Yet market researchers point out that the number of hits is irrelevant - the value of hits lies in who (such as a kid playing around on the family computer versus a qualified buyer) retrieves the data and how that retrieval affects the user's awareness, attitude, or behavior. At a meeting of a large bank's top management team, one executive proudly announced that the firm's newly installed Web page was already getting 50 hits a day. He didn't seem to notice that 5 of today's hits had just been made in the demo that preceded his remark.

Web pages contain far less information than CD-ROMs because of the limitations of data transfer by modem. A CD-ROM drive can easily process and send to a PC full motion video, and designers want to include as much movement and color as they can. Internet advertisers are always advised to minimize movement and color. Otherwise, it can take minutes just to reach a single page and hours to transmit the same information that on the Toyota CD-ROM can be zipped through in 20 minutes or so.

Shoppers in New York's Union Square have been dazzled and amazed by therealistic 3-D images of products from Bradlees department store that float above them on the sidewalk outside the shop. The "suspended volumetric displays" look virtually solid. The response of passersby has been so positive that Bradlees was able to sell 3-D "virtual" advertising space to manufacturers. Even if such advertising doesn't sell more goods than does conventional advertising, it grabs much more attenion

All this means that on-line advertising is not a simple electronic extension of broadcast TV, home shopping, the Yellow Pages, and newspaper ads. The keys to success seem to be (1) "narrowcast" - find ways of getting your message to the specific individuals and communities that are most likely to respond actively to it rather than passively; (2) focus on navigators, not surfers, on the Internet; (3) focus very carefully indeed on using multimedia for communicating information rather than exploiting its striking visual and auditory effects for "eye candy"; and (4) provide more than just a passive reading of what's on the screen; the attraction of the on-line world is interaction and exploration.

Q3. What are the features that you may look for while selecting development tools for Animation using series of pictures, Video editing and Simulating a practical session in multimedia? [15]

The features of development tools are as under :-

a) Integrating multimedia elements.
b) Script language programs.
c) Icon-based programs.
d) DLL'S for extending features.
e) Supporting CD-ROM and laser disc sources.
f) Supporting Video for windows.
g) Hypertext.
h) Cross platform capability.
i) Run-time player for distribution

Now let us study each of the features in detail.

a) Integrating multimedia elements : As we all know important different media elements of a multimedia presentation. As there are many multimedia elements, a authoring software's has to support all the different media elements. Authoring programs provide developers with a great degree of control over each multimedia element than presentation programs. Authoring softwares are also geared towards education and training applications as well as business presentation.

b) Script language program : Authoring softwares has the feature to write scripts for software to build features that are not supported by the software itself. These type commands linked together in a word processing typescript. The script language specifies multimedia elements, sequencing, hotspots, etc. nearly all the authoring softwares are backed up by powerful scripting programmes. This scripting program is object oriented. Here no editing of media elements can be done. They can only be used for handling the elements & increase interaction. Most of the scripting languages are interpreted instead of compiled. The runtime speed gains over other authoring methods are minimum. It also supports more & complete medias.

c) Icon based programs : Authoring a complete multimedia projects is very complex & this icon based programs are available where graphical icons are used to control the features. The main features of icon based programs are :-

➢ Icon-based programs are easier to learn than script programs.

➢ Working on a icon based program is also easy as editing anything can be done easily by just clicking on the icon.

Icon based authoring programs are also object oriented development programs where multimedia elements are represented by icons.

Icon based programs use less time for development. Many of these tools are also optimized for developing CBT's. The main part of such program are the icon palette, containing the possible functions/interactions of a program and the flow line, which shows the actual links between the icons. However, the high end packages, such as Authorware or icon author are extremely powerful and suffer least from runtime speed problems.

d) DLL's for extending features : With advance technologies developing authoring programs can call on special features available in the Windows is Dynamic Link Libraries (DLL's). These DLL's with special features are automatically installed with software itself. Programming languages like C, C++ allow the user to create their own DLL's.

e) Supporting CD-Rom & laser Disc sources : Saving the arrays of different media elements is often not practical to get the quality and speed. Authoring softwares allows full control of drives.

Authoring softwares supports MCI command language that helps direct control of CD-Rom drives. Multimedia presentation that depend on large amounts of sound or video clips require high end PC with great storage option & memory. This CD-Drive and DVD player as a video source. Authoring softwares provide seamless control on this hardware.

f) Supporting video for windows : Videos stored on the hard disk is sometimes the right media for your project. Authoring softwares has the capability to support most multimedia elements including video for windows latest softwares from macromedia like authorware and director permits the loading of video clips from video for windows and animation clips from auto desk.

g) Hypertext : Hypertext is nothing but text working like a button. Hypertext capabilities can be used to link graphics, animation or frame and of course other text. Hypertext interfaces allows users to select individual hot words on a screen, which are then linked to other pages or layers or text etc. A perfect example of hypertext application is windows help.

Hypertext systems are useful when presenting large amount of textual information. Many hypertext authoring programs provide graphical links for animation, sound and video as well as text.

h) Cross platform capability : This is a very important feature. A multimedia project has to play on all different platforms. This is very important to expand your audience. A very important consideration with authoring programs is the capability of presenting on Macintosh or other hardware platforms. Now days all the authoring softwares are capable of work on different platforms.

i) Run-time player for distribution : Run-time software is often included in authoring software to explain the distribution of your final product. Advance authoring programs provide specialized packing and run time distribution for use with devices like CD-Rom & other hardware. While making professional presentation that all the DLL's & run time modules are packed with the presentation.

Q4. A multimedia teaching aid is to be developed for teaching Binary Search Tree data structure. How will you design this multimedia? Give details on the objectives, target audience, resource requirements and advantages of making the above multimedia. Which of the multimedia components would you like to include in your above tutorial? Give reasons. [15]

There are many search methods but the binary search tree method are very popular in professionals. A tree which have there left and right subtree are called binary search tree. The binary search tree is a binary tree which is either empty or contains a node whose keys satisfies the conditions:

(a) The key in the left child of a node (if any) proceeds the key in the parent node.

(b) The key in the right child of a anode (if any) succeeds the key in the parent node.

(c) The left and right subtree of the root are again binary search trees.

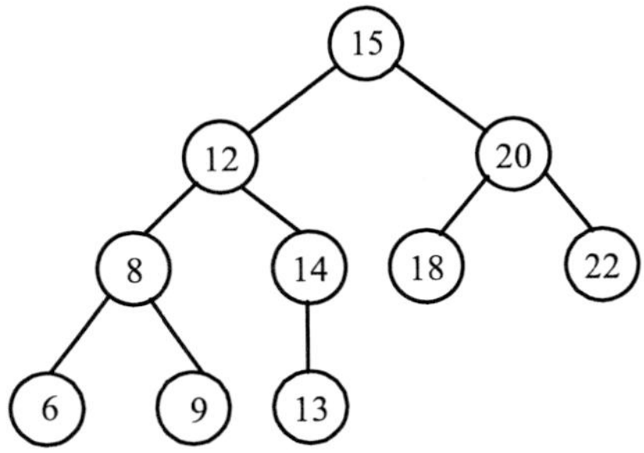

During the initial design phase all aspects of the multimedia projects are carefully planned before the production start. This is the phase or stage where director, the interface designer, the content designer and the main programmer have to take decision on key elements of the production.

1. Flow chart : This is the map that show how all the elements in the titles are connected. They are the blueprint of the output.

2. Scripts : The script is just like a movie work in conjunction with the flowchart to provide a printed version of all the text.

🗁 **Objective :** To give demonstration on the topic binary search tree to the students, so that they would easily understand the concept of one of data structure element that is binary search tree.

🗁 **Target audience :** Our target audience are here the students which has curriculum of studying the data structure like PGDCA/MCA/BCA students.

🗁 **Resource Requirements**

(a) Definition of BST, its objective and rules of designing the BST.

(b) Use of hyperlinks so that students can view the different aspects of BST in a better manner.

(c) There requires proper software, authoring tools of multimedia in which one can design for particular problem.

(d) Algorithm to design and search the element in BST can be linked with help of hyperlinks and any programming language.

(e) If LAN exists than every student should be able to view the topics.

(f) Proper FAQ should be designed so that students can ask for their problem.

Advantages of Making this Multimedia

(a) Data structure is one of the important topic for students because it helps a lot while designing of programmes by designing multimedia software on this topic helps to those also who cannot understand the things so easily.

(b) Students will have practical views on this topic.

Based upon the proceeding considerations, the following components of a Multimedia system that need to be designed :

✓**Content :** Specify the information needs and interaction requirements of the users in the different tasks, i.e. what kind and level of details of information do the users want to receive ? How do they want to select and access that information ? This amount in some forms to task content and structure analysis, where the "task" includes non job – related activities, such as browsing a system for leisure purposes.

✓**Structure :** Specify the structure between different pieces or chunks of information and how the user might gain access to this information.

✓**Access :** Specify the information navigation and access techniques i.e. how will the user know then related information is available and how to access it ? Do users always know how to locate themselves in the information space and to find the way back to where they come from ? Is the user allowed to make new connection between arbitrary or selected pieces of information ?

✓**Style :** Specify the way each component of information will be presented to the user. In which modality will the information be presented (textually, verbally, graphically, by animation, by audio or video sequences, still images etc.) ? will be shown only once and disappear or remain for closer inspection or repeated presentation ? Can it be interrupted or hidden ? Can the user switch between different presentation modes depending upon preference or circumstances ?

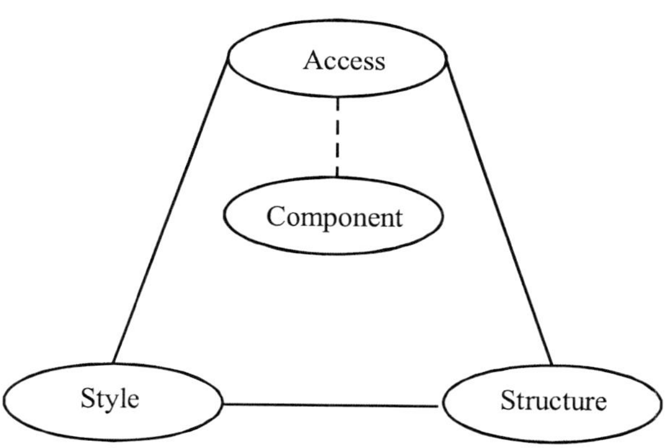

Because any person can get easily this multimedia based teaching aids. Finally, this is fruitful for any person.

Q5. Describe how multimedia can be used in the following: **[15]**

(a) A Conference

(b) A Library

(c) A Museum

(a)A Conference : The activities in an office such as meetings, group discussions, training are some areas where we need the concept such as brainstorming, sharing of idea, problem solving etc. for real-time meetings that involve geographically dispersed group of people, we can avail the choices as:

✓ Audio conferencing

✓ Video conferencing, or

✓ Document conferencing.

🗁 **Audio conferencing :** This technology allows 'out-of-town' people to participate in a formal meeting. This technology can also be used by a group of people to meet frequently whatsoever is the physical distance among them. Audio conferencing is an effective means of communication for reporting about a project status. It can be used to solve problems quickly. One of the disadvantages of audio conferencing is that such conferences are restricted to only voice, so this conference can be preceded by sending email of documents that are to be used during the conference. The second disadvantage is that the person who is not proficient in spoken words cannot participate well in such conference.

🗁 **Video Conferencing :** Video conferencing is being used successfully by several organizations abroad. Video conferencing resembles an office meeting; thus, require setting of time, preparing rooms and place, agenda etc. However the biggest drawback is the cost of the equipment.

Video conferencing brings people together naturally and simulate a real life meeting environment. Today video conferencing has been brought to the computer however; it is not easy to use, as the participant has continuously look at the camera on the top of his machine.

🗁 **Document Conferencing :** Document conferencing, also called audio-graphic conferencing technology, allows people to meet using their PCs and telephone lines. The telephone lines connect the participants so they can share audio information and the data they have stored in their PC. In addition, it allows online editing of a document by several participating people in the conference. This conferencing technology has been used in the education filed. It extends the boundaries of the classroom and reach out into the community. A document that can be used in the conference may consist of text, graphics, sound or even video clippings.

(i) Large screen display

(ii) Information of vacant seats.

(iii) Information of total strength.

(iv) Infirmation of unidentified objects.

(v) Emergency attention to all viewers.

A conference is a live connection between people in separate locations for the purpose of communication, usually involving audio and often text as well as video.

At its simplest conferencing provides transmission of static images and text between two locations. At its most sophisticated, it provides transmission of full motion video images and high-quality audio between multiple locations.

(b) A Library

Multimedia is very useful in library. The multimedia system is able to mange all the functionality of the library. It is used to maintain real time information about book, (topics, authors, title, availability) to display publicity on the information panel.

It easily integrates text, images, sound, music, animation, interactive controls, color and other graphical elements to create stunning multimedia productions. Neo Book can be used to produce electronic magazines (e-zines) that can be distributed over the Internet, interactive educational and training material, CD-ROM interfaces, electronic books, reference works, brochures, catalogs, entertainment titles and much more.

Multimedia CD-ROMs is a new learning method, which is not only user friendly but also saves storing space. Another additional advantage is the increased shelf life of the desired book in the CD. The multimedia is very useful in library system because the all information regarding books and catalogs are stored in CD-ROM in the way of video and audio form.

(c) A Museum

In the Museum it can be placed at the reception lounge various types of museum like Rail Museum, Doll Museum, Science Museum. These above museum guide every information to their own stream. It can guide various information and other relevant topics and one of the most important whether somebody damaging the museum things or not.

Multimedia can be used in just about any situation where computers are being used to deliver information, and a number where they are not traditionally used.

A museum is a place where art effects and ancient objects, paining is kept. Thus Museum becomes a huge place & this place is very useful for knowledge enhancement. Here also multimedia can have a very major role to play. As multimedia is used for distribution of knowledge and information & Museum is a place where one goes for knowledge and information. Multimedia here can be used for different ways.

- A complete road map of the museum.
- Proper distribution of different zones of the museum.
- Details regarding each ones.
- Complete details of the different thing which are displayed i.e. the history of object.
- Value addition i.e. extra information regarding the topic.
- When & where did the object was found.
- What the object was made up of and how it was made.

CS-66: MULTIMEDIA
DEC-2003

Note : *There are **five** questions in this paper. Question no. **1** is **compulsory** and carries 30 marks. Attempt any **three** from the rest.*

Q1(a). What is morphing? How is it similar to/different from Warping?

First of all morphing and warping are two different techniques of animation. The suitable work would be effects used for production. There is a lot of difference in both.

Morphing: Morphing takes two images and seamlessly changes one image to another. The second image actually seems to grow out of the first one. Morphing can also be used to show the pace of changes more clearly than photos. Morphing is used in Ads & Movies. Morphing is quite different than Warping.

Warping: Warping is variation of the morphing where one image is used to show various changes that is take place. It uses the key points of one image to create different effects, instead of mixing up two images.

(b)What are multimedia pedagogues? How do they support the teaching and learning?

Multimedia for Teaching and Learning Audio-visual material can provide useful aids for learning when integrated into computer-based teaching systems. However, a teaching system is only useful if the learner remains active and motivated.

Truly interactive systems can evolve into multimedia pedagogues and can facilitate a shift in teaching and learning. Background In recent years, the term multimedia has evolved to describe the storage and display of audio-visual material as well as text and graphics in computer systems. Teachers have been using 'multiple media' presentations to enhance the learning experience of their students, such as slide shows, television broadcasts and videos, for as long as the technology has been available. An example T.V. is used in imparting education to widest student community by IGNOU through its Gyan Darshan Channel which uses slide shows, animation etc. to clear the concepts.

Pedagogues are useful teaching aid only if they simulate and motivate the students. A multimedia tutor can provide multiple numbers of challenges to the student to simulate his interest in a topic. The instructions provided by pedagogue have moved beyond providing only button level control to intelligent simulations, dynamic creation of links, composition and collaboration and system testing of the user interaction.

Here some of the multimedia pedagogue which supports the teaching and learning are :

Simulations : Simulation is an important area of pedagogy where a student is engaged in situations of problem solving. It has two part :

(i) Scenarios based simulations : Scenario based simulation uses video, graphics and sound to engage the student in a particular problem situation. The scenario based tutors have limited answers and suggestions to offers.

(ii) Knowledge based simulations : Knowledge based simulations are more intelligent as far as behaviour is concerned and are adaptive to student needs. Knowledge based simulations are difficult to design.

The Cardiac Tutor : It is a knowledge based simulation, which teaches the student about the cardiac resuscitation. The knowledge about cardiac resuscitation was collected iteratively from various exerts in the area.

This tutor has been designed to present a graphical view of an emergency patient. The goal for the student is to save the patient. The tutor also provides clues to the student. These clues can be :

- Spoken Advice
- Emergency Room Sound
- Graphical Indications

Multimedia Compositions : A composition created by a student on multimedia platform require lot of activity to perform. These activities are :

- Creation of Text.
- Organisation, that is making the items.
- Access of documents which involves searching of patterns and indexing.
- Communication which helps in basically sharing the work and ideas. A well-connected multimedia interface allows integration of several media forms for a particular piece of information such as text, process description or graphics.

Multimedia and Explanatory Systems : The multimedia system also have a very important property, that is, they adapt their responses to the student needs. Thus, providing explanation to various situations, which have been put for the pedagogy to solve.

The advantage of this planner over a normal hypertext based presentations are :

- The student can themselves choose the media to display information.
- A piece of information can be reused for answering different question as the objects are defined in the forms of a shared base of information.
- Capabilities of having natural link still exist.

Technical Challenge for Developers : If we people will use the potential of multimedia technology then we will have to deal with the following challenges :

- We've to move to knowledge based multimedia system, which will customize the presentations based on the situation they are responding to.
- In future, there will have to be trends of having network based multimedia.
- More advanced authoring tools need to be developed which provide easy representation for implementation.

Conclusion Multimedia learning environments, or multimedia pedagogues as we might call them, must be shown to be educationally effective and to provide students the same or better quality of experience as they have with traditional teaching methods. At best such systems will enhance and improve the students' quality of learning. When they work well, they may also educate in new cutting-edge ways, allowing faculty to spend less time in lectures and more time working with individual students. The global network will enable easy access to information. Multimedia and artificial intelligence technology should play a central role in bringing this information to new levels of realism and usefulness, enabling learners to gain access to more knowledge and to a variety of media forms. In sum, desktop multimedia has the potential to make computer education as effective as one-to-one human tutoring yet as compelling, affordable, and widespread as television.

(c) What is hypertext? Describe its applications.

When a hypermedia project includes large amounts of text of symbolic content, this content can be indexed and its elements then liked together to afford rapid electronic retrieval of the associated information. When words are keyed or indexed to other words, you have *hypertext system;* the "text" part of this term represents the project's content and meaning, rather than the graphical presentation of text. Hypertext is what the World Wide Web is all about.

When text lives in a computer instead of printed pages, the computer's powerful processing capabilities can be applied to make the text more accessible and meaningful. The text can then be called *hypertext;* because can be accessed in nonlinear way, quickly and intuitively.

🗁 ***Applications of Hypertext :*** Since hypertext is a medium, it is natural to use it in connection with computer-oriented applications. Hypertext can be used to prototype the user interface for almost any other computer program as most initial prototyping consists of linking together screen designs and presenting them to the user in an order determined by simple user actions.

(a) Online documentation: Online documentation may be the most natural of all hypertext applications. Hypertext is the obvious method for helping user in the situation when they require good access tool to help them retrieve the sections of the manual that are relevant to their current needs.

(b) User Assistance: Hypertext provides a mechanism for integrating several forms of user assistance, including the online manual, an introductory tutorial, online help system, and even the error messages. Because users only get massages when they are in some kind of trouble, the error messages are a print candidate for providing users with assistance.

In an integrated user assistance facility based on hypertext, it would be possible for the user to link an error message to the location in the help system that gives further assistance on the problem. Also if the user wanted further assistance than could be provided by the help system or the manual then it may become possible to link further, to the appropriate location in the tutorial component, to get a computer-aided instruction lesson.

This type of integrated user interface does not exist in current computer system and can be made possible with the hypertext facility.

(c) Software Engineering: The hypertext has a great potential for providing links among the large number of specification and implementing documents that are produced during the software development life cycle. For example, it would be possible to start from a required document and link to that part of the design specification that meets a given requirement. One can then link from the design specification to the actual code. A developed organisation would require to follow a software engineering methodology supported by an integrated set of computerized tools in a complete CASE (Computer Aided Software Engineering) environment, in order to derive full benefits from this form of hypertext links among the various documents in the software lifecycle.

It is also possible to use hypertext in a lifecycle-oriented approach by including linking facilities in structure-oriented editors for program code. For example, it is possible to click on a variable to get to see its definition and associated comments, or to link from a procedure call to opening a window with the text of the procedure.

(d) Describe the basic feature of any one of the following authoring tools:
(i)Macromedia Director
(ii)Authorware Professional

(i) Macromedia Director

Now the latest version for macromedia Director is Director MX. It is most powerful tool for multimedia presentations and kiosk application than CBT or interactive catalogs that require more database work. The features of their product are as under:

- Precise time control due to central scoring component.
- Cross-platform compatibility.
- Strong animation features.
- Extensive architecture to add functionality.

The interface of director includes a stage or movie, a playback screen and all elements imported as cast members. The animation done in director consists of frame comprising individual channels. It can hold sound, custom palette, text, etc as an sprite linked with cat. An ultimate time-based control can be achieved as all sprites can be accessed during each frame of movies sprites are only copies of the cast member so that they can be transformed in each frame. Each channel number represents a stage layer so the spites can be moved between layers by simply shuffling them up. The strongest feature of director is its cross-platform compatibility. It is compatible for windows as well as Macintosh platforms. A Broad range of file formats. From graphics, sound, movies etc. Each time a object is imported the object becomes a last member with a specific number on it. In director one can have 32000 cast members. Director allows a non-programmer to arrange cast members frequently and put them in motion, but interactive movies need some coding. This coding is known as lingo. Though director can create complex multimedia events such as CBT, a bit of programming knowledge is still required.

Director is extremely useful tool that exports the logical metaphor to achieve spectacular results.

(ii) Authorware

Macromedia's Authorware is a dependable industrial-strength environment that allows multiple people to contribute to an application. Artists can load a library with media, programmers can provide templates for complex interactions, and interface designers can put everything together. And one non-programming designer can even do the entire job alone.

Authorware 3 allows authoring of programs in identical environments on either the PC or the Macintosh and produce runtimes for either. Authorware's icons hold a wealth of programming information that never requires the user to think like a programmer.

Some icons in Authorware can manipulate media on the screen. They can display and erase graphics, move or animate objects. Play AVI and Quick Time digital movies as well as WAV sound files, and access videodisk and videotape players.

The new framework icon automates hypermedia interactions and provides a default navigation structure. With a 10-page document in rich text format (RTF), it is easy to import it into the first "page" of framework using Authorware. Authorware can create a new display page for each hard page break in RTF (Rich Text Format) file. Eight buttons are used to move between pages, pop up a pick list of pages, search documents and exit the framework.

Authorware 3 has added text styles that you can apply to any text (labels, menu, options, scrolling text boxes).

Designing in Authorware is also allowed. Authorware elegantly provides full data integrity for it's naming of icons and variables. Change a variable name and it changes everywhere it's used.

Q2. What are the various hardware components needed for multimedia display and development? Describe the usage of these components.

A typical multimedia computer usually include devices like **CD-ROM** player, sound card such as Sound Blaster, Master Blaster and some times a microphone and a range of multimedia software. And probably with either MIDI (Musical Instrument Digital Interface) a standard interface can be in hardware or software which is used for playing a digital instrument through PC interface on the card as an add on utility. Let us look into the requirements of hardware for a multimedia PC. Figure 1 gives the diagram of such requirements.

One cannot record video using such a system. For doing recording one require additional equipments such as digital video camera. However, once various components of multimedia are recorded in the required format, this machine can be used to put various pieces together to

form a multimedia information system. The software tools required for such production are discussed in the next chapter. Many multimedia machines however are equipped to record sound. Let us explore more about the hardware related to multimedia technology

The CPU : The CPU which is recommended for a multimedia computer should be Pentium processor on a PC or other advanced chips such as PowerPC etc. Apple Macintosh and Silicon graphics have their own set of powerful processors for multimedia. However, the CPU of multimedia computer should be at lest 486 with math co-processor attached otherwise the response time of multimedia will be poor. The co-processor chip greatly reduces the load of the CPU. The powerful co-processor chip added for supporting graphics is called graphics accelerator. The memory capacity for such a machine should be 8 MB or above. A 16 MB memory enhances the performance of a multimedia machine by 50% over 8 MB machines.

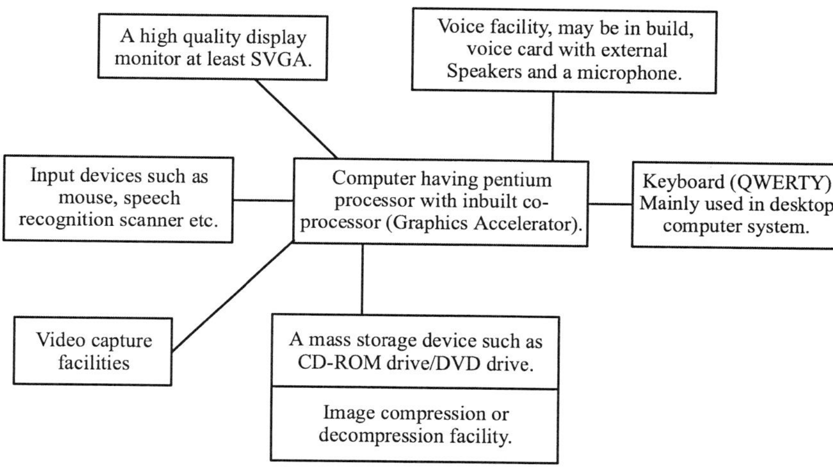

Figure: Requirements of Multimedia Computer

The Monitor : The multimedia PC should be equipped with a monitor having Super video Graphics Arrays (SVGS) card. The basic advantage of having SVGA is that it has a better resolution, thus the display will be of better quality for the graphics and pictures. A typical representation which may be used in multimedia can be 720×640 or 1200×680 etc.

Input-Output Devices : Keyboard and Mouse are two important components for any multimedia PC. Since multimedia computer are accessed using a graphical user interface, therefore mouse is an essential input device for it. Here special mention is to be made about two important input-output devices. These are the sound speakers, which produce sound output and microphones, which are used for on-line recording of sound using various multimedia software. In addition to this, multimedia also supports MIDI interface, thus a digital musical instrument can be connected to it on thee socket provided for it. This, a audio interface normally allows data transmission using DMA channels, that is it does not require the intervention of the CPU while transferring digital data to memory.

Some of the never machines are coming up with a TV board which is installed inside the computer and allows connection of VCR/Video Camera/Cable connection. This

TV board can be operated with the help of software, which are normally provided with this board. Thus you can watch TV programmes on the multimedia machine. However, please note that this interface does not allows digital recording of video on to your computer. This interface is meant only for the purpose of display. If you want to capture these video frames a video capture board is to be added in the multimedia PC.

CD-ROM is a very important storage device, which has become an essential component of multimedia computer of its mass storage capacity and portability. A CD-ROM drive is a common hardware component of a multimedia computer. We will be providing more details on in the next subsection. A scanner can also be used along with a multimedia PC for scanning the pictures and putting them in digitised form in the computer.

CD-ROM : Multimedia uses digitised audio and video not only take huge amount of storage space, but also required high speed storage media, which can large amount of data back and forth quickly to keep audio and video playing recording smoothly.

Because of this requirement most of multimedia packages user hard disk drive, which offer high speed, high data throughput, and plenty of storage devices like 1 GB or more. Sometimes two or more hard disk drives are used as array to work together so that they act like a single hard drive.

However using array of two or more disk for multimedia storage, can no doubt boost the processing speed for the multimedia element, but these are not durable in nature. Magnetic optical disk media offer large amount of storage in a durable package. CDROM is widely used for multimedia storage as it has an amazing amount of flexibility and potential as multimedia storage and distribution medium. One CD-ROM can hold up to one and half hour of digital audio or around 700 to 750 MS of computer data for that matter.

As far CD-ROM is concerned, the main feature of it is huge storage space and very high immunity from damage. It is easy locate different pieces of data in CD-ROMs, so that comparatively simple software can be used guide the laser beam to find what is required.

Sound Card : Sound output from a computer has been feature of machines usually used for sending warning error message or games. If better quality and capabilities for sound output or inputs are required, then there must be a device, which can be added to the basic machine. This device is know as Sound Card, which is asses to the basic machine by inserting it in free slot. The most common reason for adding a sound card to a PC is to be able to use multimedia fully by recording and playing the back the digital audio. While selecting an add on sound card, quality of sound from the loudspeaker has to be taken into consideration and the software provided with a sound card should be adequate enough to suit your requirements for handling sound effects in multimedia

Laser Disc : Like CD-ROM, a laser disc uses the same recording media. It can record and play back high quality digital audio files. As compared to the CD-ROM, a laser disc can play back four channels at a time (two digital and two analog channels) whereas CD-ROM can play only two channels at a time. CD-ROM stores digital data on only one side of the disk, whereas the laser disc stores an analog video signal on both side of the disc. But the biggest difference between them is that laser disc stores video in analog form.

The disadvantages of using a laser disc are like any other video source. The only plus point being that you can access video from any location on the disk. The older multimedia system used to have a laser disc under computer control for playing video they used to have a separate TV screen in addition to a computer screen. Laser Disc is old technology; the DVD has replaced it.

🗁**DVD :** DVD is the cohesion of multimedia and digital video player, movies and interactivity. By employing the latest advances in digital technology, DVD can hold up 25 times more digital info than a CD-ROM and DVD can be used to create innovative cutting edge video-discs with all sorts of data including director's cuts, photo galleries, interview with actors in fact practically anything today's video producers can imagine. Using DVD technology. Besides multilingual capabilities of DVD the producers can create a limitless range of interactive titles, instead of watching a video in the linear fashion as with traditional videotape.

Originally it was felt that DVD is the short for Digital Video Disc now it is more commonly referred to as "digital Versatile Disc" as it has many potential applications than video. The new multimedia storage format of choice, DVD is more that just a high quality video formatting DVD-ROM can combine hours of stunning video, audio and music with computer data and instructions to offer high-capacity media-rich games with exceptional video quality, specialized educational and entertainment programs, software libraries, and training programs, digitized photo collections and, of course, high quality interactive encyclopedias and interactive experiences, all on a single disk. Even today's most popular games consoles have DVD at the core of their technology. A single-sided, single-layer DVD can contain up to 133 minutes of video enough to handle 95% of all movies, without the interruption of flipping the disc over changing discs. DVD was designed to be the next generation of home video entertainment. DVDs offer digital sound and picture and high video resolution. However, our object is to use it as rich multimedia source.

DVD is the first standard designed specifically with the consumer and computer electronic industries in mind. Consumers will be able to enjoy the benefits and enhanced performance of DVD and PC users can turn their PC into genuine multimedia machines. The main advantage for PC uses is the enormous capacity of 4.7 to 17 GB that DVD offers. More storage intensive graphics and video sequences can be incorporated into software applications. A PC equipped with the necessary hardware and appropriate playback software can then DVD-Video discs. Thus PC users can take advantage of the consumer side of DVD.

For the computer world, the main type of DVD disc used is called the DVD-ROM. This is a real only disc similar to the CD-ROM. In order to real DVD-ROM discs, PC users will also need a special DVD-ROM drive. With this equipment, PC users can access any data in standard PC formats or even video in MPEG-1 format, It is possible to use a PC for cross platform applications with a wide variety of audio video material.

🗁**DVD-ROM drives :** DVD-ROM driver are designed to read both CDs and DVD discs. The drives have seek time ranging from 150-200 ms, access time between 200 and 250 ms, and data transfer rates of 1.2 to 1.4 Mbps with burst transfer rated of up to 17 Mbps. This is the data equivalent of an 8x CD-ROM drive. Hence, when reading CD-ROMs, DVD-ROM driver transfer data at 3x speed. For PC users, upgrading to a DVD-ROM does not involve complicated installation procedures or exotic hardware. Connectivity is similar to CD-ROM drive DVD-ROM drive are available with standard interfaces such as EDIE (ATAPI) and SCSI-2. Audio connections allow playback of audio CDs. With the correct audio deciding equipment, a PC can produce DVD-audio quality sound.

DVD-RAM for writing and deleting many times : Another DVD product for PCs is DVD-RAM. These discs and drive have a capacity of 2.6 GB can be rewritten many times. It includes functions and applications similar to those of floppy discs or MO (magneto optical) discs. DVD-RAM is an efficient rewrite-able medium for handling and storing any data the requires a large capacity, such as moving pictures. Because ultra precise writing is necessary, even a fingerprint left on the disc's recording side before writing would change the optical intensity so that accurate writing could not be achieved. Therefore, a DVD-RAM (rewrite-able) disc must be contained in a special cartridge.

Q3. Describe the usage of multimedia in the following applications:
(a) A web-based information portal
(b) An interactive audio
(c) A distributed learning platform

(a) web-based information portal

Multimedia is gaining popularity on the web with several technologies to support use of animation, video, and audio to supplement the traditional media of text and images. These new media provides more design options but also require design discipline. Unconstrained use of multimedia results in user interfaces that confuses users and make it harder for them to understand the information. Portals software should not only be capable of searching across multiple sources, it should also provide tools that enable the search results to be imported into the hub environment.

Some of these tools may be visible to end users to help them to manage their own search results. The portal system will use agreed mechanisms conforming to z39.50, LDAP, RSS, OAI protocols and standards. You can create your Web page portal using by Microsoft personal web server 4.0 server. You can connected to a corporate network. You can share document with your co-workers from your own computers. You can also test your web site before you upload it to an Internet Service Provider (ISP). To create a web page programs such as Microsoft Front Page express can be used.

(b) An interactive audio

An Interactive audio especially for students and teachers is a great use is distributed learning. This system provides the real time communication.

The main benefit of audio is that it provides a channel that is separate from that of the display. Speech can be used to offer commentary or help without obscuring information on the screen. Audio can also be used to provide a sense of place or mood as done to perfections. Mood setting audio should employ very quiet background sounds in order not be complete with the main information for the user's attention.

Whenever you need to inform the user about a certain work of music, it makes much more sense to simply play it than to show the notes or to try to describes it in words. Speech is also perfect for teaching users the pronunciation of words. Non-speech sound effects can be used as an extra dimension in the user interface to inform users about background events.

Good quality sound is known to enhance the user experience substantially so it will worth investing in professional quality sound production. The classic example is the video game study where user claimed that the graphics were better when the sound was improved, even though the exact same graphics were used for poor quality sound and the good quality sound experiments.

(c) A distributed learning platform

The process of learning and motivation for learning are influenced by a variety of factors, which are not necessarily accessible to analysis. However, these factors are in the semiconscious or subconscious area of the human cognition. One of the essential components of the learning process is social interaction. The informal peer learning is as important as formal teaching.

Distributed learning means using a wide range of information technologies to provide learning opportunities beyond the bounds of the traditional class room. Some example of distributed learning technologies include the World Wide Web, e-mail, video conferencing, group ware, simulations, news groups, chat rooms. A distributed learning environment facilitate a learner-centered educational paradigm and promotes active learning. Distributed learning supports a "Pull" model of education in which a person engaged in learning activities at his or her owns pace and at a self-selected time. This is in contrast to the traditional "Push" model of education in which the learners synchronize their needs and schedules to the delivery of the instructor.

The development of high performance computing and communications is creating new media such as the World Wide Web and virtual reality with the help of multimedia.

The innovative kind of pedagogy empowered by these emerging media, messages and experiences make possible a transformation of conventional distance education which replicates traditional class room teaching across barriers of distance and time into an alternative instructional paradigm distributed learning.

🗀 **Collaboration and multimedia Learning: Benefits and Pitfalls :** Today, multimedia-learning materials are available on various platforms. Just like multimedia a collaborative learning environment integrates text, graphs, audio and video. However, the traditional CBT systems operate in standalone mode that is user interactivity is restricted to the CBT only, whereas the possibility to interact with instructors and peers is offered by collaboration using multimedia communication. Thus, by using communication network and collaborative learning in groups is possible.

🗀 **The main elements of such kind of environment of learning are :**

✓ **Collaboration :** The traditional CBTs require the student to work in self-study mode. But work without a tutor may be ineffective. Thus, instead of offering courses on CD-ROM or videotape a new learning environment is need which focuses on bringing several learners together for better attainment of learning goal. Communication should be possible in any direction, learners can ask their tutor or talk to other learners.

✓**Distance Cooperation :** The collaboration of such kind has no geographical boundaries. The only mean required is the availability of telecommunication or Internet facility. The availability of communication facility is a must for any collaborative environment.

✓**Deferred or Real Time Communication :** This system will provide possibility to communicate with the colleagues and tutor in a time frame which is not immediate. For example, a learner may be allowed to answer a question at a later time i.e. not on the spot. A new type of learning process may take place with benefits for some learning situations. Thus, students can learn in a group situation no in real time but later, thus allowing more contemplation and depth.

✓**Distributed Data :** Learning data, such as learning material, videos, graphics, text files etc. are no longer needed to be stored on the local computer, but can be distributed over the network. All participants may share the same information, which can be modified at a common place. However, a student should not be allowed to modify the data. Thus proper data security measures need to be incorporated for such learning.

✓**Multimedia Interface :** A usual way to communicate is to talk to and see our communication partner. This natural way of interfacing may be provided by multimedia environment using audio and video communication technology.

The network provides a convenient a effective and efficient way to distributive learning platform main elements of learning are :

(i) Collaboration

(ii) Multimedia interface

(iii) Distribute data

(iv) Distance co-operation

Q4. Suppose you are asked to develop a multimedia tutor for the topics of "Computer Fundamentals". Describe the process of multimedia development for the above tutor. Give description on each step of developers in the context of above application.

The following points to develop a Multimedia tutor for the topics of "Computer Fundamentals".

(i) First of all you have to plan a structure in your Mind to develop the project.

(ii) The specimen of audience (what you say and how you say will depend on the type and age group of student).

(iii) Outlining the Programme.

(iv) Develop a flow chart.

(v) Making a dynamic Question, answer sessions so the students question can be justified.

(vi) Plan the production of text, graphics, animation, audio and video.

(vii) Preparing the time schedule and the budget of project.

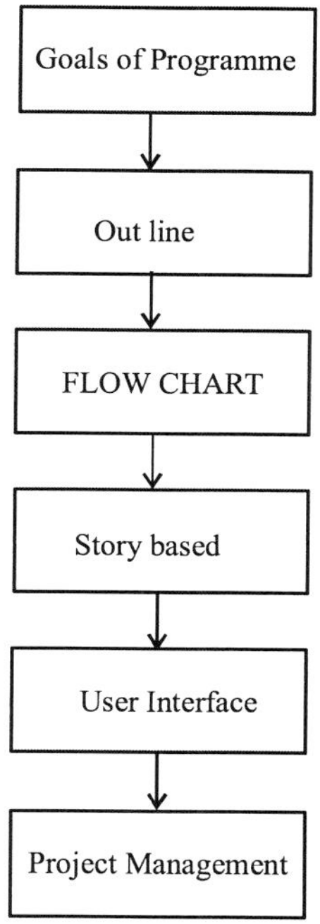

Multimedia is very useful in any development of the tutorial. When we develop any tutorial then planning is the necessary thing. Firstly it provides the analysis of the tutorial.

During the analysis phase of a development effort, all the member of the team gradually constructed a set of assumptions about the interactive product you are developing. It is sound practice to confirm those assumptions before undertaking the bulk of the design work of the product. The assumption should be confirmed with your client and with any vendors that may be collaborating on the project. The "Assumption check list" is a tool that can help you confirm the assumptions underlaying your multimedia development effort.

The assumption check list presumes that time has passed between the initial estimate of project scope and the approval to begin the project.

There are various steps involved in this assumption which are :

Step 1 : Meet with the client and determine :

- Are the goals and objectives still on target ?
- Is the audience still the same ?
- Is the review of each proposed element same ?
- Are the plans for marketing the product same ?
- Are implementation plans same ?

Step 2 : Review your estimates of project scope, including :

- Materials required

- Time needed
- Project cost

Step 3 : If required, rethink the project goals :

If serious questions about project scope or other assumption arise, don't hesitate to raise a red flag. It is better to rethink the multimedia development project now than to cancel it later.

(i) Cognitive characteristics :

- General aptitudes
- Specific aptitudes
- Functional literacy
- Computer literacy
- Learning style
- Prerequisite content knowledge

(ii) Social characteristics :

- Attitudes toward
- Relationships with poor
- Attitude toward authority
- Ethnic background
- Education level

(iii) Personality characteristics :

- Motivation to use this program
- Motivation to learn
- Attitude toward learning
- Attitude toward technology
- Self esteem

(iv) Physical characteristics :

- Visual abilities
- Auditory abilities
- Tectile abilities

Whenever you write objectives, review the verbs to select the ones most appropriate to computer fundamental tutor. This is by no means a complete list of all the possible verbs and its primary value may be in spurring your imagination in writing better objectives for the tutor. So it will be adaptable to change.

Q5. Compare and contrast the features of various authoring tools available. Indicate which type of application a given authoring tool is more suitable for. Give proper justification in support of your answer.

Let us briefly clearly the type of authoring tools available in the market.

✓ **Time-based authoring :** They use time scale to decide duration of message on the screen. Some of the authoring tools in this category are macromedia action, animation works interactive etc.

✓ **Card-based or page based authoring tools :** These tools allow information to be put in as stack of cards can further be linked with each other in predefined sequences. Even the cross linkages along with branching facility are also possible in such packages. Examples in this category are hyper card by Apple, asymmetric tool book and many presentation software.

✓ **Icon-base authoring tools:** These tools allow creation of an Icon based flow script, which is then converted to an application. Examples in the category are macromedia authoring professional, icon Author etc.

✓ **Theatrical authoring tools :** These types of tools refers to media elements as independent cast members, which are assembled using score which is a sequencer in terms of time, linking and animation. Complex visual effects can be applied on these scores to create powerful presentations. Macromedia director is one such package.

Now the question is which authoring software is most suitable for what applications? There are no standard guidelines, however, the following are some suggested usage.

Business applications	:	Time based authoring tools Icon based authoring tools
Education	:	Icon based authoring tools Theatrical based authoring
Games/cyber art	:	Preferably Theatrical based authoring

🗁 Interactivity in an Application :

Most of the authoring tools of multimedia allow the following type of navigational structures:

✓ Linear or sequential mainly used in business and educational applications.

✓ Hierarchical, like a tree structure, used in educational and business applications

✓ Non-linear, like a graph, users select the path of its own, used in various encyclopedia development

✓ A combination of the above tools.

In most of the system interactivity is built by creating menu-based options through questions and their feedback.

CS-66: MULTIMEDIA
JUNE-2004

Note : *There are **five** questions in this paper. Question no. 1 is **compulsory** and carries 30 marks. Attempt any **three** from the rest.*

Q1(a). List five multimedia facilities needed by Distributed Learning Environments. Further, list any five uses of multimedia in education. **10**

Methods of encouraging distributed learning environment that are self-paced yet can evaluate and document learners at their own time and place' understanding of key concepts are highly desirable. In most subject matter areas there are key concepts and principles that must be taught over and over again to large numbers of students or which are difficult for students to grasp without the use of various **multimedia facilities** like *sound, graphics, interaction, hyper-text or moving images used in Radio, T.V., WWW, Video Conferencing, Audio Conferencing*. In these situations, lecturer time could be saved and students would be more likely to comprehend difficult concepts if they were given a well-designed learning resource. It has been observed that computer-assisted learning tools and, in particular, distributed multimedia, have definite advantages over other media of instruction- they can provide a multisensory learning environment, promote a more active form of learning, offer more independent learning, and provide simulations of complex scientific or social processes that are difficult or even impossible to demonstrate in classroom situations. That they could access in their own time and use at their own pace.

Following are the five examples of use of multimedia in education :

Multimedia is very important in all the fields but from education point of view it has done wonders. Education with the help of entertainment is provided by multimedia. This is also known as edutainment, i.e. fun with education. Now let us understand the whole process of education & see where multimedia is useful.

(i) The field of computer assisted learning has reached a new high in popularity due to the Web. A variety of different products trying to meet the needs and supporting of Web Based Training (WBT) exists. In contrast to the traditional classroom equipped with the blackboard and a piece of chalk (and perhaps a projector for transparencies) there is the electronic world with its challenges like virtual universities or virtual classrooms. And there is more and more courseware on the Web.

(ii) With a large screen projector and a multimedia playback system, teachers can use multimedia as a way to enhance their standard lesson plan and stimulate questions. On the other hand students will be able to further explore the topics using standard multimedia platform. The assignments, which require students to make their own interpretation of facts, can be represented in the multimedia topics.

(iii) For teaching books are required & thus the use of multimedia also begins here. Right from the designing of books to the content multimedia is used. To enhance the learning experience proper text highlights, graphics are used.

(iv) Apart from the books now a days. One gets the facility of learning through CBT. To develop this CBT different elements of multimedia like text, graphics, animation etc. are used. This CBT is useful for the students and also to the tutors. With latest technology of distributed computing multimedia education can also be helpful over the network.

(v) Lets take one example of an encyclopedia. Now we all know that encyclopedia is used for all round education. Encyclopedia has all the information of everything. They come in the sets of 5 to 10 books. Now just imagine that if these books were boring black & white text only. Naturally the interest automatically goes. But the books now being more graphical and colourful becomes very simple to learn & fun to read also. You can get the whole book on an interactive CD. This is very exciting & great fun as its like playing game when you are learning. This has many advantage as compared to a text book as per the following ways:

- Very interactive
- Very colourful & attractive.
- Made more powerful by adding sound & video where needed.
- Easy to browse through the content.
- Its fun and easy just like game.
- Visual presentation helps to remember more.
- Entertains you even when you are learning that is edutainment.

(b) Calculate the size of digital recording for a 20 second stereo recording at 22:05 KHz and at 16-bit resolution. **10**

Digital sound is sampled, that is at regular intervals a sample of the sound is taken and stored. The frequency at which the sound is sampled is called the sampling rate, and is usually in the range 11KHz-44Khz. The sample size is the amount of information stored at each sample point. This is usually 8 or 16 bit. A higher sample size means the sound will be more accurately reproduced, but the digital file size will of course be larger. The total size of a **mono** raw (uncompressed) digital sound file will therefore be **sample_rate*sample_size*duration (s)**. And the total size of a **stereo** digital sound file will therefore be **sample_rate*sample_size*duration (s)*2**.

20 Seconds stereo recording at 22.05 kHz and at 16-bit resolution will be :

22050*20(16/8)*2 (Where 1 khz = 1000 hz)

1764000 bytes for stereo (CD quality sound).

(c) Give two applications each of 'Hypertext' in the following areas : **10**

(i) Software Engineering

1. The hypertext has a great potential for providing links among the large number of specification and implementation documents that are produced during the software development life cycle. For example, it would be possible to start from a requirements document and link to that part of the design specification that meets a given requirement. One could then link from the design specification to the actual code.

2. It is also possible to use hypertext in a less lifecycle-oriented approach by including linking facilities in structure-oriented editors for program code. For example, it is possible to click on a variable to get to see its definition and associated comments, or to link from a procedure call to opening a window with the text of the procedure. The Smalltalk code browser links related pieces of code in somewhat this manner.

(ii) User Assistance

1. Hypertext provides a mechanism for integrating several forms of user assistance, including the online manual, an introductory tutorial, an online help system, and even the error messages. Because users only get massages when they are in some kind of trouble, the error messages are a print candidate for providing users with assistance.

2. In an integrated user assistance facility based on hypertext, it would be possible for the user to link an error message to the location in the help system that gives further assistance on the problem. Also if the user wanted further assistance than could be provided by the help system or the manual then it may become possible to link further, to the appropriate location in the tutorial component, to get a computer-aided instruction lesson. This type of integrated user interface does not exist in current computer system and can be made possible with the hypertext facility.

(iii) Dictionaries and Reference books

1. Several dictionaries and large reference books have been converted from a traditional paper form to a hypertext format.

For pure environment the user can click on the picture of the dog to have it replaced by another kind of dog. There are hypertext links to "dog words" and to other pats, as well as the links to other words from the definition. All features encourage the child to explore the dictionary and learn new words.

2. One of the biggest advantages of hypertext encyclopedias and dictionaries, compared to a printed work, is that they can show moving images and play sound. For example, Microsoft Bookshelf contains a dictionary with sound recordings of how the words are actually pronounced. Printed dictionaries for deaf users portray hand and facial gestures through line drawings with arrows to show movement, so multimedia dictionaries are clearly a superior format for communicating this dynamic language. Also, the computer format has added benefits such as the ability for less experienced users to view a sign at much slower speeds than normal conversation. Also in reference books we can put whole matter in hypertext form which will provide facility to visit to any chapter directly. Moreover sound can be provided in background related to that chapter's introduction etc.

(iv) Newspapers and Magazines

1. News delivery is an obvious candidate for online services since events can be reported as they occur instead of having to wait for the scheduled publication time of a newspaper or magazine. Online versions of large newspapers help the articles to be accessed around the clock. Some added value derives from search where one can find, for example, all news stories about a certain company over the last month before deciding whether to invest in it or how to solicit it as a customer. Also information filtering can be used to design personalized electronic newspapers with exactly those news-stories that are of interest to the individual reader.

2. The ability to link between articles from several magazines is a value-added feature of the hypertext versions of the magazines. Even the discussions between readers is a value-added feature for the hypermedia versions of the magazines: if somebody is reading, say an article about an upgrade to a spreadsheet application, that person is likely to be interested in the experience other readers have had when installing the upgrade.

(v) Law

Hypertext has two main applications in the legal field. The first is to support legal research and is mainly used by professional lawyers. The second is support of legal document creation and management and is used by both lawyers and people who wish to avoid paying legal fees. Legal texts are filled with cross-references and are therefore well suited for hypertext support. Typically, a lawyer's brief might refer to several count rulings, each of which would refer to further rulings and to the applicable statutes. Having each of these references available online saves the lawyer's much time in ruling in researching the law. A special aspect of law is the new statutes or higher court ruling may invalidate earlier decisions, meaning that something may be legal one day but illegal the next.

This time varying nature of the law two consequences for legal hypertext systems. The first is that a lawyer who accesses one overruled cases would better be informed that it is no longer a valid law. Legal information services achieve this purpose by inserting bi-directional links from the new law to any earlier nodes referring to the same issue. Lawyers can then follow the links in the opposite direction in a process known as Shepardizing after the printed books that originally supplied these inverse links. The second implication is that layers will sometimes need temporal scrolling of the law to discover what the rules were at some earlier point in time when the action under consideration took place. For example, if a client is taken to count over an old income tax return, the defense should be based on the tax rules for the year question.

Another legal applications is the use of multimedia visualizations by trial lawyers to illustrate their version during a trial. Since visualizations are so compelling, hurries can often be convinced that something has really happened because they saw it happen (on the computer).

(d) Give the following multimedia file formats **5**

(i) CGM

(ii) PCD

(iii) VOC

(iv) AVI

(v) MFF

(i) CGM : Computer Graphic Metafile, is 16 Color graphics. An international Starndard for moving simple graphics between familites of Corel Draw and most major graphics package.

(ii) PCD : Performance Centered Design, is used in Image (Kodak Photo-CD).

(iii) VOC : Video Object Component, is Audio file (Creative Labs Sound Blaster) this format found in many PCs and offers good compression.

(iv) AVI : Audio Video Interleaved, is a format which is used to play full-motion video and audio in a small window at about 15 frames / sec.
(v) MFF : MIDI File Format, is MIDI format designed for Microsoft Windows.

Q2. List and describe the five components of multimedia. Give two software drivers required for multimedia support. Further, list three communication devices used in multimedia applications. 15

Following are the five componenets of multimedia with their description :

(i) Textual Information : All multimedia productions contain some amount of text, and even some might contain a large amount of textual matter. The text can have various types fonts and type sizes to suit the professional presentation of the multimedia software. The standard software interface which is now a days provided on multimedia is the windows interface. This interface allow large amount of fonts to be stored in multimedia.

(ii) Images : Another important and interesting components of multimedia is graphics. One of the basic facts in multimedia production is that people do not like reading large amount of textual matter on the screen. Also, it is a myth about human nature that a subject is better explained to them when represented in pictorial or graphical form, instead of textual matter i.e., graphics are used more often than text to explain a concept present background information etc.

Unlike text that is represented in universal ASCII format, graphics does not have any single agreed format. To start with these are two different ways in which graphs or images can described, Bitmap and vectors.

(a) Bitmap Images : A bitmap images assumes an image to consist of two-dimensional squares, which are called the PIXEL (Picture Element) or dots on the screen. The size and the quality of such a image depends on the pixel density and number of colors it user. A standard image with 16 colours will be ideal solution for a low cost multimedia package. These bit map files can be edited easily, however, require large memory space for editing purposes. As bitmap images are stored as large files and you require large amount of disk space to deal with it. There are various formats such as PCX, TIF, BMP, and GIF etc., in which images are stored.

(b) Vector Images : Other formats for storing images vector or object oriented format. In this format, an image is formed as a set of straight or curved lines instead of dots. A line can be represented by a mathematical equation, whose number can be stored as a set of binary codes. This form of coding is potentially more economical for disk storage space. The drawback is that it requires software to produce the image that is time consuming. CAD package use this type of images. A vector image file is always of the same size no matter how large a image is. Thus, for display clarity this type of images should be projected on better resolution display units.

(iii) Animation : There are several technology and sources available to produce image or graphics for multimedia package. Image can be created by using a Paint program, by scanning photographs using a scanner and by drawing artwork. You can generate 3D graphics and animation using various sophisticated software. You can combine these images using image manipulation programs that can combine many different types of graphics files, to create new images.

(a) Morphing : Morphing takes two images and seamlessly changes one image to another. The second image actually seems to grow out of the first one. Morphing can also be used to show the pace of changes more clearly than photos. Warping is variation of the morphing where one image is used to show various changes that take place. It uses the key points of one image to create different effects, instead of mixing up two images.

(b) In 3-D animation mathematical model of 3-D object is created to realistically portray with depth. Now it has become a common media element in film, video and multimedia packages. 3-D animations follow mainly three steps; modelling, animation and rendering.

(c) In a 2-D animation an object can move up (called Y axis) and sideways (called X axis). But in the case of a 3-D model, a third axis is used; depth or the Z-axis. Once an object is created along these three axes, colour, shading and light source can be added to the image to make it more realistic.

(iv) Digital Audio : The most common reason for using digital audio in computer is to be able to use multimedia in its full potential. The most common requirement is to be able to input sound such as a spoken commentary on image or a document.

The sound is a repeated pattern of pressure in the air and a microphone converts a sound wave into an electrical wave. The shape and frequency of the electrical wave is identical to the shape and frequency of the sound wave and the clarity of what we hear is entirely to the dependent on the shape and frequency of the sound wave. Sound can also be recorded and reproduced using digital signals and the errors can be reduced drastically in digital recording of the sound. For replaying the sound, audio has to be converted into digital form to produce digital audio in order to use it in the multimedia. And the digital audio system will then reconvert the entire digitised audio into analog form, which can be heard on the speaker. This two-way transformation of audio is know as analog-to-digital conversion and digital to analog conversion respectively. But the storage space required for digital audio is huge, somewhere around more that 1 MB for one minute of audio. The entire process of digitization is simple process of converting analog or electrical signal of audio to computer data file in the digital format. The microphone (which is normally used for recording) convert the voice into electrical signal or analog audio signal. Then the analog signal is passed into the audio input of a digital card or sound card. Once inside, the signal is fed into the analog to digital converter, which convert the analog audio signal to digital form and store it as computer data file. Playing back a digital audio file is just the reverse process of converting analog to digital. Once the digital audio file is sent to the sound card for playback the file is channelled through a converter and the digitised version of the original file is converted into analog and put into speaker. As constant or frequent conversions can reduce the sound quality, it is always advisable to keep all audio in digital format while working on a multimedia program.

A Digital signal processor is always embedded in the sound card to provide additional capabilities without affecting the CPU. A simple recording of digital sound can be done and may be compressed if desired. A common digital sound file existing in personal computers are know as. WAV files. The MIDI sound saves disk space as it only stores the instructions about how to play a musical instrument. It prestores the sound relating to the sound notes of various instruments and reproduces it when a voice signal asks for it. Several software which are used for creation of digital sound files (may be as. WAV file) are media player for windows.

(v) Digital Video : Digitised video is one of the many technologies used in the development of interactive multimedia. It is one of the ways to play back and record video in multimedia program. It offers a wide range of flexibility as compared to standard video signal.

It is one of the ways to play back and record video in multimedia program. It offers a wide range of flexibility as compared to standard video signal. Video projects are created in two main phases : production and post production.

Digital video editing involves converting video taped footage into data that can be stored on, and accessed from a computer hard disk. Digital video editing is non linear. Permitting any video clip, sound, edit, or effect to be removed without over-writing or changing the original clip. A non linear, open architecture digital video system is based on multi-step process that includes logging and digitizing source video, editing and post production and transferring final output to the video tape, CD-ROM, DVD or hard disk. These process are :

- Logging
- Capturing or digitizing
- Visual effects
- Composing
- Animation
- Titles
- Motion control
- Transitions
- Image processing and
- Digital video applications

Unlike regular video, quality of image would not degrade from copy to copy as digital video is make up of digital code and not an electrical analog signal. However, the final output depends on how the video image are converted to digital form during the development phase. Video signal comes from an external source such as TV or VCR or camera to the video-digitizer-card inside the system. The process of converting analog video signal to digital format is called 'sampling'. Using this process, the converter card in the system converts the analog video signals into digital data streams so that these signals can be stored in the binary data structure format of 1s and 0s. the digital data file is them compressed to a considerable amount using some compression program. During this process the digitizer fuses the digital video into a digital movie format and saves all the sections of the compressed movie in the hard disk. Once the conversion and compression process is complete, the file can be played back on the computer screen. These digitised files can also be edited according to requirement using various video editing software. However, you may find that the video if used as full screen video may be jerky in certain machines. The main reason for this is that to present a moving picture, we have to store and process enormous amount of data, as we need to show 30 frames of continuous pictures per second considering one frame itself requires lot of data a moving pictures requires 30 times of it per second. However, standard such as Moving Pictures Expert Group (MPEG) have specified compression standards, which have enabled a full screen video. MPEG compression only records the frames and tries to predict the remaining frames from this key frame by comparing the changes of missing frame from key frames. Another technology, which is using this kind of compression, is video conferencing. ".AVI" files in windows basically contains interleaved data for audio/video. This compressed data can be decompressed and passed through a digital to analog converter to produce the video. These components of a multimedia system are integrated after they have been stored digitally by using Authoring software, which provide the necessary interactivity in the overall mix of information.

Software Drivers : (i) Creative Labs Sound Blaster PCI 256 driver, this is used for Audio Card manufactured by Creative Labs, supports 4 channel output.

(ii) DirectX, this is used for providing enhanced quality support for multimedia applications.

Three Communication Devices :

(i) Modem : Modulator / Demodulator transforms a digital bit stream into an analog signal (modulator), and analog bit stream into Digital signal (demodulator). It can be connected to your computer externally at the serial port or internally as a separate board. Internal modems often include fax capability. Modem speed is measured in baud, is the most important consideration. Because the multimedia contains the graphics, audio resources, video samples which are usually large in size. So, high speed modems are preferable.

(ii) DTH Set top Box : which is a device used to implement Direct to Home technology to accept various available channels over the cable network.

(iii) Telephone : which is used to connect modem to the Internet, without telephone one cannot transmit or receive data from computer via modem (NOTE : these days wireless modems are also available most common example of which is "Reliance Mobile", which works as modem without telephone line). Your all multimedia files are received by the computer through telephone having modem inbetween the telephone line and computer for modulating and demodulating the data.

Q3. List any five applications of multimedia in the following areas: 15

(i) Business

Multimedia is widely used now a days in various applications and business is one of them. As the market competition is increasing with the introduction of better products in the market everyday, it has become absolutely necessary to provide service and timely information to your client in a brief, necessary and more understandable manner in a short time. Multimedia provides various ways to maintain a competitive edge for a company especially in training, market speculation, and public relation.

Now let us see five applications of Multimedia in business.

1. The global team : Multimedia technology with communication technology has opened the door to form global work group team, members may be working anywhere and do there work. These team members can be in different cities and may also speak different languages.

2. Voice mail : Voice mail is a tool which communicates voice over lines. This can be phone lines or the Internet. A voice mail system is not dependent. The only draw back for a voice mail is that it only hurdles audio information, voice mail system is time & location independent but it offers no interactivity.

3. Multimedia based fax : Fax is more famous and more used rather than the voice mail for the following reasons.

(i) Used to send detailed information.

(ii) Easier to use.

(iii) Handles graphic information

(iv) Provides a printed copy of information.

(v) Also fax is non interactive option for the user. Even a fax modem can be used to send & receive fax.

4. Audio conferencing: This technology allows out of town people to participate in a formal meeting. This technology can also be used by a group of people to meet frequently whatsoever is the physical distance among them. Audio conferencing is quite effective means of communication as it is used to discuss anything regarding everything. The only disadvantage regarding this type of conferencing is that one cannot see the other person. This may also cause problem if the other person is not well conversant & is not able to speak clearly. Audio conferencing technology was just available only in the conference room.

5. Video conferencing: Video conferencing is generally used in large corporate sectors. In foreign countries the use of video conferencing is a high success. Video conference is just like any office meetings thus require setting of time, preparing rooms & place, agenda, followed by discussion etc. Video conferencing brings people together naturally & tries to simulate a real life meeting environment. Video conferencing works with the help of a TV & a camera. The same hardware should be available with all the people who are participating in video conferencing. They are looking at the camera & the other person can see in the T.V. Now a days video conferencing can be done through a PC also. But setup for a video conferencing is high. It is very expensive. Video conferencing is done through high speed network connection also known as broadband technology.

Advantages :-

✓ Save time & money for big corporate houses when they have to go out of country to attend meetings.

✓ Very effective & powerful means of communication.

6. Document conferencing : The other name of document conferencing is Audio-graphic conferencing. A PC & a telephone line is required for document conferencing. The PC is the information hub and telephone connection is used to connect two PC. Due to these telephone connections two people can share information from each others PC which is stored in it.

Apart from sharing information it also allows online editing of a document by several participating people in the conference this conference facility has been adopted by many big companies, specially in the IT industry and the education industry. In the education industry it has been great catalyst with the help of this technology it is possible to bring the education classroom or the corporate environment to the community. A document that can be used in the conference may consist of text, graphics, sound or even video clips.

Advantages:

✓ As now even the common men have a PC at their home, it becomes very easy to go for document conferencing.

✓ This is very easy to use.

✓ It is less expensive.

✓ Basic setup is not very high.

✓ Every common man can use it.

Website Hosting and Publishing: Website is one of the very important place where multimedia is used streaming Audio, Video, millions of people daily enjoys like on demand audio and video from rich, media web sites. Streaming media is a method of making audio, video and other multimedia available in real-time with no downloads. Streaming media elements have five elements namely.

✓ Encoders & tools

✓ Data types

✓ Servers

✓ Networks

✓ Players

E-commerce based application: Electronic commerce is an upcoming model of new selling and merchandising tools in which buyers are able to participate in all phases of a purchase decision, while stepping through process electronically rather in physical stores. The multimedia technologies may be used for presentation of information through the web for such systems.

(ii) Communication

The advances of computing, communication and creation of relevant standards have lead to the beginning of an era where people getting multimedia facilities at home. Many be in the form of an Interactive T.V or through the World Wide Web. Cable TV and telephone companies dot com companies, publishing industry etc. are the main infrastructure providers for these facilities. The networking technology along with the improved compiling and compression technologies are delivering interactive services profitably. The entertainment cable, telephone, and internet passed industries companies are trying to design wide variety of such multimedia services.

These services may include:

✓ Basic Television Services

✓ Interactive entertainment

✓ Video on demand

✓ Home shopping through e-mail

✓ Financial transactions using e-commerce

✓ Interactive single and multimedia games

✓ Digital multimedia libraries

✓ Electronic versions of newspapers, magazines etc.

Today Personal Computers are the tool that promotes collaboration. They are essential to any multimedia workstations. Many high-speed networks are in place that allows multimedia conferencing, or electronic conferencing. Such facilities are even available today through Internet also. Today, we have to depend on our telephone to link us with others, whether it is a phone call or a group audio conference or dialup Internet connection. However, tomorrow it will be sort of based link that link us with other. A Computer-based multimedia conference allows us to exchange audio, text, image, and even video information. It also facilitates group development of documents and other information products. Let us discuss more about these concepts in greater details.

(iii) Publishing Industry

Today publishing industry has changed drastically because of availability of Multimedia. The publications which are meant for family such as newspapers, family magazines etc. are readily available on-line, that is in multimedia form giving real life experiences.

For example, the on-line-news clippings are not only read but can also be experienced by seeing the video film associated with it. Examples in this category are: Microsoft Multimedia, the life and composition of Bethovan etc. where a rich mix of sound, visuals, and moving is provided for publication.

The publishing industry is being transformed through the use of multimedia and high speed networks. The market for media products is expanding rapidly as homes and businesses are connected to fibre networks. The publishing industry is divided into three major markets : education, entertainment and professional publishing.

Entertainment publishing can focus on the home or mobile system using all media professional publishing is probably the largest sector of the three and includes information whose value to companies ranges from the very short term such as stock prices, through the medium term such as company reports and world news to the long term such as directories of people and organizations. Publishers must commission and collect material, package it and distribute it to the target niche or broad markets. Given the volume of medium, the breadth of the market, and the value of the information to be published, fibre and wireless networks are two to routes for both the collection and distribution of material.

Electronic publications consisting of user controlled education, interactive novels or stories, or educational/information based activity are eligible. School publishing materials are intended for class room use at the elementary through postgraduate level these are making interactive and intellectual for the user.

The publishing meant for children has changed tremendously with the advent of multimedia. Today many encyclopedia and books providing a sort of edutainment are available. The advantages of using multimedia on these books are evident from the type of media rich experiences these CD-ROM based product provide. For example, an Atlas encyclopedia may not only allow you to pinpoint the location of Delhi in India but also shows you a Road map of Delhi showing several historical sites. A dictionary meant for children not only shows the meaning of the words but can also show its characteristics for example a tiger may be defined as a wild animal and along with that a movie in which tiger is shown in his natural habitat. Thus this kind of media rich experiences are much more entertaining and provide better learning environment for children.

In fact, we believe that for increasing general awareness of a child, multimedia is the best tool available us today. However, still the reading habits, listening habits, playing attention etc. are the capabilities on which the education will rely upon.

For professionals, today many a products are available in the market. For example, how to tackle many management-oriented issues, can be presented in multimedia form. Professionals, however, can use multimedia technology for on-line video-conferencing, on-line document editing etc. functions.

As far as academics are concerned multimedia publishing is a boon or get information from World Wide Web. Today, if a researcher wants to refer to conference proceedings, all he has to do buy a CD produced for it. This CD normally contains abstracts, paper presentations, reports presentation etc. The other advantage an Academician gets by having such a detail on CD is that his search through the material can be faster, as in general, several indexes are being provided in the CDs. Thus, Multimedia publishing has a great potential and will be the technology, which has tremendous potential.

Q4(a). What is an authoring tool? List four characteristics needed for selecting a multimedia authoring software. How is Quick Time related to other authoring tools? Explain this with a diagram. 10

Also known as *authorware,* a program that helps you write hypertext or multimedia application. Authoring tools usually enable you to create a final application merely by linking together object, such as a paragraph of text, an illustration, or a song. By defining the objects' relationships to each other, and by sequencing them in an appropriate order, authors (those who use authoring tools) can produce attractive and useful graphics applications graphics. Most authoring system also support a scripting language for more sophisticated applications.

Four characteristics to select a authoring software:

✓ **Importing :** It should be able to import carious media elements, which may have been developed using other software package.

✓ **Creating :** It should allow some basic features for creation of text, graphics and may be sound if not video.

✓ **Integrating :** It should allow you to define sequences and provide linkages

✓ **Delivering:** It should allow developing self-running application and encryption of application data.

Quick time : Quick time is a software developed by apple that supports time-based multimedia on the Macintosh. It has also been ported for windows environment. The given figure describes how the different development environment relate to one another.

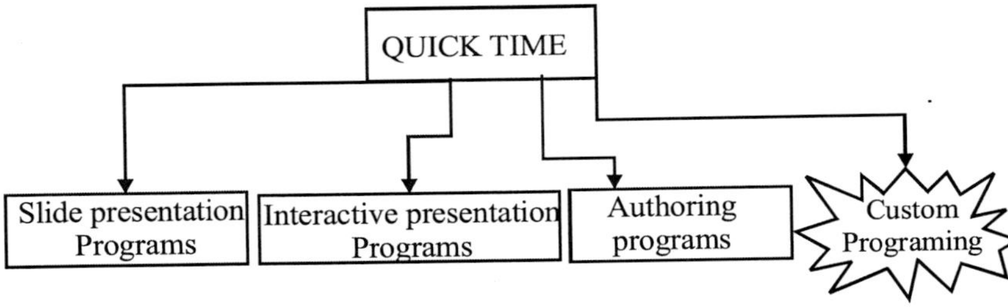

Importance of Quick Time : Quick time adds support for time-based media to the basic Macintosh system architecture. The most common media that require this kind of support are video, animation and sound. It is important that quick time supports sound because quick time can synchronize round tracks with video track. Quick time provides synchronization between the animations that would otherwise play at different speeds when played on different machines.

Quick time stores video digitally i.e. it converts the frames of video to digital images that are stored in the computer's hard disk. The advantage of storing video this way is that computer can very quickly and easily access other information on a hard disk. Another advantage is that once the frames are stored on the hard disk they can be manipulated using a number of difficult editing applications.

The disadvantage of storing video this way is that the computer has to do a lot of work to display the video sequences.

To achieve digital video, the computer needs two things :

✓ The computer must be capable of handling video's large amount of data. This is accomplished by streaming in which the computer displays one frame as it read the following frame from the disk.

✓ The computer needs kind of timing mechanism that keeps video and sound synchronized. Timing is particularly important when the people are displayed speaking on the screen, as without synchronization their lips won't move in synch with the sound. Quick time fulfills both needs.

Quick time has many features but the two most important are its compressors and its timing mechanism. The compressors enables the program to reduce the frames to a manageable size, so the computer can stream the information from the disk. The timing mechanism ensures that multiple tracks maintain synchronization.

(b) Compare any five features of DVD-ROM and CD-ROM. **5**

Refer to Study Material, Chapter-1, Page no. - 12, Q9

Q5. List the eight phases in multimedia application development. Explain, taking the example of IGNOU, how the multimedia application can be used to facilitate the course delivery to its students. **15**

The process of developing a multimedia application is the same as creating any other software application. One must create project specifications, select a development team, start developing code, test the code, and develop documentation.

One must also collect media elements, or clips, determine the hyperlinks glossary, and create an on-line help system.

Eight phases in Multimedia applications development :

(i) Selecting a project
(ii) Designing the project and developing a prototype on paper
(iii) Selecting an Authoring Tool for the Job
(iv) Structuring the Text-based Data
(v) Collecting Media Elements
(vi) Tagging and Coding Documents
(vii) Including Documentation and On-Line Help
(viii) Testing the Product

Multimedia application can be used at various places to facilitate the course delivery system to IGNOU students :

(i) Maintaning records of study packets sent in the computer through Multimedia based application software. Which will greatly facilitate the maintaining huge amount of database at MPDD(Material Production and Distribution Division) of IGNOU. The system will also provide various reports at the cilck of a mouse like packet sent, packet remaining, packet not received etc. This system will increase the speed of work.

(ii) Students can be provided with multimedia based tutorials besides the conventional study material, which will greatly enhance the understanding power and increased ability to grasp concepts within less time, as most of the students are working and have less time to study at home. Providing CDs will enbale to access the courese material at their office easily.

(iii) Multimedia will provoke radical changes in the teaching process during the coming decades, particularly as current student base go beyond the limits of traditional teaching methods.

(iv) An increased use of multimedia involves student themselves. Students put together interactive magazines and newsletters they make original art using image editing tools.

(v) Course delivery through video conferencing can also be used to clear the problems of the students. Where a student can ask his / her doubts and get answers from the experts in the subject.

Feedback is the breakfast of Champions.

Ken Blanchard

You can Help other students.
" Inform any error or mistake in this book. "

We and Universe
will reward you for Your Kind act.

Email at : feedback@gullybaba.com
or
WhatsApp on 9350849407

CS-66 MULTIMEDIA
DEC 2004

Note : *There are* ***five*** *questions in this paper. Question no.* ***1*** *is* ***compulsory*** *and carries 30 marks. Attempt any* ***three*** *from the rest.*

Q1(a) Explain the need of audio and video components in multimedia applications. How does audio/video enhance the impact of multimedia applications ? **[5]**

Video and sound help in communicating a lot of information in a small time. Sound is a very exciting part of multimedia application. You multimedia should be equipped with good supportive sound, however, please do not use excessive sound in your application. It may be annoying to the user. Video enhances the impact of multimedia application, especially in area involving difficult concepts. However, please note that good quality digital video clips can be displayed only if there exist good hardware and software configurations in the client machine.

Some of the usage of audio and video in multimedia may be for :

✓ The background sound

✓ Sound/video recordings of an eminent person.

✓ Narration of historical facts

✓ Narration of an industrial process preferably through video

✓ A welcome message showing a walk through a building museum, historical place etc.

(b) Compare the features of DVD-ROM and CD-ROM. **[3]**

<u>**CD-ROM Vs DVD-ROM**</u>

	CD-ROM	DVD-ROM
Diameter	120 mm	120 mm
Thickness	1.2 mm	1.2 mm (0.6mm per layer)
Track Pitch (distance between successive turns of a spiral	1.6 μm	0.74 μm
Min. Pit length	0.83 μm	0.40 μm
Laser Wavelenght	780 mm	640nm
Layers	1	1,2 or 4
Data Capacity	0.65 GB	4.7 GB
Data Capacity (per layer)	0.650 GB	4.7 Gigabytes 92 hours 15 minutes) - Single side, single layer 8.5 Gigabytes (4 hours) - Single side, dual layer 9.4 Gigabytes (4 hours) 30 minutes0 -Double side, single layer 17 Gigabytes (8 hours) -Double side, double layer

(c) List five fundamental rules required for interface design in multimedia applications. Explain them with the help of an example. [6]

Following are the fundamental rules for interface design :

✓ Keep low cognitive load. Keep a simple, consistent screen design

✓ Do not divide the learner's attention; you must use various media elements such as text, graphics, and sound to reinforce a concept rather than introducing different types of concepts.

✓ You may use color, special effects, and sound to direct the learner's attention to important areas of the presentation. However, use them only if it is essential.

✓ The information, which a learner may need to undertake an activity must be available on the screen, for example, the reference information for answering a feedback form must be available.

✓ Encourage frequent revision/rehearsals by the learner.

✓ Encourage reinforcement of learning by using concrete words and different media to repetition the message.

(d) List the basic hardware requirements for any multimedia system. [4]

A typical multimedia computer usually include devices like **CD-ROM** player, sound card such as Sound Blaster, Master Blaster and sometimes a microphone and a range of multimedia softwares. And probably with either MIDI (Musical Instrument Digital Interface) a standard interface can be in hardware or software which is used for playing a digital instrument through PC interface on the card as an add-on utility. Let us look into the requirements of hardware for a multimedia PC. Figure follows gives the diagram of such requirements.

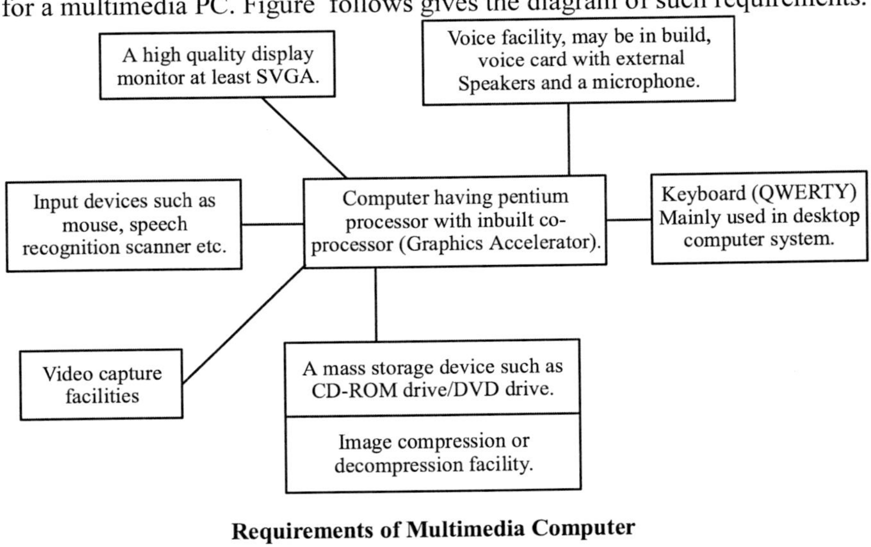

Requirements of Multimedia Computer

One cannot record video using such a system. For doing recording one require additional equipments such as digital video camera. However, once various components of multimedia are recorded in the required format, this machine can be used to put various pieces together to form a multimedia information system. Many multimedia machines however are equipped to record sound. more

✓ **The CPU :** The CPU which is recommended for a multimedia computer should be Pentium processor on a PC or other advanced chips such as PowerPC etc. Apple Macintosh and Silicon graphics have their own set of powerful processors for multimedia. However, the CPU of multimedia computer should be at lest 486 with math co-processor attached otherwise the response time of multimedia will be poor.

✓ **The Monitor :** The multimedia PC should be equipped with a monitor having Super video Graphics Arrays (SVGS) card. The basic advantage of having SVGA is that it has a better resolution, thus the display will be of better quality for the graphics and pictures. A typical representation which may be used in multimedia can be 720×640 or 1200×680 etc.

✓ **Input-Output Devices :** Keyboard and Mouse are two important components for any multimedia PC. Since multimedia computer are accessed using a graphical user interface, therefore mouse is an essential input device for it.

✓ **CD-ROM :** Multimedia uses digitized audio and video not only take huge amount of storage space, but also require high speed storage media, which can store large amount of data back and forth quickly to keep audio and video playing recording smoothly.

✓ **Sound Card :** Sound output from a computer has been feature of machines usually used for sending warning error message or games. If better quality and capabilities for sound output or inputs are required, then there must be a device, which can be added to the basic machine. This device is know as Sound Card,

✓ **Laser Disc :** Like CD-ROM, a laser disc uses the same recording media. It can record and play back high quality digital audio files.

✓ **DVD :** DVD is the cohesion of multimedia and digital video player, movies and interactivity. By employing the latest advances in digital technology, DVD can hold up 25 times more digital info than a CD-ROM and DVD can be used to create innovative cutting edge video-discs with all sorts of data including director's cuts, photo galleries, interview with actors in fact practically anything today's video producers can imagine.

(e) Explain the usefulness of multimedia in medical applications. [5]

The basic properties of multimedia that is information delivery through multiple media with the use of Communication technology make us realize that this application is a distributed, collaborative application. Since a medical consultation system is extremely critical as decision make by doctors are life critical, therefore, the data manipulations and user interaction in such a system are extremely broad and quite demanding.

This application is a distributed multimedia based project, which is being developed at University of Pittsburgh medical center. At present this system is used at seven hospitals and many diagnostic and research laboratories. Mednet provides the following services :

- A real-time monitoring and multiparty consultation
- Collaboration during brain surgery.

The intra-operative monitoring places a real-time control about the condition of the patient. Mednet is different from the other picture taking teleconferencing systems as it provides real time monitoring and collaboration.

(f) Give the pictorial representation of the planning process of multimedia, and explain it. [7]

Please Refer to JUNE05, Q5(a)

Q2(a) What is a Macromedia Director ? Explain its features. Also mention any three types of applications that can be developed by using it. [6]

It is most powerful tool for multimedia presentations and kiosk application than CBT or interactive catalogs that require more database work. The features are the following:

- ➢ Precise time control due to central scoring component.
- ➢ Cross-platform compatibility.
- ➢ Strong animation features.
- ➢ Extensive architecture to add functionality.

The interface of director includes a stage or movie, a playback screen and all elements imported as cast members. The animation done in director consists of frame comprising individual channels. It can hold sound, custom palette, text, etc as an sprite linked with cat. An ultimate time-based control can be achieved as all sprites can be accessed during each frame of movies sprites are only copies of the cast member so that they can be transformed in each frame. Each channel number represents a stage layer so the spites can be moved between layers by simply shuffling them up. The strongest feature of director is its cross-platform compatibility. It is compatible for windows as well as Macintosh platforms. A Broad range of file formats. From graphics, sound, movies etc. Each time a object is imported the object becomes a last member with a specific number on it. In director one can have 32000 cast members.

(b) Explain the role of multimedia in a CBT (Computer Based Tutor) to teach any Computer Science course. [5]

Multimedia is very important in all the field but from education point of view it has done wonders. Education with the help of entertainment is provided by multimedia. This is also known as edutainment, i.e. fun with education. Now let us understand the whole process of education & see where multimedia is useful. For teaching books are required & thus the use of multimedia also begins here. Right from the designing of books to the content & the outer look multimedia is used. To enhance the learning experience proper text highlights, graphics are used. Apart from the books now a days. One gets the facility of learning through CBT. To develop this CBT different elements of multimedia like text, graphics, animation etc. are used. This CBT is useful for the students and also to the tutors. With latest technology of distributed computing multimedia education can also be helpful over the network.

The use of multimedia in education are many ways. Lets take one example of an encyclopedia. Now we all know that encyclopedia is used for all round education. Encyclopedia has all the information of everything. They come in the sets of 5 to 10 books. Now just imagine that if these books were boring black & white text only. Naturally the interest automatically goes. But the books now being more graphical and colourful becomes very simple to learn & fun to read also. You can get the whole book on an interactive CD. This is very exciting & great fun as its like playing game when you are learning. This has many advantage as compared to a text book as per the following ways:

- Very interactive
- Very colourful & attractive.
- Made more powerful by adding sound & video where needed.
- Easy to browse through the content.
- Its fun and easy just like game.
- Visual presentation helps to remember more.
- Entertains you even when you are learning that is edutainment.

Thus we can see that multimedia definitely helps in education.

(c) List and explain the legal issues related to copyright in multimedia applications. [4]

Please Refer to JUNE05 Q5(b)

Q3(a) Identify the various types of multimedia to teach the practical component for any Science course. Design a rough sketch for the user interface. [5]

Multimedia is the use of two or more types of media. One of the more common uses of the term multimedia is tying these media via a computer, i.e., multimedia personal computers. Electronic multimedia courseware ties training to state-of-the-art computer technology. Electronic multimedia courseware links audiovisual, graphic, automation, and programmed instruction disciplines for individual and group instruction. The most important characteristic of electronic multimedia is the immediate feedback trainees receive in interacting with the computer.

A summary of different multimedia types which can be used to teach the practical component for any Science Course is given below :

We have taken example of teaching photosynthesis.

Animations :

Simple animations: animated gif

The image is a set of slides which have each been given a length of time to display.

Click Refresh to see it again. They can repeat as many times as you like, but have no sound track. Here, we can make different images of photosynthesis step by step which will increase the ability of students to learn it faster.

✓ **Interactive Graphics: Shockwave :** Some graphics appear to be interactive because they change when the mouse passes over or when clicked, but this is often a simple change of one image for another. However, Shockwave files can be truly interactive, and it is possible to build in an amazing range of routes to explore an image: an entire video game complete with sound effects can be contained in one Shockwave file. Here, we can develop a button as clicking on it the rays of sun start falling on the plants and photosynthesis process starts.

Sounds :

Audio:

Streaming: Real Audio, Windows Media Audio, MP3 and Advanced Streaming Format, to name just a few are often used as ways to distribute lower quality versions of wave files. Here, we can use it as file size of these files are very less and it will be easier for us to distribute it over Internet.

Moreover, audio will be placed to increase the ability to learn faster.

Besides that video can also be used but we will use **Interactive Graphics: Shockwave.**

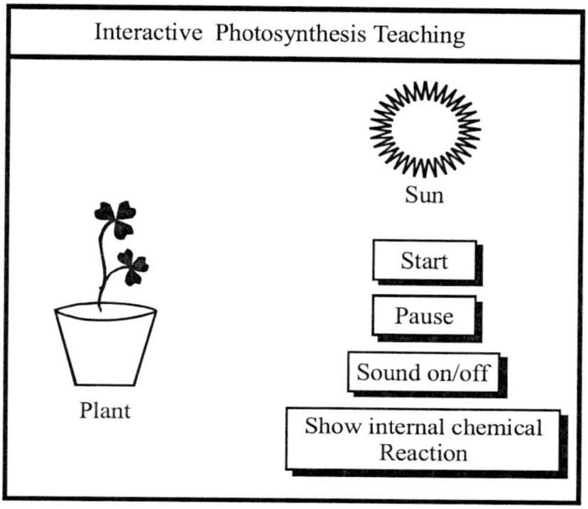

User Interface

(b) List and explain, three types of authoring tools available in the market. [6]

Authorware Professional

Macromedia's Authorware is a dependable industrial-strength environment that allows multiple people to contribute to an application. Artists can load a library with media, programmers can provide templates for complex interactions, and interface designers can put everything together. And one non-programming designer can even do the entire job alone.

Authorware allows authoring of programs in identical environments on either the PC or the Macintosh and produce runtimes for either. Authorware's icons hold a wealth of programming information that never requires the user to think like a programmer.

Some icons in Authorware can manipulate media on the screen. They can display and erase graphics, move or animate objects. Play AVI and Quick Time digital movies as well as WAV sound files, and access videodisk and videotape players.

The new framework icon automates hypermedia interactions and provides a default navigation structure. With a 10-page document in rich text format (RTF), it is easy to import it into the first "page" of framework using Authorware. Authorware can create a new display page for each hard page break in RTF (Rich Text Format) file. Eight buttons are used to move between pages, pop up a pick list of pages, search documents and exit the framework. Authorware 3 has added text styles that you can apply to any text (labels, menu, options, scrolling text boxes).

Designing in Authorware is also allowed. Authorware elegantly provides full data integrity for it's naming of icons and variables. Change a variable name and it changes everywhere it's used.

It is most powerful tool for multimedia presentations and kiosk application than CBT or interactive catalogs that require more database work. The features of their product are as under:

- Precise time control due to central scoring component.
- Cross-platform compatibility.
- Strong animation features.
- Extensive architecture to add functionality.

The interface of director includes a stage or movie, a playback screen and all elements imported as cast members. The animation done in director consists of frame comprising individual channels. It can hold sound, custom palette, text, etc as an sprite linked with cat. An ultimate time-based control can be achieved as all sprites can be accessed during each frame of movies sprites are only copies of the cast member so that they can be transformed in each frame. Each channel number represents a stage layer so the spites can be moved between layers by simply shuffling them up. The strongest feature of director is its cross-platform compatibility. It is compatible for windows as well as Macintosh platforms. A Broad range of file formats. From graphics, sound, movies etc. Each time a object is imported the object becomes a last member with a specific number on it. In director one can have 32000 cast members.

✓ **ImageQ:** ImageQ is another multimedia authoring software package. Although, it is a windows 3.1 application but it can also play back on windows 95, create slide show presentations well and provides a way to distribute them easily. It lacks the intuitive programming language and strong interface necessary for truly productive multimedia applications development.

ImageQ presentations comprise a series of background image and associated control scripts that add user interface controls, overlay images, and underlying programming to each slide. It uses a multiple-document interface to manage one or more presentations simultaneously.

The slide strip window for each presentation contains either thumb nails or file information for each slide image and provide the means of navigating through the presentation at design time. Although the image in the slide strip are, miniature versions of the background image they do not show any of the users interface element that the user has added such as button and list boxes. The user must create these through code, which ImageQ will interpret only at runtime-a major deficiency that other authoring system (such as Icon Author and Director) avoid by offering design tools to arrange interface controls visually without code.

While ImageQ does not provide the robust slide design tool that competing products include, it does import a wide variety of graphics formats. Once the images have been imported into an ImageQ presentation, they can be kept in their native formats or saved as .BMP or .HKF files.

Whenever images are imported into an ImageQ presentation, it involves only creation of thumb nails slide references, the image themselves remain as separate files. The list of filenames and the control and transition setting are stored with an IMQ extension, which serves as the main file for the presentation.

ImageQ's programming language is awkward to work with, because it uses unconventional syntax and event handlers. For example, ImageQ uses lines like "and X to Y", put 150 into X for adding the two values in a single statement and assigning the value to 150 to X, respectively.

Though ImageQ lacks and programming tools, it does well with distribution. It is easy to build portable presentations as alone .EXE files that includes the ImageQ runtime. ImageQ is really a presentation package in an authoring system's clothing. Its real strength lies in ability to create traditional slide shows with prebuilt images and distribute them with no royalty. Yet the product's lack of interactive design tools and its clumsy programming languages ultimately make it a poor choice for robust multimedia applications development.

(c) What is a simulation ? List and explain, the categories of simulations. [4]

Simulation is an important area of pedagogy where a student is engaged in situations of problem solving.

There are two categories of simulations :

(i) stand-alone, and

(ii) integrated.

In *stand-alone simulation activity*, simulation program runs independently from the system of interest; the purpose can be: decision making, training to enhance decision and/or motor skills, understanding and education, and entertainment. Planning is only one of the applications of use of simulation in decision making.

In *integrated simulation activity*, the simulation program operates together with the system of interest either to support or to enhance real system operation.

Q4(a) Explain the need for understanding the psychology of a learner during interface design. [7]

The individual style of learning has got different dimension. Some people learn by graphic learning while others learn primarily by reading, seeing, or visualizing. Some of the learner learns more effectively through physical movement or touching, these are called kinesthetic learners thus need of understanding psychology of a learner is important. To get a general feeling of the learning styles of the users, you may ask the following question to the intended audience of the multimedia: "How do you learn? What kinds of books do you prefer?

Do you like the Books with lots pictures and diagrams? Do you learn better by watching video? etc.

You will discover that the intended audience of your multimedia package follows a variety of learning styles, that is, they learn and prefer to learn in different ways. The design of your application must incorporate different multimedia building blocks that in turn appeal to different learning styles. Therefore, you must use effectively text, audio, graphics, animation, and digital video such that you multimedia application is more meaningful to the people having different learning styles.

(b) Explain how multimedia can improve the quality of advertising of a product using the Internet. [8]

Multimedia is a natural for advertising - natural images, special effects, animation, 3-D. There are three main areas of current opportunity: CD-ROM, the Internet, and customer point-of-contact use of multimedia.

As manufacturers seek to gain greater competitive advantage through the application of Information Technology there will be need of increasing use of Multimedia and high networks.

The multimedia nature of the Internet is suitable for high-impact advertising. The Internet has become an integral part of the media mix for many advertisers, and new forms of advertising have filled the World Wide Web landscape, including animated banner ads, sponsor logos, interstitials, “advertorials,” “advertainment,” and 3-D visualization. Where multimedia is highly used to make all these animated banner ads, sponsor logos, interstitials, “advertorials,” “advertainment,” and 3-D visualization which enchances the quality of advertising of a product by leaving an impact in the minds of the Internet users. Being a modern way of advertising it results in leaving good views about the quality of the product which is advertised on the Internet by using Multimedia.

Q5(a) What is digital audio ? Write two differences between conventional audio and digital audio. [5]

✓ **Digital Audio :** The most common reason for using digital audio in computer is to be able to use multimedia in its full potential. The most common requirement is to be able to input sound such as a spoken commentary on image or a document.

The sound is a repeated pattern of pressure in the air and a microphone converts a sound wave into an electrical wave. The shape and frequency of the electrical wave is identical to the shape and frequency of the sound wave and the clarity of what we hear is entirely to the dependent on the shape and frequency of the sound wave.

	Analog audio		Digital audio
1.	When we hold a microphone up in the air it connects the charges in the air & converts them into electric voltage. This is known as analog signal.	1.	Digital audio is a technological process whereby an analog audio is first converted into a continuous stream of numbers. This is known as digital audio.
2.	Analog audio when plotted on a paper it would look like a graph.	2.	But where as digital audio give the output in series of 0 & 1.
3.	The recording is done on a magnetic tape for further play modes.	3.	The recording done on a hard disk or any media which supports digital format.
4.	The output device for an analog sound is a simple speakers.	4.	The output device of a digitized audio is amplified speakers which are built in.
5.	The quality of the sound output is less.	5.	Here the sound quality is excellent.
6.	Editing analog audio piece is quite difficult & time consuming & less accurate.	6.	Digital audio editing gives high quality output with less complexity & less time consuming. Accuracy level is high.

(b) Explain the term "collaboration" in terms of multimedia. [5]

Collaboration : The traditional CBTs require the student to work in self-stud mode. But work without a tutor may be ineffective. Thus, instead of offering courses on CD-ROM or videotape a new learning environment is needed which focuses on bringing several learners together for better attainment of learning goal. Communication should be possible in any direction, learners can ask their tutors or talk to other learners.

The term "collaboration" is one of the commonly used terms is multimedia applications today. The verbal meaning of this word is the actual meaning in the context of multimedia, that is collectively doing a particular work but for this collaborative work physical presence may not be required.

(c) Explain the role of multimedia in E-commerce applications. [5]

Electronic commerce is an emerging model of new selling and merchandising tools in which buyers are able to participate in all phases of a purchase decision, while stepping through those processes electronically rather than in a physical store or by phone (with a physical catalog). The processes in electronic commerce include enabling a customer to access product information. Select items to purchase, items securely, and have the purchase setting financially. The multimedia technology may be used for presentation of information through the web for such systems. e.g. The products details can better be presented by use of multimedia like using animation, graphics and sound. A product's presentation can be made better which ease the consumer in understanding the product and make them comfortable with online purchase.

E-Commerce applications are available for Business-to-business transactions, Business-to-consumer transaction and for the Intra-Company (Enterprise) transactions

The basic requirements for an e-commerce based application are to develop an on-line catalog and handle transactions on-line. This can manage large product assortment and complete sales at lower costs.

CS-66 MULTIMEDIA
JUNE 2005

Note : *Question number 1 is* ***compulsory.*** *Attempt any* ***three*** *from the rest.*

1(a) What is multimedia ? Explain three major components of multimedia. **[5]**

Multimedia is an integration of various media, which convey the information with computing technology. Various media such as text, graphics, animation, sound, audio, video etc.

Multimedia is a computer itself or a computer software product. In practically we can say that multimedia is a combination of both hardware and software. Another much used term is "hypermedia". The term hypermedia refers to the information structure of the content. If the texts, pictures, and sounds are linked to each other by associative links the applications may be called "hypermedia".

Multimedia systems support the physical and logical coexistence and interactive use of heterogeneous media classes such as print, audio and video in specific application environments.

One of the key features of multimedia is "**Interactivity**". Hypermedia and virtual reality applications are based on multimedia systems. Hypermedia extends the **media-oriented features** of multimedia systems by the concept of hyperlinks, i.e.; logical structures that provide means for organizing media objects in a flexible, logically coherent, network-oriented and non-sequential way. Virtual reality extends the interaction **oriented features** of multimedia by the concept of cyberspace, i.e. modeling objects and their behaviour in virtual environments. The basic advantage of multimedia over the conventional form of media, which uses sound, graphics, and text etc. is the interactive feature of multimedia.

The maojor components of multimedia are:

✓ The text can be used for adding emphasis.

✓ Graphics provides a visual impact. It is generally said that a picture is worth a thousands words. Thus, graphics can be used for enhancing a presentation.

✓ Voice tries to enhance a presentation to the extent that a presentation moves on to the form of persuasion. Many people want to listen about a particular topic rather than reading about it.

✓ The animation can be used effectively for attracting attention. Animation also makes a presentation light, thus, can be used for presentation of several complex subjects. It is also a tool, which helps in focusing attention; for example, a chart if drawn through animation may be focused on to quickly.

✓ The video part of multimedia can be used as a powerful communicator providing clear-cut instructions.

(b) Explain the role of software in multimedia. List four major recent softwares in the multimedia industry. [4]

Using multimedia always means using multimedia software. Multimedia applications need good operating system as their platform. Currently the operating system is typically windows 95/98. It is important that the operating system provides smooth handling of sound, video, graphics, and network communication.

Making multimedia applications or "multimedia components", requires special software. Graphics programmes such as Photoshop are specialized for processing and manipulating bitmaps, while Corel Draw is a programme for vector graphics. Cake Walk and Cool Edit are applications for making and manipulating music and sound.

Similarly other multimedia related software also work on the same type of working environment, but they have their own features to experiment upon. Some of the recent software used in multimedia industry are:

✓ **Photoshop** ⇒ Industry standard digital imaging software.

✓ **Director** ⇒ Authoring multimedia for CD-ROM & the Web.

✓ **Premiere** ⇒ Digital video and post-production tool.

✓ **Sound Edit** ⇒ Sound capture and editing for multimedia, music or the net.

✓ **Flash** ⇒ Vector-based animation tool.

✓ **Frontpage :** Authoring tool for intranet and the WWW.

✓ **Alias | Wavefront** ⇒ 3d tools for games, films.

(c) Identify, and briefly explain, four important multimedia services which are used with the advances in communication technology. [4]

✓ **Voice mail** ⇒ Voice mail is a tool which communicates voice over lines. This can be phone lines or the Internet. A voice mail system is not dependent. The only draw back for a voice mail is that it only hurdles audio information, voice mail system is time & location independent but it offers no interactivity.

✓ **Multimedia based fax** ⇒ Fax is more famous and more used rather than the voice mail for the following reasons.

(i) Used to send detailed information.

(ii) Easier to use.

(iii) Handles graphic information

(iv) Provides a printed copy of information.

(v) Also fax is non interactive option for the user. Even a fax modem can be used to send & receive fax.

✓ **Video conferencing** ⇒ Video conferencing is generally used in large corporate sectors. In foreign countries the use of video conferencing is a high success. Video conference is just like any office meetings thus require setting of time, preparing rooms & place, agenda, followed by discussion etc.

✓ **E-commerce based application** ⇒ Electronic commerce is an upcoming model of new selling and merchandising tools in which buyers are able to participate in all phases of a purchase decision, while stepping through process electronically rather in physical stores. The multimedia technologies may be used for presentation of information through the web for such systems.

(d) Explain what an Everest Authoring System is. List, and explain, its four major features. [6]

Everest Authoring system 1.5 is best suited for the developers of CBT applications who seek a powerful but easy to use windows-based authoring environment. As far as CBT environments go Everest (a window 3.1 application that also plays back on windows 95) features

1. Storing multimedia support,
2. Enough object orientation to improve that productivity over competing product.
3. Great technical support

Everest's nearly seamless multi paradigmatic approach includes such features as

1. Visual programming with icons,
2. Direct manipulations of interface elements and
3. Procedural programming

Everest has successfully integrated these element making applications development easier.

The everest developer environment opens with multiple views of an application. In Everest's application creation, the user starts off with a library and names an initial screen. Dragging a layout object icon from the toolset onto visible as an icon on the Icon script, also occupies the attributes window, in which the user can choose a background colour on bitmap, select a screen size, and specify up to 434 more properties.

Also interface and media object icons can be dragged into the screen; like list and combo boxes, edit boxes, text displays; bitmap placeholders, sliders an gauges, buttons of all types, video and audio, OLE and animation.

These objects can be a made to move around, visually resize them and their properties set by clicking on them in either the visual screen or the icon script. The placeholder objects can be left empty or their contents can be specified immediately.

(e) What are Annotations ? Explain the role of annotations in the applications of hypertext, using an example. [4]

✓ **Annotations** ⇒ A special link type is the annotation link to a small, additional information. The reading of an annotation typically takes the form of a temporary excursion from the primary material to which the reader typically takes the form after having finished with the annotation. Annotations are quite similar to footnotes in traditional text and can be implemented, as Guide pop-up windows that disappear as soon as the user releases the mouse button. Annotations can be accessed through an icon.

Hypertext writers can use annotations in the same way they would use footnotes in traditional text with the exception that hypertext annotations are less intrusive because they are not shown unless the research asks for them. Many hypertext systems allow readers to add new links to the primary material even they do not always allow the reader to change the original nodes. **For Example** : if we make a time table of a school which is viewable on the website of the school. As the caleder shows that English will be tought on Monday from 1.00 P.M to 2 P.M but it does not show which teacher will be taking the lecture. Here, we can provide that details to the user by using Annotations, user will be shown a small window containg all other details like teacher name, class room number etc. as soon as the cursor is placed on English.

(f) Explain the need of interface design for developing content material. How does psychology of learning affect the design process ? Discuss three major rules in designing the computer based instruction material. [7]

The term multimedia interface design refers to the means through which a user interacts with application content or information. Through the interface you may be provided with navigation buttons, text fields, instruction, graphics, animation, audio recourses and other means of help users achieve the goals of application. Since one of the main use of multimedia is in education and training, therefore, the basic concepts of how learning takes place is helpful and even necessary in designing a meaningful and useful multimedia application interface. In the following subsection let us explore the basic principles of the psychology learning and its application to interface design.

✓ **Interface design and the psychology of learning** ⇒ Multimedia involves multi-sensory experiences. Multimedia content reaches users in many different forms, therefore, providing an enhanced learning environment. But how does we learn in a learning situation?

The first step in the cyclic process of learning is attention to information. The human brain obtains information through senses, fundamentally through our eyes and ears. However, the information is accepted only if one is paying attention. The information so gathered is transferred to the local working memory. This local memory is to be continuously refreshed: otherwise the information so gained may be lost. This process is called rehearsal. The rehearsal process may cause transfer of information to short term memory to the long-term memory of the human. This process is termed as encoding. For using encoded information it must be retrieved from the long-term memory and delivered to the working memory for the processing, thus completing the cycle of learning. The following figure shows the learning cycle.

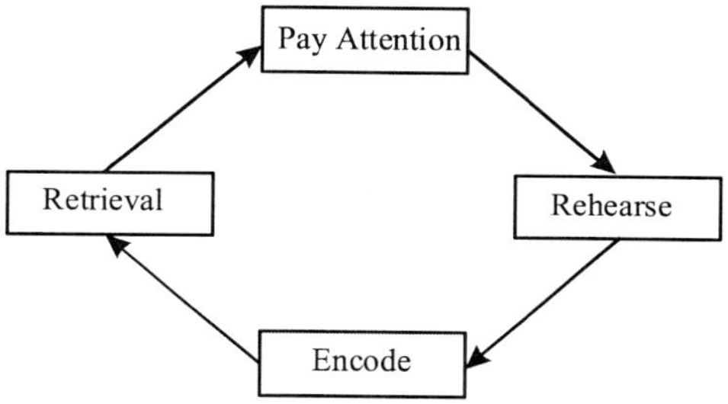

A well-designed multimedia programme demands the simultaneous attention of several senses through process of appealing to more than one sense simultaneously, facilitating the rehearsal process. Even the process of retrieval is facilitated for the concept being presented by the power of multiple media. Thus, multimedia enhances the retention of knowledge.

Another important issue for multimedia application design is the amount of information that can be assimilated at given time: this is referred to as the cognitive load. Too much information in a multimedia presentation may overload users cognitive abilities, thus, making learning less effective. This will defeat the basic design objectives.

Three major rules in designing the computer based instruction material:

✓ Do not divide the learner's attention; you must use various media elements such as text, graphics, and sound to reinforce a concept rather than introducing different types of concepts.

✓ You may use color, special effects, and sound to direct the learner's attention to important areas of the presentation. However, use them only if it is essential.

✓ The information, which a learner may need to undertake an activity must be available on the screen, for example, the reference information for answering a feedback form must be available.

2(a) Explain the role of DVD-RAM for writing and deleting the content, with a suitable diagram. Compare it with CD-ROM, on the basis of at least two features of each. [10]

Another DVD product for PCs is DVD-RAM. These discs and drives have a capacity of 2.6 GB that can be rewritten many times. It includes functions and applications similar to those of floppy discs or MO (magneto-optical) discs. DVD-RAM is an efficient rewriteable medium for handling and storing any data that requires a large capacity, such as moving pictures. Because ultraprecise writing is necessary, even a fingerprint left on the disc's recording side before writing would change the optical intensity so that accurate writing could not be achieved. Therefore, a DVD-RAM (rewriteable) disc must be contained in a special cartridge. Although the DVD-RAM standard has been ratified and published by the DVD consortium, DVD-RAM drives will only appear on the market in early 1998.

Temperature and humidity changes

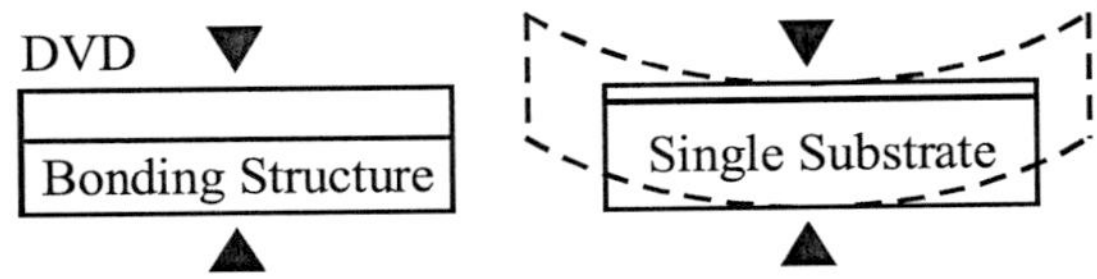

DVD has a symmetrical structure which resists from warpage, because the discs are bonded together.

Comparision of CD-ROM and DVD-RAM : 1.2 to 1.4 Mbps with burst transfer rates of up to 17 Mbps. This is the data equivalent of an 8x CD-ROM drive. DVD spin rates are about three times faster than those of single-speed CDROM drives. Hence, when reading CD-ROMs, DVD-RAM drives transfer data at 3x speed.

DVD-RAM can write or erase data on the disks while CD-ROM can only read that is the major difference between the two. While both can read the data from the disks.

(b) What is an explanatory system ? Explain how multimedia can be used to develop an explanatory system. **[5]**

The multimedia system also have a very important property, that is, they adapt their responses to the student needs. Thus, providing explanation to various situations, which have been put for the pedagogy to solve. There are called explanatory system.

The advantage of this planner over a normal hypertext based presentations are:

- The student can themselves choose the media to display information.
- A piece of information can be reused for answering different question as the objects are defined in the form of a shared base of information.

• Capabilities of having natural link still exist.

Learning environments should be built on a framework of well-articulated, diverse learning outcomes. This component of the learning environment is squarely in the province of the instructional designers and content experts. Ideally it should be set in place before serious learningware development occurs. Here comes the role of Explanatory systems which are capable to explain the different ideas. Taking an example of teaching a C++ to the students where Mutimedia can be used to develop explanatory system where we will use text, graphics, and animation to provide education to the students. The system will be capable to behave /explain different parts or concepts of the C++ language.

3(a) Explain four major application areas for multimedia. **[4]**

Following are the major multimedia applications :

✓ **Entertainment :** The entertainment industry has used this technology the most create real life like games. Several developers have used graphics, sound animation of multimedia to create variety of games. The special technologies such as virtual reality have made these games just like experiences of real life. Our such example is flight simulator which creates a real-life imaging

✓ **Edutainment :** Edutainment is nothing but educational entertainment. Many computer games with focus on education are now available. Example, in this case is an educational game, which plays various rhymes for little kids. In addition to playing rhymes, the child can paint the pictures, increase reduce size of various objects etc. Similarly many other edutainment packages, which provide a lot of details information of kids, are available. Microsoft has produced many such CD-based multimedia such as Sierra, Knowledge Adventure etc. Which in addition to play provide some sort of learning component. The latest in this series is a package, which teaches about the computer using games playing. There are many more

companies which have specialized in entertainment sector you may explore the list of such companies on the net.

✓**Business Communications :** Multimedia is a very powerful tool for enhancing the quality of business communications. The business communications such as employee related communications, product promotions, customer information, and reports for investors can be presented in multimedia form. All these business communications are required to be structures such that a formal level of content structure exists in the communication. Other common business application involving multimedia requires access to database of multimedia information about a company. The multimedia technology of today can easily support this application as natural language enquiry systems do exit for making queries.

✓ **Knowledge Transfer :** This kind of application involves transmission of a piece of information with the maximum impact, that is the transfer of information in such a fashion that it facilitates the retention. This application is meant for academic and business both.

In academies, the knowledge transfer is used as the building block, whereas, in business it is the effective transfer of information which might be essential for the survival of a business. Multimedia based teaching is gaining momentum as powerful teaching aids are quite common. Multimedia is one of the best ways to provide short-term training to the workers in a business houses. It gives lot of flexibility in providing training.

(b) Describe two ways in which simulation can improve the quality of an interactive system for teaching and learning. [5]

Simulation is an important area of pedagogy where a student is engaged in situations of problem solving.

Following are the ways in which simulation can improve the quality of an interactive system for teaching and learning :

1. *Learning with Scenarios.* This strategy uses a real-world scenario as the vehicle for instruction in interactive system for teaching and learning. Presentation of a scenario involves demonstrating the operational activities and teaching the correct methods required to solve the problem.

2. *Learning by Doing.* Within the context of the scenario, the system coaches the student in step-by-step operations required to perform the task. Thus, again increasing the quality of interactive system as the quality of learning is also increasing.

3. *Practising with Contents Feedback.* The student performs activities without prompting by the tutor.

(c) Identify a type of multimedia suitable to teach the practical component of computer based courses, and explain it. Also design a diagram for the user interface. [4]

Multimedia is the use of two or more types of media. One of the more common uses of the term multimedia is tying these media via a computer, i.e., multimedia personal computers. Electronic multimedia courseware ties training to state-of-the-art computer technology. Electronic multimedia courseware links audiovisual, graphic, automation, and programmed instruction disciplines for individual and group instruction. The most important characteristic of electronic multimedia is the immediate feedback trainees receive in interacting with the computer.

A summary of different multimedia types which can be used to teach the practical component for computer based Course is given below :

We have taken example of teaching C++ language.

Animations :

Simple animations: animated gif

The image is a set of slides which have each been given a length of time to display.

Click Refresh to see it again. They can repeat as many times as you like, but have no sound track. Here, we can make different images of pointer e.g. use in memory referencing, in doubly linked list etc. which will increase the ability of students to learn it faster.

✓ **Interactive Graphics: Shockwave :** Some graphics appear to be interactive because they change when the mouse passes over or when clicked, but this is often a simple change of one image for another. However, Shockwave files can be truly interactive, and it is possible to build in an amazing range of routes to explore an image: an entire video game complete with sound effects can be contained in one Shockwave file. Here, we can develop a button as clicking on it the major concepts of OOP wil be displayed with animation.

Sounds :

Audio:

✓ **Streaming :** Real Audio, Windows Media Audio, MP3 and Advanced Streaming Format, to name just a few are often used as ways to distribute lower quality versions of wave files. Here, we can use it as file size of these files are very less and it will be easier for us to distribute it over Internet. Moreover, audio will be placed to increase the ability to learn faster.

Besides that video can also be used but we will use Interactive Graphics: Shockwave.

When we are assigning the job of creation of windows tutor that time we consider the interface design :

- Keep low cognitive load.
- Keep a simple, consistent screen design.
- Don't divide the leaner's attention.
- Encourage frequent revision/rehearsal by the learner.
- Avoid repetition in interactions.
- Encourage reinforcement of learning by using concrete words and different media to reinforce the message.

4(a) List two major categories of multimedia development tools. Also mention the programs which act as multimedia development tools for these categories. **[5]**

Major categories of multimedia development tools :

✓ **Analysis Tools** ⇒ These tools help the designer analyze what the needs and goals for the project scope are.

✓ **Design Tools** ⇒ The design tools given here are useful for planning how the project will be developed, including user characteristics and specific objectives.

✓ **Management Tools** ⇒ These tools are used for the management of the multimedia development process as a whole.

✓ **Production Tools** ⇒ The tools in this area are helpful in the actual production of the multimedia product. ProductionShoe 2.0 is a program used by shoes manufacturers.

✓ **Evaluation tools** ⇒ Evaluation tools included here supports the task of generating evaluations by various different means. ShareBroker 1.0 is program used to evaluate the performance of the share. It also forecast the future of the share.

(b) Explain four major features of authoring system. **[4]**

There are four basic features or all authoring software:

✓ **Importing** ⇒ it should be able to import carious media elements, which may have been developed using other software package.

✓ **Creating** ⇒ it should allow some basic features for creation of text, graphics and may be sound if not video.

✓ **Integrating** ⇒ it should allow you to define sequences and provide linkages

✓ **Delivering** ⇒ it should allow developing self-running application and encryption of application data.

(c) What is a hypertext ? Explain two major computer applications and business applications of hypertext. **[6]**

Hypertext is nothing but text working like a button. Hypertext capabilities can be used to link graphics, animation or frame and of course other text. Hypertext interfaces allows users to select individual hot words on a screen, which are then linked to other pages or layers or text etc. A perfect example of hypertext application is windows help.

Hypertext systems are useful when presenting large amount of textual information. Many hypertext authoring programs provide graphical links for animation, sound and video as well as text.

✓ **Computer Applications** ⇒ Many tutorials to be studied on computer only are launched which contain large amount of pages linked through hyperlinks. And on Internet where the major use of hypertext can be seen. We can not imagine cyber space without hypertext.

✓ **Business Application** ⇒ It is difficult to find a business of any kind today without a World Wide Web address. Some of these Web pages are nothing but empty storefronts, but some firms have recognized hypertext's potential for disseminating information on their products in ways that can be individualized to customer needs. Many websites selling almost everything can be easily find on the Internet.

5(a) Give the major steps in the planning process of any multimedia programme/application, with the help of an appropriate diagram. [7]

A multimedia development team consists of many different skills oriented people, who include a producer, education consultant, media consultant, media designers, media specialists, webmaster etc. However, the whole team works for a single objective that is creation of an effective multimedia application. Therefore, one of the major issues for multimedia production is to plan an application. Let us discuss it in grater details in this section.

To start the authoring process of multimedia application development without planning all the components of the project is a major mistake as it may lead to an insufficient application being developed. A multimedia project should be planned through following stepwise process:

✓ Develop the Multimedia programme/application concept.
✓ Outline your programme.
✓ Development of flowchart.
✓ Develop programme storyboard.
✓ Consider copyright issue.
✓ Plan the production of text, graphic, animation, auto, and video,
✓ Prepare the project budget and time schedule.

This planning process is also presented in figure given below.

(b) Explain the criticality of the copyright issues in the development of multimedia. [3]

While designing multimedia application, copyright issue plays a crucial role because of two fundamental reasons.

✓ Multimedia involves use of multiple media each of that media element may be protected under the copyright laws.

✓ Original multimedia works are also protected by copyrights.

The copyright laws protect the following types of works:

✓ Printed or Electronic text of the form of prose, poetry, news paper articles, magazine articles, books, computer software, etc.

✓ Musical works such as songs, advertisements recording of music, sounds, or words etc.

✓ Dramatic works such as plays, sits etc.

✓ Dances and mime works.

✓ Pictorial, drawings, graphics, and sculptural works such as photographs, posters, maps, paintings, drawings, graphic arts, display ads, works of fine arts etc.

✓ Motion pictures and others audiovisual works including multimedia.

Therefore, it is important that during the planning phase you sort the copyright issues relating to getting permissions of using copyright material from its owner. Please make sure that you have the licensed copies of all the software that are required for the development of multimedia.

(c) Write three major functions for multimedia authoring tools. Classify the authoring tools available in the market. [5]

Table Features of multimedia authoring tools

Item	Authorware	Director	Flash	Live-Motion	GRiNS Editor
Vendor	Macromedia	Macromedia	Macromedia	adobe	Oratrix
Method	Icon-based	Timeline-based	Timeline based	Timeline based	Timeline-based
Usage	Multimedia aggregation	Multimedia representation	Animation creation	Animation creation	SMIL authoring
Player	Authorware Plaer	Shockwave	Flash Player	Flash Player Quick Time Player	Real Play GRiNS Player

Following are the some of the packages with their features :

(i) Photoshop → Photoshop is a software which is a product of Adobe. Adobe Photoshop is an image editing software. It can be used to make layouts, editing images and creating visual effect too. Photoshop is a bitmap image software. It has great options related to masking. One can get different colour modes to work with. One can also create outwork in vector based software like illustrator & edit it out in Photoshop. Another software for graphic creation and manipulation is CorelDraw.

(ii) Sound Forge → Sound forge is a software which is used for digital sound recording and digital sound effects. This software works with sound card and one can have all the features which facilitates in manipulating sound.

(iii) 3DS Max → 3DS Max can be used extensively for 3D animation and special effects. Thus this software can be used to create 3D animation as per our story board. One can apply state of the art effects like camera, light, textures. These effects look very realistic.

(iv) Flash → Flash is a product of Macromedia. It is a vector shape animation product. It is used basically for web animation. But due to its good interactive option and compatibility it is also used in authoring. It also supports action script that gives enhance output as per requirement.

CS - 66 : MULTIMEDIA
DECEMBER-2005

Note : Question number 1 is compulsory. Attempt any three questions from the rest.

Q1(a). What is multimedia? Explain at least five applications of multimedia in distance education. **[6]**

Refer to Chapter-1 Q. No.3,18, Page No.23

Following are the five applications of Multimedia in Distance Education

(i) As this is the age of Internet the first use of multimedia should be to integrate the learning and Internet with multimedia. It means providing Internet based learning systems where multimedia is used to clear doubts, or separate forum can be created on all topics where students can share their views.

(ii) Students can be provided with multimedia based tutorials besides the conventional study material, which will greatly enhance the undertaking power and increased ability to grasp concepts within less time, as most of the students are working and have less time to study at home. Providing CDs will enable to access the course material at his office easily.

(iii) Multimedia will provoke radical changes in the teaching process during the coming decades, particularly as current student base go beyond the limits of traditional teaching method

(iv) Course delivery through video conferencing can also be used to clear the problems of the students, where a student ask his/her doubts and get answers from the expert in the subject.

(v) An increased use of multimedia involves students themselves. Students put together interactive magazines and newsletter they make original art using image-editing tools.

(b) What is the need of interface design? Explain five fundamental rules for interface design in multimedia applications. **[10]**

Refer to June-2005, Q. No.1(f), Pafe. No.174.

Refer to Dec-2004, Q. No.1(c), Page No.184.

(c) What is copyright? List and explain two legal issues related to copyright in multimedia application development. [5]

The oxford dictionary defines copyright as the 'exclusive right given by law for a certain term of years to an author, composer etc. to print, publish and sell copies of his original work. u/s 14 of the copyright act 1957 copyright means the exclusive right to do or authorise others to do certain act in relation to 1) literacy, dramatic or musical work, 2) artistic work, 3) cinematograph film, and 4) sound recording, the exclusive right for doing the respective acts extends not only to the whole of the work but to any substantial part thereof or to any translation or adoption thereof.

Following are the two legal issues related to copyright in multimedia application development :

(i) The object of copyright is to protect the author of the genuine work from exploitation. Copyright subsist only in prescribed form not only in ideas i.e. unless preserve form to store either writing, print or store in cd or cassette, it must be tangible form not intangible form. Computer programmes and databases are regarded as literacy work under the act u/s 2(o) 'computer' include any electronic device having information processing, capabilities. 'Computer programme' is a set of instruction expressed in words, codes, schemes, or in any other form, including a a machine readable medium, capable of causing a computer to perform it include both programme and source code. There are there important element to decide weather it protected under copyright or not are labour, skill, and judgement. If own intellectual creation with applying labour on it comes protected under copyright act. Thus all multimedia work covered under copyright act if originally created by the author and in protected form- not idea in mind. But apply such idea on computer or on paper or print them data form or expression form. So there is no issue as all computer work if original print or expressible form then comes in cr act.

(ii) The answer for second issue all the work in intangible form is not accepted it is in abstract form not in idea. idea's in mind not protected by cr act until they are in tangible form.

(d) What is hypertext? Explain any two application areas of hypertext. [5]

Refer to Chapter-3, Q. No.2, 3, Page No.57,

(e) List and explain two input and two output devices for multimedia systems. [5]

Refer to Chapter-1, Q. No.8, Page No.7,

Multimedia Input Devices are :

(i) Digital cameras ; digital camera phones, Digital Video DVD recorders : this is one category of input devices through which we can input various types of sound recorded or video recorded into computer to produce final multimedia applications.

(ii) Game controllers

(iii) Virtual reality (VR)

(iv) Voice recognition

(v) Text-to-speech

(vi) Brain wave input

Multimedia Output Devices are :

(i) Sound speakers, which produce sound output and microphones, which are used for on-line recording of sound using various multimedia softwares.

(ii) Monitor to see the final or output of multimedia.

Q2(a). What is a multimedia component? Explain any four components (except video) of multimedia with an example of each.. [10]

Refer to Chapter-1, Q. No.12, Page No.14

(b) What is digital video? Explain the use of digital video in developing multimedia applications. [5]

Refer to Chapter-4, Q. No.10, Page No.83

Q3(a). What is authoring software? Explain three features of authoring software. [8]

Refer to Chapter-4, Q. No.11, Page No.84

(b) Explain the need for planning in a multimedia application. Explain the need of logic flow chart for development of interactive multimedia applications with an example. [7]

Need for Planning in a Multimedia Application : During the initial design phase all the aspects of the related multimedia project is carefully thought about and planned, well before the production start. Every key element involved is discuss. There are various tools available to plan the project. A flowchart is one of them. If is one of the commonly used tools to prepare a blue print of the plan during the design phase. It shows how all the elements involved in the project are related to each other, with adequate information about their controlling features.

Like any other video program or movie, multimedia programs require a script a script on the subject involved. The script and flowchart works together to provide a printed version of text, graphics and sound to be used in the production of the multimedia program.

Refer to Chapter-4, Q. No.6, Page No.76.

Q4(a). Explain at least six features of ImageQ. **[6]**

Refer to Chapter-3, Q. No.9, Page No.69.

(b)What is a sound card? Explain the process of sound card installation. **[5]**

Refer to Chapter-1, Q. No.8, Page No.9.

Installing Sound card : While installing a sound card one should keep in mind that it should not conflict with any other external devices installed in the computer system. Installation of sound card might require some default settings to be changed to make it compatible with the computer system.
Once all setting are done correctly, place the card in a free slot a check all the connected cables to ensure that all connections are fitted properly. After this task is over, run the designated installation software that comes with sound card or motherboard if sound card is inbuilt. After the program makes necessary modifications in the registry files it activates the sound card and when the computer is switched on. These days it becomes very easy to install sound card, as it is inbuilt in motherboard and sound card driver can be installed at the time of installing the driver of the motherboard. There is no need to plug or unplug any circuit on the motherboard.

(c) What are annotations? Explain the role of annotations in the applications of hypertext with an example **[4]**

Refer to June-2005, Q. No.1(e), Page No.174

Q5(a). Explain the statement "Multimedia productions are tailored to specifically meet the users needs" with an example. **[7]**

Ans. Somewhat similar in idea to a television program, whether educational or business oriented, multimedia productions are tailored to specifically meet your needs, whether your needs include employee training, customer service, or product development and marketing. The basic facilities needed for multimedia include video capture, video editing, sound, photograph editing, picture digitization, morphing creation of 2D and 3D models, and animation and authoring.
Example : if you need multimedia application for your company, which has to

be installed at the reception counter. Company needs a multimedia application which can be accessed easily and will be interesting to browse through. As sometimes the waiting time for the persons at reception to meet the officer goes up to 20 minutes, so company wants to provide the introduction of the company, organizational structure, and last 20 years turnover, and benefits to become the associate of the company in brief. Now the multimedia application will be developed which can be accessed easily, to increase the interest good color combinations will be used, touch screen facility will be there. So, this is the example of tailored made production of multimedia for this company by the multimedia production company.

(b) Explain any two multimedia features which can be used in business. [4]

Refer to Chapter-1, Q. No.6, Page No.4.

(c) Explain any four rules to be used in designing the computer-based instructional materials. [4]

Following are the rules to be used in designing the computer-based instructional materials :

(i) For imparting procedural skills simulation can be used. Simulation should be as close as possible to the actual study environment.

(ii) Do not divide the learner's attention; you must use various media elements such as text, graphics and sound to reinforce a concept rather than introducing different types of concepts.

(iii) You may use colors, special effects, and sound to direct the learner's attention to important areas of the presentation. However, use them only if it is essential

(iv) The information, which a learner may need to undertake on activity must be available on the screen. For example, the reference information for answering a feed form must be available.

(v) Encourage frequent revision/ rehearsals by the learner.

(vi) Avoid-repetition in interactions.

(vii) Keep low cognitive load, Keep a simple, consistent screen design.

CS - 66 : MULTIMEDIA
JUNE-2006

Note : Question number 1 is compulsory. Attempt any three questions from the rest.

Q1(a). Define the term Multimedia. List four softwares used in multimedia industry.

Refer to Chapter-1 Q. No.18, Page No.23

Thus in multimedia software goes hand in hand. There are different softwares available for different purposes. Some of them are as under:

- Photoshop for image & graphic editing.
- Premier & after FX for production.
- Director & authorware for authoring.
- Sound Forge for sound editing.
- DS max for special effects & 3D animation.
- Flash for web animation.
- Apart from the above softwares there are many other softwares available for multimedia applications.

(b) Explain the role of a logic flow chart for multimedia application, with an example.

Ans. Logic Flowchart : Logic flowchart is a flowchart that represents the flow of logic in a program. It is very important, especially if the title is interactive. It provides a road map of the proposed application for the authoring team. The flow chart illustrates the choices that the user will have in each screen. The degree of complexity of these flow charts depends on the type of application to be developed.

A flowchart illustrates the steps in a process. By visualizing the process, a flowchart can quickly help in identifying bottlenecks or inefficiencies where the process can be streamlined or improved. A flowchart is a map of the multimedia project showing the storyboard elements and their links. The ideal flowchart is a clear, easy-to-follow specification of the project's topics, categories, levels and links.

The flowchart design is an outcome of the navigational structure considerations. A well thought out flowchart addresses the three navigational factors:

Access : The route the viewer must take through the production must be transparent to the viewer and be kept at a minimum.

Access Levels : The route the viewer must take through each level of the production is to be kept at a minimum. Keep the paths simple.

Graphic Path Indicators : Keep a uniform structure for the navigation graphics

Example : The flowcharts, which illustrate games, are among the most complex flowcharts. The flow chart shown below extends the example project about programming language.

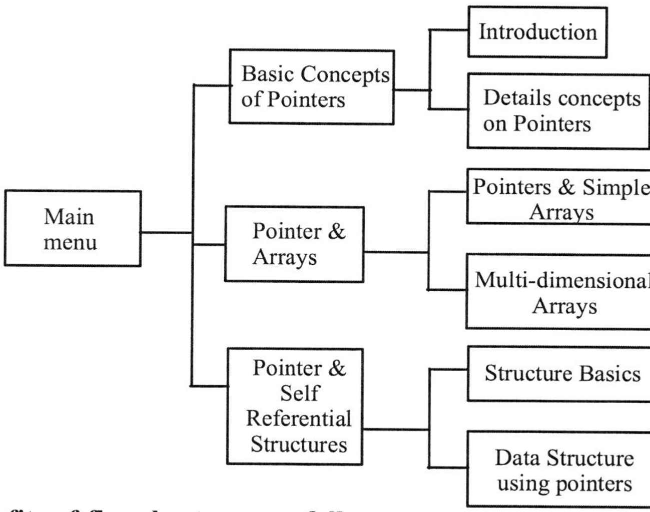

The benefits of flowcharts are as follows :

(a) Communication : Flowcharts are better way of communicating the logic of a system to all concerned.

(b) Effective analysis : With the help of flowchart, problem can be analysed in more effective way.

(c) Proper documentation : Program flowcharts serve as a good program documentation, which is needed for various purposes.

(d) Efficient Coding : The flowcharts act as a guide or blueprint during the systems analysis and program development phase.

(e) Proper Debugging : The flowchart helps in debugging process.

(f) Efficient Program Maintenance : The maintenance of operating program becomes easy with the help of flowchart. It helps the programmer to put efforts more efficiently on that part

(c) How is multimedia used in business communication? Explain this with an example.

Ans. Multimedia is used in business communication with the help of following

(i) Voicemail or VMS, is a centralized system of managing telephone messages for a large group of people. In its simplest form it mimics the functions of an answering machine, uses a standard telephone handset for the user interface, and uses a centralized, computerized system rather than equipment at the individual telephone. Voicemail systems are much more sophisticated than answering machines in that they can:

(a) Answer many phones at the same time.

(b) Store incoming voice messages in personalized mailboxes associated with the user's phone number.

(c) enable users to forward received messages to another voice mailbox

(d) send messages to one or more other user voice mailboxes

(e) add a voice introduction to a forwarded message

(f) store voice messages for future delivery

(g) transfer callers to another phone number for personal assistance

Example : Suppose two employees (Sachin and Rahul) are working on a project. Sachin has some information that Rahul should have, but doesn't want to phone her and talk to her — he just wants to give her the information. Rather than phone him, Sachin calls the voicemail system, logs on with his number and password, and records a message to Rahul in his own voice. He tells the voicemail system to send it to Rahul by keying in his mailbox number (same as his extension) or spelling her name using Touch-tone keys. The message is immediately put in Rahul's voice mailbox without his phone ever ringing. The message waiting light on his phone immediately comes on telling him there is a message. Sachin can send this message just to Rahul, to Rahul and any number of additional employees, or to group lists which contain any number of pre-programmed names and numbers. The same message can be sent to thousands of people.

Voice mail's introduction enabled people to leave lengthy, secure and detailed messages in natural voice, working hand-in-hand with corporate phone systems. The adoption of voicemail in corporations improved the flow of communications and saved huge amounts of money. GE, one of the pioneer adopters of voicemail in all of its offices around the world, claimed that voicemail saved, on average, over $1,100 per year per employee.

(ii) Electronic mail or **e-mail,** is a store and forward method of composing, sending, storing, and receiving messages over electronic communication systems. The term "e-mail applies both to the Internet e-mail system based on the Simple Mail Transfer Protocol (SMTP) and to intranet systems allowing users within one organization to e-mail each other. Often these workgroup collaboration organizations may use the Internet protocols for internal e-mail service.

Most e-mail systems include a rudimentary text editor for composing messages, but many allow you to edit your messages using any editor you want. You then send the message to the recipient by specifying the recipient's address. You can also send the same message to several users at once. This is called *broadcasting*.

(iii) Multimedia based Fax : FAX provides a non-interactive to the user. Today's multimedia are equipped wit FAX-modem cards and the FAX message gets stored electronically in these machines.

(iv) Audio Conferencing : Audio Conferencing service allows multiple participants to converse with each other regardless of their location through the normal fixed line telephone or cellular phone. An audio conference subscriber can add two or more participants in a particular conference. The customers can schedule their audio conferences through the Web or through IVR.

(v) Video Coferencing : Videoconferencing is conducting a conference between two or more participants at different sites by using computer networks to transmit audio and video data. For example, a *point-to-point* (two-person) video conferencing system works much like a video telephone. Each participant has a video camera, microphone, and speakers mounted on his or her computer. As the two participants speak to one another, their voices are carried over the network and delivered to the other's speakers, and whatever images appear in front of the video camera appear in a window on the other participant's monitor.

(vi) Application sharing : Application sharing is a feature that allows two people to work together when one of the individuals doesn't have the same application, or same version of the application. In application sharing, one user launches the application and it runs simultaneously. Both users can input information and otherwise control the application using the keyboard and mouse. Although it appears that the application is running on both PCs, it actually is running on only one, yet each user operates as though the application were running on both PC's. Files associated with the application can be easily transferred, so the results of the collaboration are available to both users immediately. The person who launched the application can lock out the other person from making changes, so the locked-out person sees the application running but cannot control it.

(d) What are Annotations ? Explain the role of annotations in the applications of hypertext, using an example.

Refer to June-2005, Q. No.1(e), Page No.174

(e) What is video conferencing ? List two differences between video conferencing and document conferencing.

Ans. Video conferencing :

Video conferencing is a communication technology that integrates voice and video to connect the remote users with each other via Internet as they are in the same room. Each user needs a computer, microphone, web cam and a broadband Internet connection for participating in the video conferencing. Users at both the ends see and hear each other in real time allowing natural conversation. Many communication companies have been dabbling in video conferencing technology.

Videoconferencing is a very useful technology for telemedicine and telenursing applications, such as diagnosis, consulting, transmission of medical images, etc., in real time. Using VTC, patients may contact nurses and physicians in emergency or routine situations, physicians and other paramedical professionals can discuss cases across large distances. Rural areas can use this technology for diagnostic purposes, thus saving lives and making more efficient use of health care dollars.

Differences b/w Videoconferencing and Document Conferencing are:

(i) Video conferencing can enable individuals in faraway places to have meetings on short notice. Time and money that used to be spent in traveling can be used to have short meetings. Technology such as VOIP can be used in conjunction with desktop videoconferencing to enable face-to-face business meetings without leaving the desktop, especially for businesses with wide-spread offices. The technology is also used for telecommuting, in which employees work from home.

On the other hand, in document conferencing, no face to face communication can be possible.

(ii) Document conferencing is mainly used in the education field. It extends the boundaries of the classroom and reaches out into the community, whereas video conferencing is mainly used in business applications.

(f) Explain the use of the Everest Authoring System. Also list four features of this system.

Ans. Everest Authoring System

Everest is specifically designed to meet the special demands of CBT, WBT and distance learning. Everest is a software tool that helps you create those teaching materials.

CBT is computer-based training, that is, training delivered via a computer. Want to teach a large group of people how to use a new software application? Operate a electrical generation power plant? Properly complete a tax form?

You can do it with CBT, and for less cost than other forms of training. Everest helps you create that CBT.

WBT (web-based training) and distance learning are CBT delivered over the Internet or an intranet. Everest lets you develop your training materials once, then deliver them anywhere via diskette, CD-ROM, intranet, and the Internet. Below are a few of the features and benefits that are found in Everest, *and not in any other authoring tool.*

(i) No conversion necessary to enable Internet/intranet delivery :

ALL other authoring tools force us to convert project into a different, special form in order to deliver it via the Internet. That's extra work for we! After conversion, we have to retest project to make sure it still operates correctly. And, if we discover a problem, we have to edit the original, then regenerate the Internet-format version.

With Everest, we simply post to wer Internet site *the very same files* we would distribute via diskette or CD-ROM. It's so much easier! And, Everest is the only system that can do it.

(ii) Performance :

Everest simply blows the doors off all other authoring tools when it comes to Internet playback speed. Everest is the only system that automatically determines the content the user needs for the next page, and silently downloads it while the user is occupied viewing the current one. When the user advances, the content (text, graphics, animation, sound, interaction, etc.) is often completely pre-downloaded and ready to go.

(iii) Internet Simulator :

Everest is the only authoring system that contains an Internet Simulator. With the simulator, we can test run wer project at a variety of communication speeds (conventional modem, ISDN, DirecPC, intranet, etc.) to observe its performance. We don't even need an Internet connection to use the simulator. It's a fantastic way to make sure wer project performs well in all environments, and Everest is the only tool that has it.

(iv) Minimal Memory :

Other systems, with their plug-in, HTML and Java requirements, consume upwards of 32 to 64 megabytes of memory to play back wer project. That high memory need limits the potential audience for wer projects. Everest requires the least memory: as little as 4M will do.

(g) Describe the Hardware requirement for a multimedia system, with a

suitable diagram.

Refer to Chapter-1, Q. No.8, Page No.7.

Q2. Briefly explain four features of Digital Video. Also explain why it is increasingly used in current applications. Explain two differences in the functions of Digital Video and a CD-ROM.

Ans. Digital video is a type of video recording system that works by using a digital, rather than analog, representation of the video signal. This generic term is not to be confused with the name *DV*, which is a specific type of digital video targeted at the consumer market. Digital video is most often recorded on tape, then distributed on optical discs, usually DVDs. There are exceptions, such as camcorders that record directly to DVDs, Digital camcorders which encode digital video on conventional analog tapes, and camcorders which record digital video on hard disks.

Features:

(i) Digital video can be copied with no degradation in quality. No matter how many generations a digital source is copied, it will be as clear as the original first generation of digital footage.

(ii) Digital video can be processed and edited on an NLE, or non-linear editing station, a device built exclusively to edit video and audio. These frequently can import from analog as well as digital sources, but are not intended to do anything other than edit videos. Digital video can also be edited on a personal computer which has the proper hardware and software.

(iii) Digital video is used outside of movie making. Digital television (including higher quality HDTV) started to spread in most developed countries in early 2000s. Digital video is also used in modern mobile phones and video conferencing systems. Digital video is also used for Internet distribution of media, including streaming video and peer-to-peer movie distribution.

(iv) Digital video cameras come in two different image capture formats: interlaced and progressive scan. Interlaced cameras record the image in alternating sets of lines: the odd-numbered lines are scanned, and then the even-numbered lines are scanned, then the odd-numbered lines are scanned again, and so on. One set of odd or even lines is referred to as a "field", and a consecutive pairing of two fields of opposite parity is called a *frame*.

It is increasingly used in current applications :

In its 18 years of activity MPEG has developed an impressive portfolio of technologies that have created an industry worth several hundreds billion USD.

Moving Picture Experts Group (MPEG) a working group of ISO/IEC in charge of the development of standards for coded representation of digital audio and video. Established in 1988, the group has produced MPEG-1, the standard on which such products as Video CD and MP3 are based, MPEG-2, the standard on which such products as Digital Television set top boxes and DVD are based, MPEG-4, the standard for multimedia for the fixed and mobile web, MPEG-7, the standard for description and search of audio and visual content and MPEG-21, the Multimedia Framework.

MPEG has recently started a number of new standard lines : MPEG-A "Multimedia Application Format" provides application-specific standards by integrating multiple MPEG technologies. MPEG-B, MPEG-C and MPEG-D provide Systems, Video and Audio specific standards, respectively, and MPEG-E "MPEG Multimedia Middleware" or M3W is the latest standard under development that will support download and execution of multimedia applications.

Differences b/w Digital Video and CD-ROM :

(i) Digital video : A progressive scanning digital video camera records each frame as distinct, with both fields being identical. Thus, interlaced video captures twice as many fields per second as progressive video does when both operate at the same number of frames per second. This is one of the reasons video has a "hyper-real" look, because it draws a different image 60 times per second, as opposed to film, which records 24 or 25 progressive frames per second.

CD-ROM : Data is stored on the disc as a series of microscopic indentations ("pits", with the gaps between them referred to as "lands"). A laser is shone onto the reflective surface of the disc to read the pattern of pits and lands. Because the depth of the pits is approximately one-quarter to one-sixth of the wavelength of the laser light used to read the disc, the reflected beam's phase is shifted in relation to the incoming beam, causing destructive interference and reducing the reflected beam's intensity. This pattern of changing intensity of the reflected beam is converted into binary data.

(ii) Digital video : A progressive scanning digital video camera records each frame as distinct, with both fields being identical. Thus, interlaced video captures twice as many fields per second as progressive video does when both operate at the same number of frames per second. This is one of the reasons video has a "hyper-real" look, because it draws a different image 60 times per second, as opposed to film, which records 24 or 25 progressive frames per second.

CD-ROM : The rate at which CD-ROM drives can transfer data from the disc is gauged by a speed factor relative to music CDs: 1x or 1-speed which gives a data transfer rate of 150 kilobytes per second in the most common data format. By increasing the speed at which the disc is spun, data can be transferred at greater rates. For example, a CD-ROM drive that can read at 8x speed spins the disc at up to 4000 rpm (compared to the 500 rpm maximum for 1x speed), giving a transfer rate of 1.2 megabytes per second. Above 12x speed, vibration and heat can become a problem. CD-ROM drives above this speed tackle the problem in several ways.

Q3.(a) What is Macromedia Director? How is it used to develop multimedia?

Refer to Chapter-3, Q. No.6(iii), Page No.66.

(b) Explain the following multimedia file formats.

AVI, BMP, JPEG, MPEG and Wav.

Refer to Chapter-1, Page No.14, 27.

Q4(a). What is a hypertext ? Explain this with a diagram. Also describe three major elements of hypertext?

Refer to Chapter-3, Q. No.2, Page No.57 and Q. No.5, Page No.62

(b) Explain the use of communication technology for multimedia services, with an example.

Communications technology refers to the transmission of data from one computer to another from one device to another. Computer systems refer to an entire working computer. All computer systems consist of various components they include the case of the computer the power supply and many other components.

Communication technology exhibits ever increasing capabilities and corresponding increases in complexity. Students need to learn how to evaluate and develop applications for the new technology.

Today, people spend more time using communication technology than they did twenty years ago. One hypothesis is that people spend more time on their own with their terminals, and less time in face-to-face interaction with other people. This is what happened when television was introduced. The study of the social aspects of technology has often regarded technology as instrumental. This means the use of technology is directed to the achievement of specific results. That is why interaction between users through computers or the telecom network may be described as an instrumental mode of communication (Rasmussen, 1990). It has also been an assumption that interaction with less face-to-face contact between transmitter and receiver renders less social information. The research in the use of telecommunication services has shown that this is not the case. On the contrary, it seems that new communication technologies and services can be regarded as expressive media and be a substitute for and an extension to human-to-human communication in an expressive mode. Access to networks and the use of communication technology is getting increasingly important for people in their personal development as social beings, in attaining their education, and doing their work

Basic multimedia communication technology tends to cover a range of multimedia devices, such as sound cards and graphic cards that allow users to create visual presentations that output sound and /or images. Multimedia generally means the combination of two or more continuous media. The two media are normally audio and video, sound plus moving pictures. For example the digital camera may be used externally to the PC, and allows the user to record images. When connecting the camera to the computer, using a cord, images will be formatted and printed. Various computers have sound cards stored within them, this allows output of sound from speakers through the use of CD's, and other formats that may have music attached to it. Sound cards allow individuals to listen to music played or stored on their computer.

Example : IPTV is a system used to deliver digital television services to the consumers who are registered subscribers for this system. This delivery of digital television is made possible by using Internet Protocol over a broadband connection, usually in a managed network rather than the public Internet to preserve quality of service guarantees. Often, this service is provided together with Video facility on demand. In addition to this, there is provision to include Internet services such as web access and Voice over Internet Protocol (VoIP). In cases when Internet service is also provided, it may be called Triple Play. Today, IPTV is creating headlines all over the world. This mass publicity is the result of numerous instances and stories depicting its humble deployments and its future. IPTV is a very useful system, through which we can receive both TV and video signals along with other multimedia services by means of wer Internet connection. In a nutshell, it is nothing but a broadband connection and a system to deliver various programs of television using the Internet protocol (i.e., language) over computer networks.

Q5(a). Explain the process of collaborative learning using multimedia, with an example.

Ans. The production of multimedia content is time consuming, expensive and often overextending for technical institutions. Just like multimedia a collaborative learning environment integrates text, graphs, audio and video. Experiments have shown that learning using CBT (Computer Based Training) is more time efficient, but for social and emotional reasons the students do not want to disclaim conventional lecturing and a script. Therefore, blended learning will enhance conventional lecturing by the aspects of eLearning. Since 1996, the Department of Integrated Circuit Design complements classical teaching in readings, exercises and labs with multimedia, CBT etc. and the students are enthusiastic.

The following reference model is a framework for CBTs

* the dedicated structure provides a basic and consistent look and feel of our CBTs
* it enables a reduction of production time by a factor of two to four of that of corresponding printed lecture material
* it provides fundamental functionality such as navigation, automatically generated table of contents, management of bookmarks, a history list, text search function, glossary, tooltips

'Computer-Based Training (CBT) is completely different today thanks to advances in hardware and software. For one thing, most CBT products can run on nearly all computers. Moreover, due to the increased accessibility to fast hardware, more companies are developing CBT programs. No longer just for broad topics with universal appeal, such as safety and supervisory skills, today's CBT software also focuses on much more specific topics such as manufacturing quality and productivity improvement.'

E.g. : LogiSyn is a computer based training program (CBT) on chip design and a representative of numerous recently created CBTs using reference model for fast and economic CBT development with Authorware. In order to measure CBT efficiency in support to, or even as a substitution for traditional teaching methods, two extensive evaluations of students participating in lectures on chip- and system design are presented. Furthermore, the concept of a reference model for low-cost low-time production is sketched: CBT design should only take two to four times longer than traditional design of printed lecture material.

(b) Explain the production process of multimedia applications, with an example.

Ans. Production Process of multimedia applications :

After the invention of the printing press, it is the advent of multimedia that has changed the way we learn and comprehend. Integration of multiple media such as visual imagery, text, audio, video, graphics and animation together multiply the impact of the message.

Multimedia differs fundamentally from the conventional media like slides and films. While, conventional media are linear (one event follows another in a sequence), multimedia is non-linear- it has the capacity for branching in different directions and establishing linkages between different sections or components of the programme. The non-linear attribute provides the end-user the luxury of viewing the multimedia presentation at their convenience and pace.

The production of interactive multimedia applications is a complex one, involving multiple steps. This process can be divided into the following phases :

(i) Conceptualization
(ii) Development
(iii) Preproduction
(iv) Production
(v) Postproduction
(vi) Documentation

(i) Conceptualization

The process of making multimedia starts with an "idea" or better described as "the vision"-which is the conceptual starting point. The starting point is ironically the visualization of the ending point - the multimedia experience that the targeted end-user will have. Conceptualization involves identifying a relevant theme for the multimedia title. Criterias like availability of content, how amenable is the content to multimedia treatment and issues like copyright are also to be considered.

(ii) Development :

♣ ***Defining project goals and objectives :***

After a theme has been finalised for a multimedia project, specific goals, objectives and activities matrix must be laid down.

Goals : In multimedia production goals are general statements of anticipated project outcomes, usually more global in scope.

Objectives : Specific statements of anticipated project outcomes.

Activities : These are actions, things done in order to implement an objective. Specific people are responsible for their execution, a cost is related to their implementation and there is a time frame binding their development.

♣ ***Defining the Target Audience :***

A very important element that needs to be defined at this stage is the potential target audience of the proposed title since, this will determine how the content needs to be presented.

(iii) Preproduction :

It is the process of intelligently mapping out a cohesive strategy for the entire multimedia project, including content, technical execution and marketing. Based on the goals and objectives, the three pillars of multimedia viz. Hardware, software and user participation are defined. At this stage the multimedia application. The Production Manager undertakes the following activities:

- Development of the budget control system
- Hiring of all specialists involved in the multimedia application process
- Contracting video and audio production crews and recording studios
- Equipment rental, leasing and purchasing
- Software acquisition and installation
- Planning the research work of the content specialists
- Development of the multimedia application outline, logic flow, scripts and
- Video and audio files production scripts and schedules
- Coordination of legal aspects of production

(iv) Production :

Once all the preproduction activities have been completed, the multimedia application enters the production phase. Activities in this phase include:

- Content Research
- Interface Design
- Graphics Development
- Selection of musical background and sound recording
- Development of computer animation
- Production of digital video
- Authoring

(v) Postproduction :

In this phase, the multimedia application enters the alpha and beta testing process. Once the application is tested and revised, it enters the packaging stage. It could be burned into a CD-ROM or published on the Internet as a website.

(vi) Developing documentation :

User documentation is a very important feature of high-end multimedia titles. This includes instructions for installing, system requirements, developing acknowledgments, copyrights, technical support and other information important for the user.

CS - 66 : MULTIMEDIA
DECEMBER-2006

Note : Question number 1 is compulsory. Attempt any three questions from the rest.

Q1(a). Discuss the hardware requirement of multimedia computers through a diagram. Also explain various hardware requirements.[10]
Refer to Chapter-1, Q. No.8, Page No.7

(b) How does multimedia support e-commerce-based application in business promotion ? [5]

Ans. Electronic commerce is an emerging model of new selling and merchandising tools in which buyers are able to participate in all phases of a purchase decision, while stepping through those processes electronically rather than in a physical store or by phone (with a physical catalog). The processes in electronic commerce include enabling a customer to access product information. Select items to purchase, items securely, and have the purchase setting financially. The multimedia technology may be used for presentation of information through the web for such systems. e.g. The products details can better be presented by use of multimedia like using animation, graphics and sound. A product's presentation can be made better which ease the consumer in understanding the product and make them comfortable with online purchase. E-Commerce applications are available for Business-to-business transactions, Business-to-consumer transaction and for the Intra-Company (Enterprise) transactions

The basic requirements for an e-commerce based application are to develop an on-line catalog and handle transactions on-line. This can manage large product assortment and complete sales at lower costs.

(c) While designing multimedia applications, how does copyright issue plays a crucial role ? [5]

Ans. Simply put, "copyright is a legal device that provides the creator of a work of art or literature, or a work that conveys information or ideas, the right to control how the work is used."

The copyright issue plays a crucial role in designing multimedia applications, by providing 4 basic protections, which are as follows:

(i) The right to make copies of the work.

(ii) The right to sell or otherwise distribute copies of the work.

(iii) The right to prepare new works based on the protected work.

(iv) The right to perform the protected work (such as a stage play or painting) in public.

Emphasis should also be laid on **"What Can be Copyrighted?"**

Tangible, original expression. This means, for example, that a verbal presentation that is not recorded cannot be copyrighted. However, anything that is tangible can be copyrighted. There are three fundamental requirements for something to be copyrighted:

Fixation :

The item must be fixed in some way. The fixation may be just about anything. For example, a piece of paper, a computer disk, a audiotape, or a videotape are all legitimate forms of fixation.

Originality :

The work must be original. Originality includes a novel or a student's e-mail message to a professor. Both are considered examples of original expression. It is not necessary for the work to be completely original. Works may be combined, adapted, or transformed in new ways that would make them eligible for copyright protection.

Minimal Creativity :

The work must include something that is above and beyond the original. Verbatim use is not considered original. Reference to the original work that is used to discuss a new concept would be considered original, however.

Creativity need only be extremely slight for the work to be eligible for protection.

What Cannot be Copyrighted?

(i) Works in the public domain:

(ii) Ideas are in the public domain.

(iii) Facts are in the public domain.

(iv) Words, names, slogans, or other short phrases also cannot be copyrighted. However, slogans, for example, can be protected by trademark law.

(v) Blank forms.

(vi) Government works, which include:

(vii) Judicial opinions.

(viii) Public ordinances.

(ix) Administrative rulings.

(x) Works created by federal government employees as part of their official responsibility.

(xi) Work is for which copyright wasn't obtained or copyright has expired . It is a common misperception that state employees and contractors performing work on behalf of the federal government cannot copyright their work. Unless it is explicitly stated in the contract between the government and a contractor, federal government contractors are permitted to copyright their works as can state employees.

(d) How do scripting languages serve as a useful tool for spreading interactive education ? [5]

Ans. Scripting languages are often the ideal tool if we want to manipulate text, manage jobs, or link together disparate components without resorting to a compiled language like C++ or Objective-C. Scripting languages are a great tool for system administrators, application developers, and pretty much any user who needs to perform complex or repetitive tasks, because they were invented to solve these types of problems more quickly than can be done with general-purpose languages.

The script language specifies multimedia elements, sequencing, hotspots, etc. nearly all the authoring softwares are backed up by powerful scripting programmes. Most of the scripting languages are interpreted instead of compiled. The runtime speed gains over other authoring methods are minimum. It also supports more & complete medias. Most of the scripting languages like PHP, Perl are widely used over Internet and there high use encourages the use of multimedia elements which further accelerates the process of learning which results in spreading of education. Thus, scripting languages serve as a useful tool for spreading interactive education.

(e) How does Quick time software work ? [5]

Refer to Chapter-3, Q. No.10, Page No.70.

Q2(a). Define the term "Multimedia Interface Design". Write at least 7 rules that need to be followed in the design of computer based instruction. [6]

Refer to Chapter-4, Q. No.1,3, Page No.72,73.

(b) Name and describe at least 7 software tools that are related to multimedia application. [4]

Ans. 7 s/w tools that are related to multimedia applications are:

(a) Image Enhance : Free image editor for Windows: bitmap and JPEG images, webcams, digital cameras and scanners, filters and effects.

(c) Construction set : Well-known program for building GIF images and animations. Runs on Windows.

(d) Microsoft GIF Animator : Free program to create animated GIF's, including comments and transparency. Windows.

(e) Maya Personal Learning Edition : 3D graphics and animation program, free for non-commercial use. Runs on Windows and MAC.

(f) VectorDraw Professional is a COM-based component for vector graphics. Aiming at enhancing developers' creativity over the graphics environment who desire full programming control. It is also designed for users with a minimum experience in the graphics background. It gives us the ability to customize all messages and dialogs (local language) and provides over 700 methods, properties and events. UNICODE support is also provided.

(g) MakeGIF 1.4 : MakeGIF creates animated GIFs from command line in batch mode. This program is visual command line processor. We can use pictures created by MS Paint, Adobe Photoshop and dozens of others programs. MakeGIF has optimization tools for making GIFs smaller.

Q3(a). Explain five application areas of multimedia **[5]**

Refer to June-2005, Q. No.3(a), Page No.177.

(b) State any five elements of hypertext **[5]**

Refer to Chapter-3, Q. No.5, Page No.62.

Q4(a). Discuss the planning process of a multimedia application with the help of a figure. Also, Explain the different phases of planning process.

Refer to Chapter-4, Q. No.4, Page No.73. **[6]**

(b) Explain the role of multimedia in entertainment and business. **[4]**

Refer to Chapter-2, Q. No.1, 4, Page No.30,34.

Q5(a). How did multimedia transform the publishing industry? Indicate at least 5 changes. **[6]**

Refer to Chapter-2, Q. No.2, Page No.32.

(b) Explain the use of four communication technologies in multimedia service **[4]**

Refer to Chapter-2, Q. No.3, Page No.33

Feedback is the breakfast of Champions.

Ken Blanchard

You can Help other students.

"Inform any error or mistake in this book."

We and Universe

will reward you for Your Kind act.

Email at : feedback@gullybaba.com

or

WhatsApp on 9350849407

CS-66 : MULTIMEDIA
June, 2007

Note : Question no. 1 is **compulsory**. Answer any **three** questions from the rest.

1. (a) Explain two applications of multimedia. Describe different types of requirements for multimedia computer system that will support your applications.

Ans. With the advancement of technology many applications are evident for the multimedia technology. The advancement of technology has opened up new field for the application development. One such field, which is having tremendous potential and falls under the broad preview of multimedia, is virtual reality, may be the tool of tomorrow. Today, virtual reality is primarily used in applications in entertainment industry but is going to be very useful tool for performing simulative, remote control applications. Virtual reality will have a tremendous impact on on-job training sector. In the following sections we well present a board categorization of multimedia applications.

✓**Entertainment :** The entertainment industry has used this technology the most to create real life like games. Several developers have used graphics, sound animation of multimedia to create variety of games. The special technologies such as virtual reality have made these games just like experiences of real life. One such example is flight simulator which creates a real-life imaging. Many multimedia games are now available on computers. The children can enjoy these experiences, for example, they can drive cars of different variety, fly aircraft, play any musical instrument, golf etc. Multimedia productions are also used in creation of many movies where the multimedia components are mixed with real life pictures to create powerful entertainment atmosphere.

✓**Edutainment :** Edutainment is nothing but educational entertainment. Many computer games with focus on education are now available. Example, in this case is an educational game, which plays various rhymes for little kids. In addition to playing rhymes, the child can paint the pictures, increase or reduce size of various objects etc. Similarly many other edutainment packages, which provide a lot of detailed information for kids are available. Microsoft has produced many such CD-based multimedia such as Sierra, Knowledge Adventure etc. which in addition to play provide some sort of learning component. The latest in this series is a package, which teaches about the computer using games playing. There are many more companies which have specialized in

entertainment sector you may explore the list of such companies on the net.
Now Refer : Refer to Chapter-1, Q.No.-8&10, Page No.-7&12

(b) List any five services that are available to people due to advancement of computing and communication technologies.
Ans. Refer to Chapter-2, Q.No.-3, Page No.-33

(c) Describe Everest Authoring System.
Ans. Refer to June-2006, Q.No.-1(f), Page No.-204

2. Give the template for audio description in multimedia application development.
Ans. The storyboard is a graphical representation of the proposed multimedia project. The storyboard is an extension of ideas presented in the programme script. It is presented with a series of temples used for various purposes. Some of the common templates, which are required to represent a complex application, are :

✓ Logic flow and branching sequence templates
✓ The storyboard template
✓ Animation sequence templates
✓ Button details template
✓ Audio/ video scripting templates

These templates are very useful information and help the developer to keep a production log or history of the work. They also help in keeping track of the production design and help in identifying the design parameters for the application development. Throughout the authoring process, the development team should discuss progress on the multimedia development project with the client or with the members of application target group.
Template for audio description is :
Now Refer : Chapter-4, Page No.-78

3. (a) Describe any two multimedia file formats.
Ans. Refer to Chapter-1, Page No.-14&27

(b) What is digital video? Explain the application of it in the development of multimedia applications.
Ans. Refer to June-2006, Q.No.-2, Page No.-206
& Refer to Chapter-4, Q.No.-10, Page No.-82

4. (a) List any five facilities that need to be supported by a multimedia network for any business industry.

Ans. Refer to Chapter-2, Q.No.-4, Page No.-34

(b) Explain the working and principle of QuickTime.
Ans. Refer to Chapter-3, Q.No.-10, Page No.-70

5. (a) List any five tips for creation of textual information in a multimedia application.

Ans. Textual Information : All multimedia productions contain some amount of text, and even some might contain a large amount of textual matter. The text can have various types of fonts and of varied sizes to suit the professional presentation of the multimedia software.

Five tips for creation of textual information are:

✓ The amount of text put in a multimedia application may be limited to short paragraphs or point wise lists.

✓ The font size should be large enough to be read easily by the multimedia user. For examples, the application, which is to be used for the training of a group the minimum point size, should be 20 points so that it is visible from a distance.

✓ The text styling and formatting should be consistent over the complete application.

✓ The special effects on text should be used to highlight important concepts or messages, but do not overdo them.

✓ Use font types (bitmapped or outlined fonts) and point sizes, which are commonly available. This will make sure that the text looks the same as it was designed.

(b) What is a Sound Card? Explain its working and principle.

Ans. Sound Card : Sound output from a computer has been feature of machines usually used for sending warning error message or games. If better quality and capabilities for sound output or inputs are required, then there must be a device, which can be added to the basic machine. This device is know as Sound Card, which is asses to the basic machine by inserting it in free slot. The most common reason for adding a sound card to a PC is to be able to use multimedia fully by recording and playing the back the digital audio. While selecting an add on sound card, quality of sound from the loudspeaker has to be taken into consideration and the software provided with a sound card should be adequate enough to suit your requirements for handling sound effects in multimedia

Working and principle : Sound cards usually feature a digital-to-analog converter, that converts recorded or generated digital data into an analog format. The output signal is connected to an amplifier, headphones, or external device using standard interconnects, such as a TRS connector or an RCA connector. If the number and size of connectors is too large for the space on the backplate the connectors will be off-board, typically using a breakout box, or an auxiliary backplate. More advanced cards usually include more than one sound chip to provide for higher data rates and multiple simultaneous functionality, e.g. between digital sound production and synthesized sounds (usually for real-time generation of music and sound effects using minimal data and CPU time).

Digital sound reproduction is usually done with multi-channel DACs, which are capable of multiple digital samples simultaneously at different pitches and volumes, or optionally applying real-time effects like filtering or distortion. Multi-channel digital sound playback can also be used for music synthesis when used with a digitized instrument bank, typically a small amount of ROM or Flash memory containing samples corresponding to MIDI instruments. A contrasting way to synthesize sound on a PC uses "audio codecs", which rely heavily on software for music synthesis, MIDI compliance, and even multiple-channel emulation. This approach has become common as manufacturers seek to simplify the design and the cost of sound cards.

Most sound cards have a line in connector for signal from a cassette tape recorder or similar sound source. The sound card digitizes this signal and stores it (under control of appropriate matching computer software) on the computer's hard disk for storage, editing, or further processing. Another common external connector is the microphone connector, for use by a microphone or other low level input device. Input through a microphone jack is often used by speech recognition software or for Voice over IP applications.

CS-66 : MULTIMEDIA
December, 2007

Note : Question number 1 in **compulsory.** Attempt any **three** questions from the rest.

1. (a) Explain the need and development in multimedia applications. List five basic hardware and software requirements for any multimedia system.

Ans. Multimedia is an integration of various media, which convey the information with computing technology. Various media such as text, graphics, animation, sound, audio, video etc.

One of the key features of multimedia is "**Interactivity**". Hypermedia and virtual reality applications are based on multimedia systems. Hypermedia extends the **media-oriented features** of multimedia systems by the concept of hyperlinks, i.e.; logical structures that provide means for organizing media objects in a flexible, logically coherent, network-oriented and non-sequential way. Virtual reality extends the interaction **oriented features** of multimedia by the concept of cyberspace, i.e. modeling objects and their behaviour in virtual environments. The basic need of multimedia, which uses sound, graphics, and text etc. is the interactive feature of multimedia.

The basic components of multimedia are :

(i) The text can be used for adding emphasis.

(ii) Graphics provides a visual impact.

(iii) Voice tries to enhance a presentation.

(iv) The animation can be used effectively for attracting attention.

(v) The video part of multimedia can be used as a powerful communicator providing clear cut instruction.

In general, by using multimedia in the applications, we can produce applications that are:

- **Efficient :**

We can replace information you read with information you can see and hear, such as a video clip.

- **Direct :**

You can deliver information using the best medium, such as a language teaching applications that plays a native speaker's voice to demonstrate pronunciation.

- **Interactive :**

It is easier to construct genuine and multilevel user interaction with pictures and sounds than with plain text only.

In a complete sense, pictures, graphics, text and sound is the essence of multimedia and it provides the user friendly environment with most flexible interactive facilities.

Now, Refer to Chapter-1, Q.No.-8, Page No-7

Now, Refer to Chapter-1, Q.No.-10, Page No-12

(b) What is animation? Explain the use of any three types of animation in multimedia.

Ans. Animation : The word animation comes from a latin word Anima meaning to breath. If anything breaths means it has life & thus animation means to bring life i.e. to make or give moments to any object or thing. This can be any object created on computer. An animation is just a continuous series of still images that are displayed in a sequence. There are mainly two types of animation used in multimedia, namely, 2D and 3D animation. 2D animation also known as cell (pixel based) animation, is the most common kind of animation, where flat images are drawn one frame at a time. This process is very time consuming but result obtained is spectacular in nature. Computer animation has increased the efficiency, and enhanced the results of cell animation with introduction of wide ranges of colour and speed. In 3-D animation mathematical model of 3-D object is created to realistically portray with depth. Now it has become a common media element in film, video and multimedia packages. 3-D animations follow mainly three steps; modelling, animation and rendering.

(a) Morphing : Morphing takes two images and seamlessly changes one image to another. The second image actually seems to grow out of the first one. Morphing can also be used to show the pace of changes more clearly than photos. Warping is variation of the morphing where one image is used to show various changes that take place. It uses the key points of one image to create different effects, instead of mixing up two images.

(b) In 3-D animation mathematical model of 3-D object is created to realistically portray with depth. Now it has become a common media element in film, video and multimedia packages. 3-D animations follow mainly three steps; modelling, animation and rendering.

(c) In a 2-D animation an object can move up (called Y axis) and sideways (called X axis). But in the case of a 3-D model, a third axis is used; depth or the Z-axis. Once an object is created along these three axes, colour, shading and light source can be added to the image to make it more realistic.

There are endless examples of the use of animation. Two examples where it is used are following :

In Analysis and Understanding

British Telecom for example uses a sophisticated program that plots on a map of the U.K. the density of telephone fault reports using different colours. When a storm was plotted on top of this map, and the whole system was animated it could be seen that the density of the faults increased at areas from which the storm had just passed. It would have been very difficult to visualise this in a different way.

Astronomers also rely on computers to do animations of high speed jets penetrating different gases in order to determine why a few galaxies flare dramatically. This research has given out valuable information about why some galaxies flare into broad plumes and why some others remain extremely straight and narrow.

In Teaching

On of the most difficult things in teaching, is communicating ideas effectively. This might be very difficult in complex situations, and here is where animation might help to convey information. For example there are many programs that show the planetary system in action in three dimensions - an idea that would be very difficult to grasp otherwise.

(c) Explain how multimedia can have impact on advertising of a product with the changing environment of mobile technology.

Ans. Multimedia is natural for advertising - natural images, special effects, animation, 3-D. There are three main areas of current opportunity: CD-ROM, the Internet, and customer point-of-contact use of multimedia.

As manufacturers seek to gain greater competitive advantage through the application of Information Technology there will be need of increasing use of Multimedia and high networks.

The multimedia nature of the Internet is suitable for high-impact advertising. Now a days, we have the facility to access or surf the Internet on our mobile phones. Specialized phones are also launched my some companies to provide full access to Internet services. The Internet has become an integral part of the media mix for many advertisers, and new forms of advertising have filled the World Wide Web landscape, including animated banner ads, sponsor logos, interstitials, "advertorials," "advertainment," and 3-D visualization. Where multimedia is highly used to make all these animated banner ads, sponsor logos, interstitials, "advertorials," "advertainment," and 3-D visualization which enchances the quality of advertising of a product by leaving an impact in the minds of the Internet users. Being a modern way of advertising it results in leaving good views about the quality of the product which is advertised on the Internet by using Multimedia. Special protocol for the mobile network is deviced called as WAP(wireless application protocol) which has now completely changed the Internet access scenario over mobile phones. It has given a good boost to Internet services. And now multimedia access through WAP (a type of mobile technology) has given a really good chance to the companies to advertise their products over the mobile networks. Now the advertisements of the products has reached in the hands of the customers (through mobile phone / other hand held devices like palmtop, laptop etc.).

(d) Explain five features of Image Q.

Ans. Refer to Chapter-3, Q.No.-9, Page No.-69

(e) What is collaborative learning? Explain two advantages of collaboration and multimedia learning.

Ans. Today, multimedia-learning materials are available on various platforms. Just like multimedia a collaborative learning environment integrates text, graphs, audio and video. However, the traditional CBT systems operate in standalone mode that is user interactivity is restricted to the CBT only, whereas the possibility to interact with instructors and peers is offered by collaboration using multimedia communication. Thus, by using communication network and collaborative learning in groups is possible.

The production of multimedia content is time consuming, expensive and often overextending for technical institutions. Just like multimedia a collaborative learning environment integrates text, graphs, audio and video. Experiments have shown that learning using CBT (Computer Based Training) is more time efficient, but for social and emotional reasons the students do not want to disclaim conventional lecturing and a script. Therefore, blended learning will enhance conventional lecturing by the aspects of eLearning. Since 1996, the Department of Integrated Circuit Design complements classical teaching in readings, exercises and labs with multimedia, CBT etc. and the students are enthusiastic.

Collaboration - Advantages :

- the dedicated structure provides a basic and consistent look and feel of our CBTs
- it enables a reduction of production time by a factor of two to four of that of corresponding printed lecture material
- it provides fundamental functionality such as navigation, automatically generated table of contents, management of bookmarks, a history list, text search function, glossary, tooltips

Multimedia learning - advantages :

- ➢ Very interactive
- ➢ Very colourful & attractive.
- ➢ Made more powerful by adding sound & video where needed.
- ➢ Easy to browse through the content.
- ➢ Its fun and easy just like game.
- ➢ Visual presentation helps to remember more.
- ➢ Entertains you even when you are learning that is edutainment.

Thus we can see that collaboration and multimedia learning definitely helps in education.

2. (a) What is a copyright? Explain three reasons for the need of copyright for multimedia applications.

Ans. The oxford dictionary defines copyright as the 'exclusive right given by law for a certain term of years to an author, composer etc. to print, publish and sell copies of his original work. Copyright means the exclusive right to do or authorise others to do certain act in relation to 1) literacy, dramatic or musical work, 2) artistic work, 3) cinematograph film, and 4) sound recording, the exclusive right for doing the respective acts extends not only to the whole of the work but to any substantial part thereof or to any translation or adoption thereof.

Need of copyright for multimedia applications :

(i) It is needed to protect the author of the genuine work from exploitation. Copyright subsist only in prescribed form not only in ideas i.e. unless preserve form to store either writing, print or store in cd or cassette, it must be tangible form not intangible form. Computer programmes and databases are regarded as literacy work under the act u/s 2(o) 'computer' include any electronic device having information processing, capabilities. 'Computer programme' is a set of instruction expressed in words, codes, schemes, or in any other form, including a machine readable medium, capable of causing a computer to perform it include both programme and source code. Thus all multimedia work covered under copyright act if originally created by the author and in protected form-not idea in mind. But apply such idea on computer or on paper or print them data form or expression form. So there is no issue as all computer work if original print or expressible form then comes in copyright act.

(ii) The copyright issue plays a crucial role in designing multimedia applications, by providing 4 basic protections, which are as follows:

- The right to make copies of the work.
- The right to sell or otherwise distribute copies of the work.
- The right to prepare new works based on the protected work.
- The right to perform the protected work (such as a stage play or painting) in public.

(b) Why is the distribution of multimedia required in case of networks? Explain two methods of distribution of multimedia software.

Ans. Distribution of Multimedia : Once all the media elements are combined together using authoring software they are bundled into package and stored in various storage media for distribution. Creating multimedia package for various platforms is one the most crucial stages that multimedia development procedure faces today. There are many platforms available for multimedia, each of which has their own advantages. To work with full potential, multimedia packages need to be available in as many platforms as possible. The main storage media used to store multimedia package is the CD-ROM and DVD. Distribution of Multimedia can also be made through Word Wide Web also.

(i) CD-ROM : Multimedia uses digitised audio and video not only take huge amount of storage space, but also required high speed storage media, which can large amount of data back and forth quickly to keep audio and video playing recording smoothly.

Because of this requirement most of multimedia packages user hard disk drive, which offer high speed, high data throughput, and plenty of storage devices like 40 GB or more. Sometimes two or more hard disk drives are used as array to work together so that they act like a single hard drive.

Magnetic optical disk media offer large amount of storage in a durable package. CDROM is widely used for multimedia storage as it has an amazing amount of flexibility and potential as multimedia storage and distribution medium. One CD-ROM can hold up to one and half hour of digital audio or around 700 to 750 MB of computer data for that matter.

As far CD-ROM is concerned, the main feature of it is huge storage space and very high immunity from damage. It is easy locate different pieces of data in CD-ROMs, so that comparatively simple software can be used guide the laser beam to find what is required.

CD-ROM is the primary off-line medium for digital advertising. On-line advertising can reach a wider audience, just as broadcast television reaches more of the population than individual newspapers and magazines. There are many on-line information services, including America Online, CompuServe, and the Microsoft Network, but it is the Internet that is the fastest-growing target for advertising in many forms. Some companies use vivid World Wide Web pages with graphics, video, and music as a sort of giant billboard that will, they hope, immediately attract the attention of the estimated (or, rather, guessed-at) 30 million people who surf the Internet and the hundreds of millions they believe will be doing so within a few years.

DVD : DVD is the cohesion of multimedia and digital video player, movies and interactivity. By employing the latest advances in digital technology, DVD can hold up 25 times more digital info than a CD-ROM and DVD can be used to create innovative cutting edge video-discs with all sorts of data including director's cuts, photo galleries, interview with actors in fact practically anything today's video producers can imagine. Using DVD technology. Besides multilingual capabilities of DVD the producers can create a limitless range of interactive titles, instead of watching a video in the linear fashion as with traditional videotape.

Originally it was felt that DVD is the short for Digital Video Disc now it is more commonly referred to as "digital Versatile Disc" as it has many potential applications than video. The new multimedia storage format of choice, DVD is more that just a high quality video formatting DVD-ROM can combine hours of stunning video, audio and music with computer data and instructions to offer high-capacity media-rich games with exceptional video quality, specialized educational and entertainment programs, software libraries, and training programs, digitized photo collections and, of course, high quality interactive encyclopedias and interactive experiences, all on a single disk. Even today's most popular games consoles have DVD at the core of their technology. A single-sided, single-layer DVD can contain up to 133 minutes of video enough to handle 95% of all movies, without the interruption of flipping the disc over changing discs. DVD was designed to be the next generation of home video entertainment. DVDs offer digital sound and picture and high video resolution. However, our object is to use it as rich multimedia source.

3. (a) List and describe five multimedia file formats.
Ans. Refer to Chapter-1, Q.No.-12, Page No.-14

(b) Explain how communication technology is used for providing multimedia applications.
Ans. Refer to Chapter-2, Q.No.-3, Page No.-33
Now, Refer to June-2006, Q.No.-4(b), Page No.-208

4. (a) What is simulation? Explain the category of simulation with example.
Ans. Refer to Dec-2004, Q.No.-3(c), Page No.-191
& Refer to June-2005, Q.No.-3(b), Page No.-178

(b) Explain the role of multimedia in E-commerce applications.
Ans. Refer to Dec-2004, Q.No.-5(c), , Page No.-193

5. (a) Compare the features of CD-ROM and DVD-ROM along with their usage.
Ans. Refer to Chapter-1, Q.No.-9, Page No.-11,
June-2001, Q.No.1(a), Page No.-155,
& Refer to June-2005, Q.No.-2(a), Page No.-178

(b) What is MEDNET? Explain two basic services provided by MEDNET.
The Biomedical and multimedia information Technology (BMIT) group is an interdepartmental and interdisciplinary group of excellence. It has a strong

research focus in the application of computer science and information technology in biomedicine and multimedia.

Through its research, this group seeks to gain a better understanding of information science and technology as applied to biomedical and multimedia problems and to facilitate the transfer of the knowledge gained for the benefit of our health care system and multimedia industry.

The medical application is MEDNET. Mednet provides the following services :

- A real time monitoring and multiparty consultation.
- Collaboration during brain surgery.

Mednet is being developed at University of Pittsburgh Medical Centre. The intra-operative monitoring places a real time control about the condition of the patient. Mednet is different from the other picture taking teleconferencing system as it provides real time monitoring and collaboration.

The term "collaboration" is one of the commonly used term in multimedia application. The verbal meaning of the collaboration is the actual meaning in the context of multimedia, that is collectively doing a particular work but for this collaborative work physical presence may not be required. How it can be achieved by mednet as in most of the surgeries the anesthesiologist, the system and other supporting staff have to be present for patient.

CS – 66: MULTIMEDIA
June, 2008

Note : Question number 1 is **compulsory**. Answer any **three** questions from the rest.

Q1. (a) What is morphing? How is it similar to/different from warping?
Refer to Q.No.-1(a), Page No.-106

(b) What is the method of storing images in vector format? Explain its advantages.

Ans. Other formats for image is vector or object oriented format. In this format, an image is formed as a set of straight or curved lines instead of dots. A line can be represented by a mathematical equation, which can be stored as a set of binary codes. This form of coding is potentially more economical for disk storage space. There are several technology and sources to produce images or graphics for multimedia package.

Advantages: We can create it by using Paint Program, by scanning photographs using a scanner, or by drawing artwork. We can generate 3D graphics and animation using various sophisticated softwares.

We can combine these images using image manipulation programs that can combine many different types of graphic files, to create new images. Defined through mathematical expressions and are resolution-independent and scalable.

(c) What is Sampling? How is it used in digital video? Explain.

Ans. Refer to Page No.-17

(d) Differentiate between Scenario based and Knowledge based simulations.

Ans. Refer to Page No.-106, 107

(e) How does the scripting language program facilitate multimedia creation?

Ans. Authoring software offers the ability to write scripts for software to build features that are not supported by the software itself. Script language programs create multimedia presentations from a series of programming style commands linked together in a word processing typescript.

The scripting languages are closet in form to traditional programming. The scripting language specifies (by filename) multimedia elements, sequencing, hotspots, synchronization, etc. A powerful, object-oriented scripting language is presently available with many authoring systems. In such languages, the program editing of elements (still graphics, video, audio, etc.) tends to be minimal or non-existent. The scripting takes longer time in development (it takes longer to code an individual interaction), but generally allow more powerful interactivity. Since most scripting languages are interpreted instead of compiled, the run time speed gains over other authoring methods are minimal.

(f) Explain the 'compressors' and 'timing mechanism' of Quick Time Software.

Ans. Quick Time has many features but the two most important are its compressors and its timing mechanism. The compressors enable the program to reduce the frames to a manageable size, so the computer can stream the information from the disk. The timing mechanism ensure that multiple tracks maintain synchronization.

Without compressors, the large amount of data would prevent even the fastest hard disk from playing a movie by the time the computer had the first from the disks the same for displaying the frame would have passed. Even with compression, Quick Time may not be capable of playing all the frames in the movie.

The computer needs some kind of timing mechanism that keeps video and sound synchronized. Timing is particularly important when the people are displayed speaking on the screen, as without synchronization their lips won't move in synch with the sound. Quick Time fulfills both needs.

Q2. List the hardware and software components essential for professional multimedia development. Also, justify the purpose and need of each of the hardware components.

Refer to Chapter-1, Q.No.-8, Page No.-7

Q3. (a) What is hypertext? Give its applications in teaching of foreign languages.

Refer to Q.No.-2, Page No.-57, 58 and Q.No.-4(d), Page No.-59, 60, 61

(b) What are the different functions provided by most of the authoring software? Explain.

Refer to Q.No.-11,12, Page No.-84

Q4. (a) "Multimedia is stronger than multiple-media as it is interactive in nature." Comment and justify the statement.

Refer to Chapter-2, Q.No.-8, Page No.-39

(b) Explain the important features of Flash Software.
Refer to Q.No.-6(a), Page No.-65

Q5. (a) What is meant by built-in programming language? Give any two examples of built-in programming languages in context to hypertext systems.
Ans. Refer to Page No.-65

(b) Explain the processes involved in planning of multimedia application.
Ans. Refer to Q.No.-4, Page No.-73

CS – 66: MULTIMEDIA
December, 2008

Note : Question number 1 is **compulsory**. Answer any **three** questions from the rest.

Q1. Discuss how multimedia can be used for the following application areas :

(i) Website of any Advertising Agency

Ans. Some companies use vivid World Wide Web pages with graphics, video, and music as a sort of giant billboard that will, they hope, immediately attract the attention of the estimated (or, rather, guessed-at) 30 million people who surf the Internet and the hundreds of millions they believe will be doing so within a few years.

If you really want to make an impact and create something truly extraordinary with your website design, then using multimedia at every stage of development is the best way to achieve this. Multimedia is the use of video, sound, music and animation, and while there are a number of website design technologies available to provide a variety of different applications, the most commonly used are Flash, Shockwave, RealMedia and Java.

Also Refer Q.No.-4(b), Page No.-192

(ii) Website of any Educational Institution

Refer 1(i) above. Also refer Page No.-92, Point (i)

More and more educational institutions are turning to interactive learning through multimedia. This has helped in international education and training of masses.

(b) What is QuickTime ? Who developed this product ? Discuss the importance of this product and how does it work.

Refer Q.No.-10, Page No.-70

(c) Discuss the following types of authoring tools along with their purpose of use:

(i) Time-based

(ii) Icon-based

(iii) Theatrical-based

(iv) Card-based

Refer to Q.No.-12, Page No.-84

Q2(a) "Some hypertext systems have built-in programming languages, so that one can customize the system to one's specific needs." With the

help of an example product, illustrate the features.
Refer to Page No.-65

(b) Discuss the following examples of multimedia pedagogues:
(i) Computer-based CD tutors
Refer to Q.No.-4, Page No.158

(ii) Applet-based practicals (simulations)
Ans. A wide range of Java class libraries are available for graphics and animation and for creating and maintaining applet GUIs.
JavaTM is a multi-threaded language, which may be exploited by multimedia applets to:
- synchronize media like sound and video sequences;
- improve performance, since media threads anticipated to be needed soon can be loaded in parallel;
- implement multi-user applications, using a thread per user.

We can develop many applet based practicals to
Applet-based practicals (simulations) students to configure models, run simulations, and analyse the results directly from within a web page. Such applets can be implemented completely inside the any supporting framework itself. Following Figure shows the results of an applet-based simulation of a simplified model of loading trucks in a container terminal.

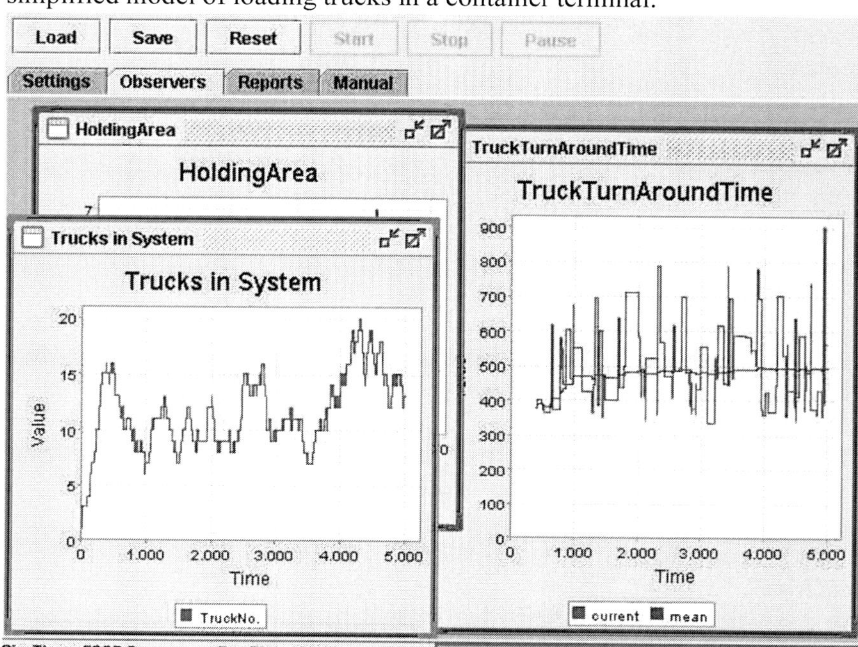

Figure : Java applet showing a simulation of trucks in a container terminal Simulation applets can be used for reference models as well as for exercises in running a simulation and the subsequent statistical analysis of simulation results.

Q3. Explain, how the following multimedia components are created and how are these used in E-learning applications :
(i) Pictures/Photographs
(ii) 3-D Graphics
(iii) Audio
(iv) Digital Video

Refer to Q.No.-12, Page No.-14. Also refer Page No.-24.

Q4. Define the term "storyboard" in the context of multimedia project. Mention the features of it and also design simple storyboard template for any instance of an application of your choice.

Refer to Q.No.-7, Page No.-76

Q5. Describe the following file format and mention the related s/w through which we can work with them:

(i) AVI

Audio Video Interleave, known by its acronym AVI, is a multimedia container format introduced by Microsoft in November 1992 as part of its Video for Windows technology. AVI files can contain both audio and video data in a file container that allows synchronous audio-with-video playback. Like the DVD video format, AVI files support multiple streaming audio and video, although these features are seldom used. Most AVI files also use the file format extensions developed by the Matrox OpenDML group in February 1996. These files are supported by Microsoft, and are unofficially called "AVI 2.0".

(ii) JPG

The name "JPEG" stands for Joint Photographic Experts Group, the name of the committee that created the standard. The group was organized in 1986, issuing a standard in 1992, which was approved in 1994 as ISO 10918-1. JPEG is distinct from MPEG (Moving Picture Experts Group), which produces compression schemes for video.

The JPEG standard specifies both the codec, which defines how an image is compressed into a stream of bytes and decompressed back into an image, and the file format used to contain that stream.

(iii) MOV

We can work with this type of file in QuikTime Movie Software. We can choose “Save As QuickTime Movie” option from the menu to save the file in .mov format / extension. - This option will save the embedded video in a *.mov file format no matter what the original encoding is/was.

(iv) PCX

PCX is an image file format developed by the ZSoft Corporation of Marietta, Georgia, USA. It was the native file format for PC Paintbrush (PCX = “PC Paintbrush Exchange”) and became one of the first widely accepted DOS imaging standards.

The PCX is a device-independent raster image format; the file header stores information about the display hardware (screen resolution, color depth and palette information, bit planes and so on) separately from the actual image information, allowing the image to be properly transferred and displayed on computer systems with different hardware. PCX files commonly store palette-indexed images ranging from 2 or 4 colors to 16 and 256 colors, although the format has been extended to record true-color (24-bit) images as well.

(v) WAV

WAV (or WAVE), short for Waveform audio format, is a Microsoft and IBM audio file format standard for storing an audio bitstream on PCs. It is the main format used on Windows systems for raw and typically uncompressed audio. The usual bitstream encoding is the Pulse Code Modulation (PCM) format. Support for WAV files was built into Windows 95 making it the de facto standard for sound on PCs. WAV sound files end with a.wav extension and can be played by nearly all Windows applications that support sound.

CS-66 : MULTIMEDIA
June, 2009

Note: Question number **1** is **compulsory**. Attempt **any three** questions from the rest.

Q1. (a) Explain, how are scenario based simulations different from knowledge based simulations.
Refer to June-2001, Page-159, 1st Para.

(b) Discuss how multimedia can be used for the following application areas:
(i) Fashion Industry
Ans. The word fashion is associated with glamour and excitement and has given rise to a whole industry. As the fashion industry is fast paced, so people with genuine interest in the fashion market and a burning desire to excel can thrive in this field. The industry offers a whole lot of new careers and is not limited to designing clothes as is commonly believed.
Fashion careers exist in the areas of art and design, communication and presentation as well as in business and technology.
The power of Multimedia usage in this industry can help much to excel this industry. Fashion designers create designs for clothes, accessories, footwear, lingerie, sportswear, children's garments, etc. on computers by using various multimedia tools. 3D view of dresses is possible by multimedia. Some high profile designers cater to individual customers or produce their own collections or work for fashion firms.

(ii) Flight and Aviation Institute
Ans. Multimedia is the best application for flight and aviation institute with the help of multimedia the institute can provide the information to the trainer in details using the multimedia system like sound, graphics, animation, video, audio and many more multimedia system that is available in information technology. Multimedia often seen at places like airports and stores is the information kiosk. Before interactive technology because widespread, these kiosks consisted of a variety of maps and perhaps an attendant who could offer more specific information. Today, **many kiosks are fully automated and interactive**. Users select from a series of onscreen choices to find the information they need.
Multimedia has the same goals and uses as other types of media. It disperses information in the most clear, helpful way possible. As people become comfortable with multimedia, they will find that it is an essential tool that can make their lives easier.

(c) How does QuickTime Software work?
Refer to Chapter-3, Q.No.-10, Page-70

(d) Differentiate between video conferencing and document conferencing. How does video conferencing play an important role in Management?
Refer to June-2004, 5 and 6th Point, Page-100

(e) Explain the role of annotations in the applications of hypertext, using an example.
Refer to June-2005, Q.No.-1(e), Page-174,

Q2. (a) Explain the production and distribution phases of multimedia development.
Refer to Chapter-1, Q.No.-13, Page-18

(b) What is hypertext? Give two applications of hypertext. Explain any five elements of hypertext.
Refer to Chapter-3, Q.No.-5, Page-62

Q3. Differentiate between the following:
(a) E mail and Voice mail
Refer to Chapter-2, Q.No.-4, 1 and 2nd Point, Page-34

(b) Vector image and Bitmap image
Refer to Chapter-1, Q.No-12, (3) & (4) Point, Page-14

(c) CD ROM and DVD ROM
Refer to Chapter-1, Q.No.-9, Page-11

(d) Animation and Digital Video
Refer to Chapter-4, 1st Point, Page-83

Q4. Design a multimedia based on-line education system. Prepare logic flow chart and story board template for this system.
Ans. Refer to Chapter-4, Q. No.-13 and 14, Page-85 to 88

Q5. (a) Explain the role of multimedia in knowledge transfer using an example.
Refer to June-2005, Q.No.-3(a), Page-177, 178

(b) Explain five major challenges for the multimedia developers.
Refer to Dec-2003, last Para, Page-107

CS-66 : MULTIMEDIA
December, 2009

Note: Question number **1** is **compulsory**. Attempt **any three** questions from the rest.

Q1. (a) What is Macromedia Director? How is it used to develop multimedia?
Refer to Chapter-3, Q.No.6(iii), Page-66

(b) Discuss how multimedia can be used for the following application areas:
(i) Health Awareness Department
(ii) On-line Entertainment Company
Refer to Chapter-1, Q.No.12, Page-44

(c) Write the hardware requirements of a multimedia Computer. Also, explain the use and importance of each hardware.
Refer to Dec-2004, Q.No.1 (d), Page-184

(d) What type of application development is best suited for Everest Authoring system? Explain the important features of this system.
Refer to June-2005, Q.No.1 (d), Page-173

Q2. (a) Explain how multimedia supports the medical collaboration and consultation system.
Refer to Dec-2007, Q.No.4 (b), Page-229

(b) How do scripting languages serve as a useful tool for spreading interactive education?
Refer to Dec-2006, Q.No.1 (d), Page-215

Q3. Design a multimedia based on-line advertisement website, which advertises for different products like mobile, jewellery, garments, food item, etc. Prepare branching sequence template and story board template for this system.
Refer to Chapter-4, Q.No.7, Page-76

Q4. (a) How is multimedia used in business Communication? Explain with an example.
Refer to Chapter-2, Page-31

(b) Explain the use of communication technology for multimedia services, with the help of an example.

Refer to Chapter-2, Q.No.3, Page-33

Q5. (a) Which multimedia software is best suited for Synchronizing sound tracks with video tracks? Write its features.

Refer to Chapter-3, Q.No.8, Page-68

(b) Write short notes on the following:

(i) Cardiac Tutor

Refer to Dec-2003, Page-107

(ii) Video Conferencing

Refer to June-2004, Q.No.-3 5th Point, Page-100

(iii) Quick Time

Refer to June-2004, Q.No.-4 (a), Page-103

(iv) Video Linguist

Refer to Chapter-3, Page-60 & 61

CS-66 : MULTIMEDIA
June, 2010

Note: *Question number 1 is* ***compulsory****. Attempt* ***any three*** *questions from the rest.*

Q1. (a) What is e-learning? Explain any five features of it. Is there any role for Multimedia to play in the success of e-learning? If yes, explain.
E-learning or CBT (Computer-Based Training), or IBT (Internet-Based Training) or WBT (Web-Based Training) comprises all forms of electronically supported learning and teaching. The Information and communication systems, whether networked or not, serve as specific media to implement the learning process. The term will still most likely be utilized to reference out-of-classroom and in-classroom educational experiences via technology, even as advances continue in regard to devices and curriculum.

E-learning is essentially the computer and network-enabled transfer of skills and knowledge. E-learning applications and processes include Web-based learning, computer-based learning, virtual classroom opportunities and digital collaboration.

Five features : (i) Employers and learners cannot afford time off to take a class. Travel itself makes traditional training too expensive and disruptive. eLearning is revolutionising the training world and the ability to erase geographical boundaries is one of the most popular features.

(ii) Novice friendly, yet still has underlying extensibility for complex interaction types.

(iii) eLearning is not only suitable for computer based courses. eLearning courses are now available in every possible subject including management and supervisory skills such as customer service, negotiation skills and time management.

(iv) Short learning curve for new content developers.

(v) eLearning is easy and engaging. It is available to everyone at any time.

There is main **role of multimedia in the success of e-learning**, or we can say that todays e-learning is based on multimedia. As elearning content is delivered via the Internet, intranet/extranet, audio or video tape, satellite TV, and CD-ROM. It can be self-paced or instructor-led and includes media in the form of text, image, animation, streaming video and audio (multimedia).

(b) Explain the process of designing a Multimedia interface.
Refer to Page No.-72, Chapter-4, Q.No.-1

(c) What is Video Conferencing? What is document conferencing? What are annotations? Explain the role of each of the above in Multimedia applications.

Refer to Page No.-5, Now Refer to Page No.-174

Q2. (a) Explain the features of a scripting language. Also, explain the role played by scripting languages in Multimedia.

Refer to Page No.-215, Q.No.-1(d)

(b) Explain any five features of the Everest Authoring System.

Refer to Page No.-204, Q.No.-1(f)

Q3. (a) Explain any five features of QuickTime software.

Refer to Page No.-70 for two features.

(iii) Editing clips through the cut, copy and paste functions, merging separate audio and video tracks, and freely placing the video tracks on a virtual canvas with the options of cropping and rotation.

(iv) Saving and exporting (encoding) to any of the codecs supported by QuickTime. QuickTime 7 includes presets for exporting video to a video-capable iPod, Apple TV, and the iPhone.

(v) Saving existing QuickTime movies from the web directly to a hard disk drive.

(b) What is extension of avi? What is extension of wav? What are the differences between them?

Refer to Page No.-236, Q.No.-5(i) & (v)

Q4. (a) Explain the role of Multimedia in communication.

Refer to Page No.-30, Chapter-2, Q.No.-1

(b) Explain any five features of Macromedia Director.

Refer to Page No.-66, Q.No.-6(iii)

Q5. Explain any 10 elements of Hypertext.

Refer to Page No.-62, Q.No.-5

CS-66 : MULTIMEDIA
December, 2010

Note: *Question number 1 is* **compulsory**. *Attempt* **any three** *questions from the rest.*

Q1. (a) What is MIDI? Explain the applications of MIDI in multimedia.
Refer to Page No.-21, Chapter-1, Q.No.-16

(b) Discuss how multimedia can be used for the following application areas:
(i) E – learning.
Refer to Page No.-236, Q.No.-3. Also refer Q1(a), June-2010

(ii) E – commerce.
Refer to Page No.-36, Q.No.-5

(c) List the basic elements of hypertext. Describe the use of links in hypertext based systems.
Refer to Page No.-62, Q.No.-5

(d) How does the scripting language programs facilitate multimedia application creation? List any two scripting languages which supports multimedia features.
Refer to Page No.-231, Q.No.-1
Now Refer to Refer to Page No.-215, Q.No.-1(d)

Q2. (a) Explain the processes involved in planning of multimedia applications.
Refer to Page No.-73, Q.No.-4

(b) Differentiate between Scenario – based and Knowledge – based simulations.
Refer to Page No.-159, First Para

Q3. (a) Explain the "compressions" and "timing mechanism" features of Quick time software.
Refer to Page No.-232, June-2008, Q.No.-1(f)

(b) List and discuss the minimum hardware and software requirements for a digital multimedia workstation/computer system.

Refer to Q.No.-8, and Q.No.-10 of Chpater-1

Q4. (a) Give the basic use of the followings multimedia software:

(i) Photoshop

Refer to Page No.-68

(ii) Designer

Used to create various designs with various effects.

(iii) Photo Magic

Magic Photo easily blends your digital photo onto another picture (a landscape picture etc). You can also add some pretty frames, cliparts, cartoon pictures or write your comments on the photo to make it more beautiful and attractive.

(iv) Director

Authoring multimedia for CD-ROM & the Web.

(v) Sound Edit.

Sound capture and editing for multimedia, music or the net.

(b) List and explain the four basic functions provided by any of the Authoring s/w. differentiate between Icon-base Authoring tools and Theatrical Authoring tools.

Refer to Page No.-84, Q.No.-11, and 12

Q5. Write short notes on:

(a) Copyright issues and their management while designing Multimedia Application.

Refer to Page No.-80, Q.No.-8

(b) Program Storyboard.

Refer to Page No.-76, Q.No.-7

CS-66 : MULTIMEDIA
June, 2011

Note: *Question number 1 is **compulsory**. Attempt **any three** questions from the rest.*

Q1. (a) Discuss how multimedia can be used for the following application areas:

(i) Online portal for kids for age below 10 years

Refer to Page No.-50 [Web-based information portal] & Page No.-51 [Distributed Learning Platform]

(b) Design a branching sequence template and story board template for a multimedia based on - line advertisement website which advertises different products like fast – food and beverages.

Refer to Page No.-241, Dec-2009, Q.No.-3

(c) Discuss briefly the use of video conferencing.

Refer to Page No.-5 [Video conferencing]

(d) Describe the following:

(i) Features of icon - based programs

Refer to Page No.-56 [Icon based programs]

(ii) Salient features of Authorware

Refer to Page No.-66 [Authorware]

Q2. Discuss the following components of multimedia and how do you create them:

(a) Text

(b) Images

(c) Digital Audio

(d) Animation

(e) Video

Refer to Page No.-14, Chapter-1, Q.No.-12

Q3. With the help of an illustration, explain the planning and design, Production and Distribution of a multimedia application.

Refer to Page No.-18, Chapter-1, Q.No.-13

Q4. (a) Explain the role and significance of multimedia in business and commerce.

Refer to Page No.-4, Chapter-1, Q.No.-6

(b) Discuss the features of Image Q and Authorware tools.

Refer to Page No.-226, Dec-2007, Q.No.-1(d) & Page No.-66 [Authorware]

Q5. Write short notes on the following:

(a) Cross - platform capability of a multimedia application

Refer to Page No.-57 [Cross platform capability]

(b) Interface design for a multimedia application.

Refer to Page No.-195, Dec-2005, Q.No.-1(b)

●●●

CS-66 : MULTIMEDIA
December, 2011

Note: *Question number **1** is **compulsory**. Attempt **any three** questions from the rest.*

Q1. (a) What is development life-cycle of multimedia contents? Also, explain the various phases involved in multimedia development.

Refer to Page No.-73, Chapter-1, Q.No.-4 & Page No.-104, June-2004, Q.No.-5

(b) What is video on demand? Explain the methods available to deliver/ distribute video on demand.

Ans. Video on Demand (VOD) or Audio and Video on Demand (AVOD) are systems which allow users to select and watch/listen to video or audio content on demand. IPTV technology is often used to bring video on demand to televisions and personal computers.

Television VOD systems either stream content through a set-top box, a computer or other device, allowing viewing in real time, or download it to a device such as a computer, digital video recorder (also called a personal video recorder) or portable media player for viewing at any time. The majority of cable- and telco-based television providers offer both VOD streaming, including pay-per-view and free content, whereby a user buys or selects a movie or television program and it begins to play on the television set almost instantaneously, or downloading to a DVR rented from the provider, or downloaded onto a pc, for viewing in the future. Internet television, using the Internet, is an increasingly popular form of video on demand.

Some airlines offer AVOD as in-flight entertainment to passengers through individually-controlled video screens embedded in seatbacks or armrests or offered via portable media players. Airline AVOD systems offer passengers the opportunity to select specific stored video or audio content and play it on demand including pause, fast forward, and rewind.

(c) Explain the working of Quick Time Software.

Refer to Page No.-70, Chapter-3, Q.No.-10

(d) Explain the role of multimedia in the area of publication, with suitable example.

Refer to Page No.-32, Chapter-2, Q.No.-2

(e) Explain the Copyright issues related to multimedia applications.
Refer to Page No.-80, Chapter-4, Q.No.-8

Q2. (a) What is hypertext? Explain this with a diagram. Also, explain its major elements.
Refer to Page No.-57 & 62, Chapter-3, Q.No.-2 & Q.No.-5

(b) Explain the differences and Similarities between Video-Conferencing and document conferencing.
Refer to Page No.-204, June-2006, Q.No.-1(e)

Q3. (a) What is Annotations? Explain the role of annotations of hypertext, using an example.
Refer to Page No.-203, June-2006, Q.No.-1(d)

(b) Describe, how are education and training fields influenced and effected by multimedia?
Refer to Page No.-92, June-2004, Q.No.-1(a)

Q4. Explain, how the following multimedia components are created and how these are used in entertainment applications:
(a) Graphics
(b) Text
(c) Sound
(d) Video
Refer to Page No.- 247, June-2011, Q.No.-2

Q5. Define the term "Story board" in the context of multimedia project. Mention the features of it and also design simple story board template for any instance of an application of academic nature.
Refer to Page No.-76, 85 & 88, Chapter-4, Q.No.-7, Q.No.-13 &14

●●●

People will naturally start trusting me when they see my reliability and consistency

Brahma Kumaris